Fine
WoodWorking
on Wood and
How to Dry It

Fine WoodWorking

on Wood and How to Dry It

41 articles selected by the editors of *Fine Woodworking* magazine

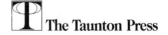

The Taunton Press

Cover photo by Richard Starr

First printing: September 1986
Second printing: December 1986
International Standard Book Number: 0-918804-54-X
Library of Congress Catalog Card Number: 86-50407
Printed in the United States of America

A FINE WOODWORKING Book

FINE WOODWORKING® is a trademark of The Taunton Press, Inc.,
registered in the U.S. Patent and Trademark Office.

The Taunton Press, Inc.
63 South Main Street
Box 355
Newtown, Connecticut 06470

Contents

Introduction

As an all-purpose material for making useful and beautiful things, nothing quite compares to wood. Freshly sawn from the log, a new board brims with possibilities, its potential limited only by the imagination of the craftsman who will work it. The same board, however, brims with water. Unless moisture is removed slowly and carefully, the wood will warp, twist and crack into so much firewood. Even when properly dried, wood and water aren't through with each other. With each change of the season, wood shrinks and swells, and unless the woodworker's design allows for this, his furniture will come to slow, certain grief.

This collection of 41 articles from the first ten years of *Fine Woodworking* magazine is a woodworker's guide to obtaining and drying his material. In it, you'll find practical articles about the nature of the wood itself plus advice on how to buy it, how to dry and store it and, for the ambitious, how to mill your own lumber using relatively simple chainsaw technology.

Paul Bertorelli, editor

Wood

A look at this fundamental material

by R. Bruce Hoadley

Wood comes from trees. Not forgetting this obvious statement will help us work with wood as it really is, not as we wish it were. For wood has evolved as a functional tissue of plants, not as a material to satisfy the needs of woodworkers.

For example, we all know that most of the wood we use comes from the trunk, bole, or stem, as it is sometimes called, not from the unseen root system below or the crown of limbs, branches and twigs that support the foliage. Some of the most prized wood does come from crotches and irregularities, such as burls or knees, but for the most part we prefer the regular grain found in straight trunks.

But sometimes we come across a board that is different from other boards. It warps severely, or pinches our saw blade as we rip it, or doesn't take a finish quite like the other boards. What we're working with is a piece of reaction wood — wood taken from a trunk that is leaning or from a branch that doesn't grow straight up (by definition most branches are made of reaction wood).

This is an extreme case, but it does illustrate why it's important to remember where wood comes from and also to know something about its anatomical structure. As woodworkers, we usually know far more about our tools than we do about our materials. But as the architect Frank Lloyd Wright once said, "We may use wood with intelligence only if we understand it."

Understanding the difference between sapwood and heartwood, between earlywood and latewood, between "hardwoods" and "softwoods," between ray cells and longitudinal cells, between ring-porous woods and diffuse-porous woods, between vessels and fibers, and so on, may give us a better understanding of why wood behaves as it does, especially when we're trying to shape it, finish it, or preserve it.

Perhaps the best place to start is at the molecular level. Wood is a cellulose material, as is cotton. And because it's cellulosic, it is hygroscopic — it absorbs water readily and swells and shrinks accordingly (therein much of the problem of the "movement of wood").

The cellulose material that wood is composed of is pretty much the same for all species. It's not until we start looking at wood at the cellular level that different woods start to look "different." (And even here this is not necessarily the case. The sapwood of many species can look very much alike. Then it's not until the sapwood turns into dead heartwood that differences among some species really become apparent).

In any event, the cellulosic material is arranged into tubular cells that run longitudinally along the length of the trunk or branch. There are three varieties of such cells — vessels, tracheids, and fibers. Vessels have a large diameter, thin walls, and are very short (but they stack together like drainage tiles). At the other extreme are fibers — narrow diameter, thick walls, and long. In between are tracheids — moderate diameter, moderate thickness, and also very long.

Because they're so large in diameter, vessels are good for conducting sap up the tree, but their thin walls don't contribute much to mechanical support. On the other hand, the thick walls of fibers make them good for support, but their narrow diameter doesn't do much for sap conduction.

In between are the all-purpose tracheids, which can provide both sap conduction and physical support moderately well. In fact, one distinction between the so-called hardwoods and softwoods is this difference in cell structure. Softwoods, or conifers, are composed mainly of all-purpose tracheids. They are believed to have evolved earlier than hardwoods. Hence their more primitive structure, with no cell specialization. On the other hand hardwoods, or deciduous trees, do have cell specialization — vessels for sap conduction, fibers for support, and tracheids for both.

The tracheids of conifers are about 100 times as long as they are wide. Thus their excellent paper-making qualities. Among

Cherry (diffuse porous)	*Black walnut (semi-ring porous)*	*Red oak (ring porous)*

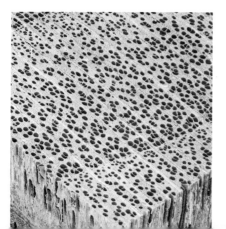 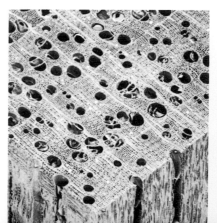 

Variations in porosity between earlywood and latewood can create problems in staining. Conifers such as Douglas fir (left) have earlywood that is lighter but more porous than the latewood. Therefore, stain reverses the grain effect, as in a photographic negative. With hardwoods like red oak (right), the earlywood pores are already darker. Lines in the light latewood are rays.

conifer species, however, there can be a three-fold range of diameters, from fine red cedar to coarse redwood. This texture range due to tracheid diameter also affects the smoothness of surface or evenness of staining that can be achieved in woodworking.

If wood were composed strictly of these longitudinal cells, whether vessels, tracheids, or fibers, it would be much less complex than it really is, and really much different, for consider how and where a tree grows.

Growth occurs in the thin layer of reproductive tissues, called the cambium, that separates the wood from the bark. This tubular reproductive sheath, several cells thick, migrates ever outward, leaving behind layers of newly formed wood (which remain fixed in place forever), and also forms new bark in front of it (which will eventually be crowded out by the newer bark cells, and by the ever-expanding girth).

The cambial cells vary in content with the growing seasons. During growth the content is quite fluid; during dormancy there is a thickening. As a result, wood cut in summer usually loses its bark upon drying, while winter-cut wood does not, an important fact for those wishing to incorporate bark into their woodworking projects.

In addition to vertical movement through the sapwood, there must be provision for horizontal sap movement. That's where the ray cells come in. They are oriented radially outward from the center or pith and are stacked vertically in groups called rays to form flattened bands of tissue. The rays not only carry the nutrients horizontally through the sapwood, but also store carbohydrates during the winter.

The rays are not great in number — typically they represent less than 10 percent of the wood volume — but they are significant for more than food conduction and storage. Their size — ranging from microscopically small in all softwoods to visibly big in many hardwoods — helps in wood identification. (For example, in red oak rays are less than one inch high; in white oak, they're one to four inches.) And structurally they influence the shrinkage of wood and the formation of checks.

Wood cells shrink and expand mainly across their girth, not their length, as they give off or take on moisture. That's why wood moves across the grain, not with the grain. But because ray cells are aligned across the grain (radially) they inhibit the longitudinal cells from expanding as much in a radial direction (towards or away from the center) as in a tangential direction (around the circumference). In effect, the radial cells act as restraining rods imbedded in the wood. That's why wood contracts or expands only half as much radially as tangentially.

The rays also form planes of weakness in hardwoods. End and surface checks, as well as internal honeycombing, will regularly develop through the rays in woods like oak.

So far we've discussed mainly the shape of wood cells, not

Eastern white pine (even grain)　　　　*Southern yellow pine (uneven grain)*

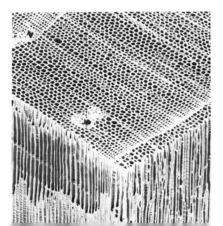

Earlywood/latewood variations are clearly visible in scanning electron microscope photographs. All the samples are oriented the same way, with the growth rings parallel to the right-hand face. Large "holes" in the pines are resin canals that help in sealing over injuries in the living trees. Pictures are from Structure and Identification of Wood, *by Core, Cote, and Day (Syracuse University Press).*

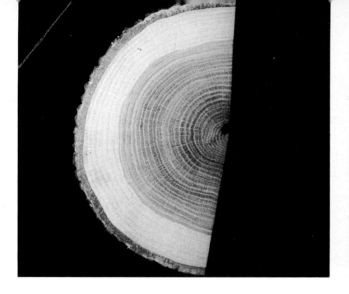

Red oak half-cross-section (before shrinkage) shows pith dot at center, dark heartwood, light sapwood, and cambium sheath where bark and sapwood meet. Rays are clearly visible in the heartwood radiating outward. At right is the section from a leaning hemlock tree. Reaction wood appears as abnormally wide latewood on lower side of rings.

whether they're alive or dead. Live cells, called parenchyma, contain living protoplasm and are capable of assimilating and storing carbohydrates. In softwoods or conifers, the parenchyma are generally limited to the ray cells, but in hardwoods, longitudinal vessels and tracheids, as well as ray cells, can be parenchyma. It differs from species to species.

But in general, most longitudinal cells lose their protoplasm soon after development by the cambium and become non-living prosenchyma useful for sap conduction or mechanical support, but not for food storage. (When such a change takes place, the cell wall structure remains unchanged. Only the protoplasm in the center cavity of the cell disappears.)

Thus the wood nearest the cambium, where sap conduction and food storage can take place, is called sapwood. As the tree grows and the oldest sapwood is no longer needed for water conduction, a gradual transition to heartwood occurs. This transition is accompanied by the death of parenchyma and loss of both food storage and conductive functions, with the heartwood serving the tree only as a supporting column.

Heartwood formation is accompanied by the deposition in the cell walls of chemical additives called extractives which can change the color of the wood. Whereas most sapwood is a cream to light yellow or light tan color, extractives are responsible for any rich browns, reddish or other contrasting dark colors the heartwood may have, as is characteristic of species like walnut, cherry, or red cedar. In some woods, such as spruce or basswood, the extractives may be insignificant or colorless so that there is little color difference between heartwood and sapwood.

Heartwood extractives can make changes other than color. Some extractives may be toxic to decay fungi and thus impart decay resistance to heartwood, as in redwood. Sapwood not only lacks decay resistance, but is attractive to stain fungi and certain powder post beetles because of the stored carbohydrates in the parenchyma cells.

In some species the original sapwood moisture content is remarkably higher, but the permeability of sapwood is usually greater, so that it loses moisture faster, but also absorbs preservatives or stains better. On the other hand, because of the bulking effect of extractives — they occupy molecular space within the cell wall — the shrinkage of heartwood may be less than that of sapwood.

For the woodworker, the heartwood-sapwood distinction is important. But what about the more general "hardwood-softwood" distinction? The names themselves are misleading because balsa wood is really a "hardwood" and hard southern pine is really a "softwood." While softwoods are generally evergreens, and hardwoods are generally deciduous, this is not always the case. The precise distinction is that the seeds of softwoods (gymnosperms — all conifers plus the familiar ginkgo tree) are naked (as in a pine seed), while for

Specific Gravity

Gymnosperms	Angiosperms
	Lignum vitae
	Ebony
Water: 1.0	Rosewood
	Purpleheart
	Domestic "Hardwoods"
Domestic "Softwoods"	Hickory
	Hard maple, Birch, Beech, Oak
	White ash
Southern yellow pine	Black walnut
Douglas fir	Black cherry
Eastern red cedar	
Hemlock, Redwood	Chestnut, Yellow poplar
White pine	Butternut, Aspen
White cedar	Basswood
0.1	Balsa

Differences in the specific gravity (the density relative to water) shows that the range of densities of domestic "hardwoods" and "softwoods" overlaps.

From *Fine Woodworking* magazine (Summer 1976) 3:12-15

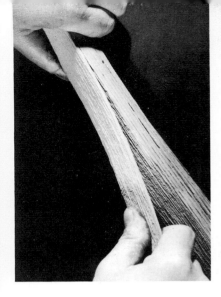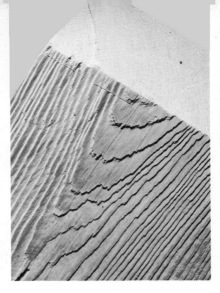

Basketmakers take advantage of weak earlywood (after pounding) of quarter-sawed ash to separate it into strips (left). Severely raised grain on pith side of flat-sawed hemlock (center) results from harder latewood being compressed into softer earlywood during planing, then springing back later. Honeycomb checks in red oak (right) can cause failure along large ray.

hardwoods (angiosperms), they are encapsulated (as in a walnut or acorn).

The hardness and softness of wood does come into play when we consider earlywood and latewood. Earlywood is that grown early in the season, when the moisture needed for rapid growth is present. In conifers, this means those longitudinal tracheid cells have thinner walls and larger cavities to favor conduction of sap. As latewood develops later in the growing season, the tracheids develop thicker walls (and in effect, denser wood). In other words, there is less airspace in latewood.

To a woodworker, what is also important is how this transition between latewood and earlywood occurs. Soft pines (e.g. eastern white, western white, and sugar) are characterized by fairly even grain, with gradual transition from earlywood to latewood. The result is fairly low average density with pleasing uniformity of wearing and working properties. By contrast, species such as the hard pines (e.g. southern yellow pine, pitch pine, red pine) Douglas fir, larch and hemlock are notably uneven-grained. In southern yellow pine there is a three-to-one ratio in the densities of the latewood versus earlywood. Thus the difficulty of machining it and the woodcarver's preference for the soft pines.

The latewood-earlywood differentiation can also present problems in staining — especially in conifers. In natural wood the latewood appears dark, the earlywood light. But earlywood is more porous, so that it absorbs stain more readily and thus stains darker than the latewood. The effect is to reverse the grain pattern, giving us the grain that would appear in a photographic negative. We've probably all seen this happen in the conifers such as pine or Douglas fir. However, in certain hardwoods, the large vessel size found in early wood makes it appear darker. Therefore, stain merely accentuates this darkness, rather than reversing it.

Hardwoods have a wider variety of longitudinal cells so there is less consistency in the differentiation between early wood and latewood. Rather than a change in the size of the tracheids, there is a change in the distribution of the larger vessels and smaller fibers. In some woods, the large vessels appear only during early growth, the fibers mainly during late growth (along with smaller vessels). This results in sharply defined rings of growth and the classification "ring-porous

hardwoods" (such as oak, elm, ash, chestnut, catalpa). As in southern yellow pine, there is a sharp difference in the densities of the earlywood and latewood.

By contrast, there are also the "diffuse-porous hardwoods" (where the pores or vessels are evenly distributed throughout the growth ring). The relative pore size, or "texture," may vary from the finest (or invisible) pores in gum, maple or aspen, to medium (or barely visible) in birch, and to coarse (or conspicuous) in mahogany. Although the vessels remain open in many species (e.g. red oak), in other species (e.g. white oak, locust) the vessels of the heartwood become blocked by bubble-like obstructions called tyloses that occur as sapwood changes to heartwood. These tyloses have a profound effect on the liquid permeability of the wood. That's why white oak is good for casks, but red oak is not.

The last distinction of interest to woodworkers is that of "reaction wood" found in leaning trees and in branches. The usual symptoms are eccentricity of ring shape and abnormally high longitudinal shrinkage, causing severe warpage in drying, as well as unexpected hidden stresses. In softwoods, the reaction wood is found on the underside and is called compression wood. It's also brittle. In hardwoods, it's found on the upper side, and is called tension wood, which machines with a microscopic wooliness resulting in a blotchiness when stained.

Perhaps all this shows that wood is no simple subject to talk about. Take the word "grain" for example. Normally, we mean the alignment of the longitudinal cells, because wood splits "along the grain." In the same context we have such terms as spiral grain, cross grain, wavy grain and interlocked grain. But grain can also refer to the uniformity of the growth ring structure. Douglas fir is an "uneven-grained" wood while basswood is "even-grained." Sometimes grain refers to the ray cell structure, as in the "silver grain" of white oak cut radially — slicing along the rays, in effect. And sometimes we refer to the "open grain" of oak and the "closed grain" of cherry when we're really talking about the texture caused by the presence or absence of large vessels. Finally, there is the "grain" of rosewood — not really grain, but figure, caused by the extractives in the heartwood.

So the word "grain" is not so clearcut and simple as it seems. Neither is the study of wood. □

Water and Wood

The problems of a difficult pair

by R. Bruce Hoadley

What is the relative humidity in your workshop? Or in your garage where you "season" those carving blocks? Or in the spare room where you store your precious cabinet woods? Or in any other room in your house or shop?

If you're not sure, you may be having problems such as warp, checking, unsuccessful glue joints, or even stain and mold. For just as these problems are closely related to moisture content, so is moisture content a direct response to relative humidity. Water is always present in wood, so an understanding of the interrelationships between water and wood is fundamental to fine woodworking. In this article we'll take a look at water or moisture content in wood and its relationship to relative humidity, and also its most important consequence to the woodworker—shrinkage and swelling.

Remember, as we pointed out in the previous article (pp. 2-5), that wood is a cellulosic material consisting of countless cells, each having an outer cell wall surrounding an interior cell cavity. A good analogy is the familiar synthetic sponge commonly used in the kitchen or for washing the car. A sopping wet sponge, just pulled from a pail of water, is analogous to wood in a living tree to the extent that the cell walls are fully saturated and swollen and cell cavities are partially to completely filled with water. If we squeeze the sopping wet sponge, liquid water pours forth. Similarly, the water in wood cell cavities, called free water, can likewise be squeezed out if we place a block of freshly cut pine sapwood in a vise and squeeze it; or we may see water spurt out of green lumber when hit with a hammer. In a tree, the sap is mostly water and for the purposes of wood physics, can be considered simply as water, the dissolved nutrients and minerals being ignored.

Now imagine thoroughly wringing out a wet sponge until no further liquid water is evident. The sponge remains full size, fully flexible and damp to the touch. In wood, the comparable condition is called the fiber saturation point (fsp), wherein, although the cell cavities are emptied of water, the cell walls are fully saturated and therefore fully swollen and in their weakest condition. The water remaining in the cell walls is called bound water. Just as a sponge would have to be left to dry—and shrink and harden—so will the bound water slowly leave a piece of wood if placed in a relatively dry atmosphere. How much bound water is lost (in either the sponge or the board), and therefore how much shrinkage takes place, will depend on the relative humidity of the atmosphere.

A dry sponge can be partially swollen by placing it in a damp location, or quickly saturated and fully swollen by plunging it into a bucket of water. Likewise a piece of dry wood will regain moisture and swell in response to high relative humidity and can indeed be resaturated to its fully

This block of catalpa had a moisture content of 114% and weighed almost 60 pounds when cut. It has been dried to 8% moisture content for carving and now weighs only 30 pounds. The gallon jugs

show the actual amount of free water (F) and bound water (B) which were lost in drying. Some bound water, equivalent to B', still remains in the wood.

Average Moisture Content (Percent) of Green Wood		
	HEARTWOOD	SAPWOOD
Ash, white	46	44
Beech	55	72
Birch, yellow	74	72
Maple, sugar	65	72
Oak, northern red	80	69
Oak, white	64	78
Walnut, black	90	73
Douglas fir	37	115
Pine, white	62	148
Pine, sugar	98	219
Pine, red	32	134
Redwood	86	210
Spruce, eastern	41	172

From *Fine Woodworking* magazine (Fall 1976) 4:20-24

swollen condition. Some people erroneously believe that kiln drying is permanent, but lumber so dried will readsorb moisture. There is a certain amount of despair in the sight of rain falling on a pile of lumber stamped ''certified kiln dried''!

It is standard practice to refer to water in wood as a certain percent moisture content. The weight of the water is expressed as a percent of the oven dry wood (determined by placing wood in an oven at 212-221°F until all water is driven off and a constant weight is reached). Thus if a plank weighed 115 pounds originally, but reached a dry weight of 100 pounds in an oven this would indicate 15 pounds of water had been present and the original moisture content would have been 15 ÷ 100 or 15%.

The fiber saturation point averages around 30% moisture content (higher in some species, lower in others). Living trees always have moisture content in excess of this level, although the moisture content (MC) may vary widely. Hardwoods commonly have original moisture contents ranging from 50 to 100%. In softwoods there is usually a noticeable difference between sapwood and heartwood; heartwood moisture content being just over the fiber saturation point whereas the sapwood commonly exceeds 100% moisture content—that is, the sapwood may be more than half water by weight.

When wood dries, all the free water is eventually lost as well as some of the bound water, depending on the relative humidity. When the bound water moisture content is in balance with the atmospheric relative humidity, the wood is said to be at its equilibrium moisture content (emc).

When lumber is left out-of-doors in well-stickered piles, protected from soaking rain and direct sun, it eventually becomes ''air-dry''. In central New England, the relative humidity (RH) averages around 77%, so air dry lumber will have a moisture content of 13 to 14%.

In heated buildings, in coldest winter weather, the relative humidity may drop quite low. The actual moisture content of thin pieces of wood or unprotected wood surfaces may be as low as 2 to 3%, only to return to 10 to 12% in muggy August weather. Therefore, for indoor uses, average moisture content should be attained to begin with. A moisture content of 6 to

8% is usually recommended for furniture manufacture in most northern and central regions of the United States. In the more humid southern and coastal regions the appropriate average equilibrium moisture content might be somewhat higher; in the arid southwest, somewhat lower. The only way commercially to get lumber this dry (that is, below air dry) is to dry it in a kiln; hence ''kiln dried'' lumber suggests this sufficient degree of drying. The drying can also be accomplished by simply leaving wood exposed indoors until it assumes the proper emc—remembering, of course, that it fluctuates as indoor relative humidity does.

Certain common terms which have been associated with drying are unfortunately misleading. ''Curing'' lumber suggests the involvement of some chemical reaction as in the

Approximate Shrinkage (as percent of green dimension) from green to oven-dry moisture content

	TANGENTIAL	RADIAL	T/R
HARDWOODS			
Ash, white	7.8	4.9	1.6
Basswood	9.3	6.6	1.4
Beech, American	11.9	5.5	2.2
Birch, yellow	9.5	7.3	1.3
Butternut	6.4	3.4	1.9
Catalpa	4.9	2.5	2.0
Cherry, black	7.1	3.7	1.9
Hickory	11.5	7.2	1.6
Maple, sugar	9.9	4.8	2.0
Oak, northern red	8.6	4.0	2.2
Oak, white	10.5	5.6	1.9
Sycamore	8.4	5.0	1.7
Walnut, black	7.8	5.5	1.4
Mahogany	5.1	3.7	1.4
Teak	4.0	2.2	1.8
SOFTWOODS			
Cedar, northern white	4.9	2.2	2.2
Douglas fir	7.6	4.8	1.6
Hemlock, eastern	6.8	3.0	2.3
Pine, eastern white	6.0	2.3	2.6
Pine, sugar	5.6	2.9	1.9
Pine, red	7.2	3.8	1.9
Redwood	4.4	2.6	1.7
Spruce, red	7.8	3.8	2.1

Cross sectional discs of red pine (left) and catalpa (right) after drying to 6% moisture content. Radial slits were sawn into green discs; width of cracks indicates the relative instability of the two species. At right, the seasoning checks in a butternut half-log illustrates that shrinkage is sometimes greater in sapwood than in heartwood.

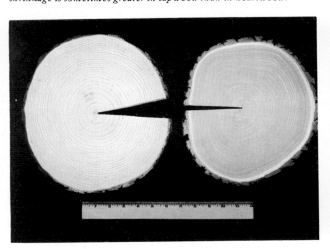

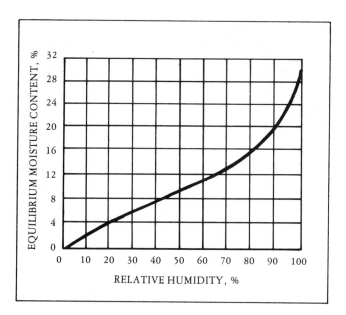

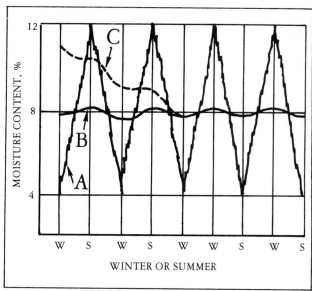

Curve at left shows the approximate relationship between relative humidity and equilibrium moisture content for most woods. At right, the curves show the seasonal indoor variation of moisture content in wood. A is unfinished thin veneers or wood surfaces, B is furniture of kiln-dried lumber and well coated with finish, and C is furniture of air-dried lumber and well coated with finish.

CALCULATING WOOD SHRINKAGE OR SWELLING

The approximate dimensional change expected in a piece of wood can be estimated by application of the following formula:

$$\Delta D = D_0 \times S \times \Delta MC \div fsp$$

where ΔD = Change in dimension
$\quad D_0$ = Original dimension
$\quad\quad S$ = Shrinkage percentage (from tables)
$\quad \Delta MC$ = Change in moisture content
$\quad\quad fsp$ = Average value for fiber saturation point, approximately 30%

Example: How much will a 14-inch wide, unfinished colonial door panel attempt to "move" (shrink and swell) if made from flat-sawed Eastern white pine?

Solution: Original dimension (width), D_0 is 14 inches.
S (from tables) is 6.0% = 6/100 = 0.06
Assuming the humidity may fluctuate such that moisture content will vary from 4% in winter to 12% in summer, then $\Delta MC = 8\%$.

$$\Delta D = (14 \text{ inches})(0.06)(8\% \div 30\%) = 0.224 \text{ inches}$$

The door panel will thus attempt to change width by nearly a quarter-inch during seasonal humidity changes. Loose framing to allow the panel to move, or finishing with a moisture-impervious finish are therefore recommended.

The formula clearly suggests ways of reducing the consequences of shrinkage and swelling. For example, reducing the dimensions (D_0) of the members: Narrow flooring will surely develop smaller cracks between boards than wide flooring. Choosing a species with a small shrinkage percent (S) can obviously help; e.g. catalpa is obviously more stable than hickory. Reducing the moisture variation is best accomplished by starting with wood of the correct moisture content and giving the completed item a coat of moisture-impervious finish.

setting of resin, or the curing of hides or meat. To some persons, the term "seasoning" suggests the addition of an appropriate chemical or some special aging process to others; it probably originated in connection with certain seasons of the year when natural drying was optimum for efficiency and quality of drying. But in reality, the drying of lumber is basically a water removal operation that must be regulated to control the shrinkage stresses that occur.

The claim that lumber is kiln dried can probably assure only that the lumber has been in and out of a kiln; it does not assure that the lumber has been dried properly (to avoid stresses), that is has been dried to the desired moisture content, or that subsequent moisture regain has not taken place. On the other hand, lumber which has been kiln dried *properly* is unsurpassed for woodworking.

The woodworker's success in dealing with moisture problems depends on being able to measure or monitor either the moisture in the wood directly, or the relative humidity of the atmosphere, or both. Direct measurement of moisture content is traditionally done by placing a sample of known initial weight into an oven (212-221°F) until constant weight is reached (usually about 24 hours for 1-inch cross-sectional wafer). Reweighing to obtain oven-dry weight enables determination of moisture loss and calculation of moisture content (moisture loss ÷ oven-dry weight). By so determining the moisture content of wafers taken from the ends of a sample board, the board moisture content can be closely approximated. Simply monitoring the sample board weight in the future will then indicate changes in moisture content.

An interesting application of this idea is to suspend a wood sample of known (or approximated) moisture content from one end of a rod, horizontally suspended on a string at its balance point. As the wood looses or gains moisture, the inclination of the rod will give a constant picture of changing moisture content. Such an improvisation can be calibrated (by adding known weights) to make a "moisture meter". Of course, there are also commercially made moisture meters, which are surprisingly accurate and simple to operate and will take the guesswork out of measuring moisture content.

Measuring and controlling relative humidity in the shop can be equally important. Simple and inexpensive wet and dry bulb hygrometers give accurate readings. Common sense will indicate where humidifiers or dehumidifiers (or some improvised means) are necessary to control humidity. One summer I suspected the humidity in my cellar workshop was high. I distributed 1/8-inch thick spruce wafers around and after several days determined their moisture content by the oven-dry technique. To my horror it was up to 21%! I immediately installed a dehumidifier and within a few weeks the emc was lowered to about 9%.

For the woodworker, then it is important either to obtain lumber of proper dryness or to be able to dry it properly (a subject we must leave to the next issue). Further, once having dried wood to the proper moisture content and built something out of it, some consideration must be given to future moisture exchange with the atmosphere. To some extent, design should allow for lumber movement, but usually the principal measure should be that of sealing the finished piece to *prevent* exchange of moisture and avoid the highs and lows of seasonal humidity fluctuation by holding close to the original average. Somehow the notion has prevailed that "wood has to breathe". Unfortunately, the term "breathe" suggests something positive or even necessary for the well being of the wood, but in reality, depriving wood of its tendency to adsorb and desorb moisture in response to humidity fluctuation is the best course of action.

Finishing materials vary widely in their ability to seal off wood surfaces and prevent moisture exchange with the atmosphere. Among the least effective is linseed oil. So-called penetrating oil finishes vary from low to moderate in moisture excluding capability depending on resin content and, as with linseed oil, give improved results when many coats are applied. Shellac is also relatively permeable to moisture. Lacquers are even better, but modern varnishes, such as the urea alkyd or urethane types, offer the best clear-finish protection against moisture adsorption. For end sealing lumber during drying or storage, aluminum paint or paraffin provide the ultimate in moisture barriers, as do commercial end sealing compounds.

Moisture extremes—either too high or too low—sometimes give rise to problems in chemical bonding of adhesives and finishes or high moisture (above 20%) may invite mold, stain or decay. But clearly the most common trouble-maker is the dimensional change—shrinkage and swelling—which accompanies moisture variation over the range below fiber saturation point.

As we begin to unravel the subject of shrinkage, three considerations should be taken into stride: *when* (over what moisture content range), *where* (in what direction relative to cell structure) and *how much* (quantitively in terms of actual dimensions). In the first consideration, as with a sponge, wood shrinks (or swells) as bound water escapes (or is picked up) in seeking its balance with the atmosphere. So only moisture change below fiber saturation point (about 30% MC) results in dimensional change, which is directly proportional to the amount of moisture lost. In considering *where* and *how much*, we must leave our sponge analogy, because a sponge has similar structure and properties in all directions; wood on the other hand, has oriented structure related to the "grain

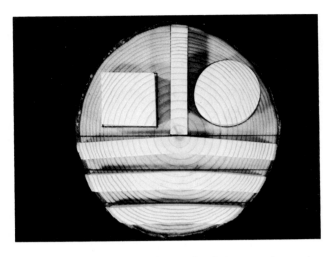

Various shapes of red pine are shown, after drying, superimposed over their original positions on an adjacent log section. The greater tangential than radial shrinkage causes squares to become diamond shaped, cylinders to become oval. Quarter sawn boards seldom warp but flat-sawn boards cup away from the pith. Camera perspective does not show full extent of shrinkage that occurred.

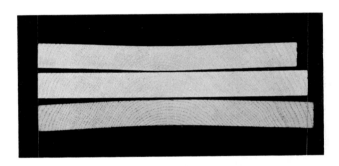

These three strips of wood were cut in sequence from the end of an air-dry red oak board. As shown by the middle strip, it measured 9-1/2-inch wide at a moisture content of 14 percent. The top strip has been dried to below 4 percent moisture content, the lower strip has been allowed to readsorb to over 20 percent moisture content and thus warps in an opposite direction.

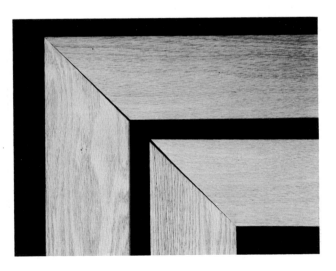

These two red oak frame corners were tightly mitered when originally assembled. The upper one was dried, the lower one dampened. Since wood is stable along the grain, but shrinks and swells across the grain, joints open as shown.

direction'' (predominant longitudinal cells) and to the growth rings. Longitudinal shrinkage (i.e., along the grain) is drastically different from shrinkage across the grain; shrinkage across the grain in turn is variable from the radial direction (perpendicular to growth rings) to tangential (parallel to growth rings).

Shrinkage in wood is commonly expressed as a percentage loss in dimension due to loss of bound water, that is, in drying from the fiber saturation point to the oven dry condition. Parallel to the grain, shrinkage is only about 1/10 of one percent, and in most cases can be neglected. However, in juvenile wood (near the pith) or in reaction wood (in limbs and leaning stems) longitudinal shrinkage may be up to ten times the normal amount, and variable—resulting in extreme warp.

The greatest concern is transverse (across-the grain) shrinkage, which averages about 4% radially and 8% tangentially. However, there is considerable variation among species, ranging from 2% to about 12% (see chart).

These values indicate the degree to which some species are apparently ''more stable'' than others. However, the greatest cause of trouble arises from the difference between radial and tangential shrinkage. As a result, cylinders of wood may become oval, squares may become diamond shaped, and flat sawn boards cup. This shrinkage difference also accounts for wood containing the pith cracking open, as anyone who has tried to dry cross-sectional discs of wood well knows. For it is impossible for wood to shrink more *around* the growth rings than *across* them without the development of stress. We also realize why edge-grain (quarter sawn) boards remain flat and shrink less across the width and are therefore preferable for many uses such as flooring.

Shrinkage in wood tissue results when water molecules leave the microstructure of the cell walls and the cellulosic structure is drawn more closely together. As sapwood transforms into heartwood, molecules of extractives (which usually give heartwood its darker color) may occupy this space and thus reduce total shrinkage. For this reason, woods with high extractive content may tend to be more stable (e.g. redwood, mahogany). At the same time, in a particular piece of wood there may be a troublesome difference between shrinkage of heartwood and sapwood, resulting in noticeable difference in shrinkage or even checking of sapwood.

The woodworker has several options and approaches, which can be applied singly or in combination, for dealing with the instability of wood. First, the wood can be preshrunk, i.e., properly dried to optimum moisture content. And secondly, the subsequent dimensional response to the atmosphere can be reduced or virtually eliminated by proper finishing. Third, sensible design can allow for dimensional change to occur without consequence; the classic example being the traditional feather-edge paneling allowed to move freely within each frame. Fourth, shrinkage and swelling can be overpowered or restrained, as the veneers making up a plywood sheet mutually do, or as the battens on a cabinet door will do. Fifth, chemical treatments may stabilize wood, although this approach is probably least convenient.

Controlling moisture content—and therefore dimensional change—involves an awareness of relative humidity and also of the dimensional properties of wood. Understanding and mastering wood/moisture relationships should be looked upon as an integral part of woodworking expertise. □

Q & A

Growth-ring orientation—*When I glue up a table top, should the growth rings all point the same way or should I alternate them?* —*Ed Stolfa, Roselle, Ill.*
R. BRUCE HOADLEY REPLIES: The drawing shows the distortion that results from each method. Orienting the rings in the same direction forces the board into an arch, which works if the top is tightly held down. Alternating the rings makes the cupping more obvious. The resulting wavy top may be hard to fasten down, but an appearance of overall flatness is maintained, and less stress will develop at the glue lines.

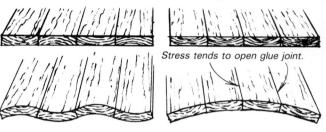

Stress tends to open glue joint.

More important, be sure that the moisture content is uniform from board to board and that the wood has reached its equilibrium moisture content (see p. 7) before gluing up.

Decay resistance—*If both are kiln-dried, which is more resistant to decay: Douglas fir or western hemlock?* —*Herbert W. Pratt, Boston, Mass.*
R. BRUCE HOADLEY REPLIES: Decay is caused by microorganisms in the wood that need moisture to live, so there should be no problem with wood that is kept dry. But in wood exposed to moisture, particularly repeated changes from wet to dry, other factors will determine any decay resistance. The most important factors are toxic substances that the living tree deposits as waste products in its heartwood, amounts of which vary widely among species. My book, *Understanding Wood* (The Taunton Press), has a table that grades natural resistance—Douglas fir is moderately resistant, the hemlocks slightly or non-resistant. This refers only to heartwood; sapwood doesn't have extractives, and is prone to rot unless chemically treated. Industry imitates the tree by impregnating lumber with preservatives that both resist moisture and inhibit the microorganisms. By the way, some of the natural deposits are quite hard, and quickly dull cutting tools.

Mahogany—*I've heard of several types of mahogany; which mahogany matches that used in 18th-century furniture?* —*Thomas Heller, Philadelphia, Pa.*
PAUL McCLURE REPLIES: The mahogany used from the 16th through the 19th centuries was either *Swietenia mahagoni* from the Caribbean Islands or *Swietenia macrophylla* from Honduras. Most of the mahogany, or cedar as it was called then, came from the coastal regions of Jamaica and Cuba. As these stands were depleted in the late 18th century, loggers turned to the coastal stands of *S. macrophylla* in Honduras. This wood was lighter in weight and darker in color, with more figure and fewer dark blotches than *S. mahagoni*.

Today, West Indian mahogany is virtually nonexistent and the timber from Cuba is banned in the U.S. Logging in Honduras is sporadically interrupted by local problems. Most of the ''mahogany'' in the U.S. and Europe today comes from Brazil, Bolivia, Columbia and Venezuela, and is actually Jequitiba (*Cariniana pyriformis*). Though a good substitute for true mahogany, Jequitiba lacks the same consistent color and the grain is more well defined; it can be used in period furniture restoration only if great care is taken in selecting lumber and finishing is painstakingly done to match.

Getting Lumber

Take log to mill, or mill to log

by Joyce and Edgar Anderson

When we started making furniture in the 1950s we could select individual boards from 10-ft. high stacks at the country's largest importer of rare woods. Two men with a forklift truck were willing to pull out from the bottom of the pile two 4-in. x 14-in. x 20-ft. Honduras mahogany planks, or to select one board each of paldao, East Indian rosewood, grenadilla and zebrawood. We could select a 5-ft. diameter walnut log from 20 logs sitting in the yard. It would be cut to our order, air-dried, kiln-dried, planed and delivered ready for use. It was very satisfactory and we would have continued to supply our needs from the lumberyard if our supplier had not started selling in 1,000-board-foot banded lots, discouraging the purchase of smaller mixed-wood orders.

At that time we were also cutting trees on our property for building our house and studio. With the help of our little bulldozer we towed logs to a ramp and rolled them onto our 1-1/2-ton truck for a trip to the sawmill four miles away. Days later, when the logs had been cut into boards, we trucked them home and stacked them outside until we needed them. Walnut and cherry were further dried inside to become the wall paneling and cabinets. Over the years nearby mills went out of business. We no longer owned a bulldozer and truck, but trees continued to be offered to us so we hired a loader and truck to take logs to a mill 30 miles away. Only trees with very good potential could justify the great expense of hauling.

We learned that the sawyer had very different criteria from ours in judging a "good" tree. His first question was whether we were bringing a backyard or fence-row tree, likely to contain buried metal. Fence-row trees need careful scrutiny. We have found bullets, bolts, rocks, concrete and old socks deeply buried in the wood. Inside a cherry tree, we found a maple board studded with nails, presumably the remains of a tree house. Although such found objects can damage expensive equipment, they can also produce beautiful wood. The blue stain from an embedded hammock hook can extend several feet along the grain and give special interest to an otherwise bland oak plank.

Because transporting a large tree section is so difficult, we have greeted eagerly the other approach of bringing the sawmill to the log. All the lumber we have acquired in the past year has been cut with the portable chain-saw mill. We are convinced this is the most practical way of all to obtain boards from individual trees. The chain-saw rig has proved such popular entertainment that people frequently call to offer their own or their friends' trees. Sometimes the tree owner helps operate the mill and shares in the lumber. Or the owner asks for a couple of pieces from the tree and we do all the cutting. We never take a good live tree that is functioning well where it stands. We have not paid money for any of the trees we have acquired.

We became familiar with an interesting ancestor of the chain-saw mill while working on a craft development program in Honduras. A two-man handsaw 10 ft. long was used in a pit-saw operation, with the logs supported on a log trestle 8 ft. off the ground. The top sawyer pulls up and guides the saw while his helper below pulls down. It is a primitive but fast and accurate way to make lumber. We have also extracted usable wood from trees by rail splitting, wedge splitting, freehand chain sawing and bandsawing.

It is almost impossible to compare the cost of FAS (firsts and seconds, the top grade) kiln-dried lumber from the lumberyard to the cost of green, log-run boards at the sawmill, or to the cost of fresh-sawn planks cut with the chain-saw mill. Some of the factors are not calculable in dollars and cents. And with green lumber one must include the time spent building foundations for the lumber pile, then stacking and stickering the boards.

Costs vary widely from area to area; all figures below are from people we dealt with in northern New Jersey in 1977. In the lumberyard, kiln-dried FAS 4/4 red oak runs about $0.90 per board foot; KD #3 common runs about $0.35. Black walnut is between $1.90 and $2.40 for KD FAS 4/4 and about $3.50 for 4-in. FAS. In some very large yards there is a minimum order (1,000 BF or $500). In others there may be a price difference of $0.15 per BF for quantity increments of under 100 BF, under 1,000 BF, and over 1,000 BF. There may be a surcharge of about 25% to select individual boards.

From the local sawmill, the range is about $0.30 to $0.50 per BF for log-run oak; drier, wider and sometimes thicker pieces command the higher prices. Walnut ranges from $0.75 to $2.00, also depending on dryness and width. Board quality at most mills is not good. It is best to pick up boards as soon as possible after they are cut, to ensure straight planks.

Some mills will also custom-cut trees brought to them. On small orders prices may range from $15 to $20 per hour, and on larger orders from $0.05 to $0.15 per BF. It is unwise to pay an hourly rate if one is not familiar with the integrity of the sawyer and the quality of his machinery; we usually arrange to pay by the board foot. Loading and trucking logs to the mill, and the boards home again, may add considerably to the cost.

The portable sawmill involves a different kind of expenditure: the initial cost of the equipment and the running costs of gasoline and maintenance. The other costs involve time. In one minute, two people operating a double-ended mill can cut approximately six to eight sq. ft. of any domestic hardwood. It takes about a day for two people to slab an average-sized tree. For each day of cutting the chain needs about two sharpenings. In two days two people have cut about 1,300 BF of 6/4 poplar, 700 BF of 6x8's and some firewood. This is about 28 man-hours to cut about 1,200 sq. ft. of wood. Board thickness makes no difference in cutting time.

It seems that over the years we have been devoting more time and physical effort, with less outlay of money, to the business of acquiring lumber. We wonder if some year soon we may find ourselves planting a tree farm. □

Joyce and Edgar Anderson, designer/craftsmen for many years, have given a summer lumbering course at Peters Valley, N.J.; Edgar has taught at Philadelphia College of Art.

Chain-saw Lumbering

Cut your wood where it falls

by Robert Sperber

I am a woodworker and have always been turned off by the "supermarket" approach to buying wood. In more and more places we must call up and order so many board feet of one kind of wood or another. We have no opportunity to choose a log and tell the mill just how we would like it cut. We can't even pick through a stack. The wood is banded together and we must take what we get. It has always seemed to me that the best way to avoid this situation would be to saw the log myself. Slicing through a log and taking that first peek inside is a great thrill and a wonderful source of inspiration.

The answer that I found is the portable chain-saw mill. It is the only solution that the individual craftsman can afford. In a few days of hard work I can cut enough wood to pay for the mill. The cutting is done by a saw chain specially ground for ripping (see page 15). Power is provided by one or two large chain-saw engines, with horizontal rollers guiding the cutting bar. There is no need to move the log; it can be cut wherever it has fallen. Rather than the log moving through the mill, as at a sawmill, the operator pulls this mill through the log.

Portable mills have been available for years, although little attention has been paid to them. Many knowledgeable people believe that the portable mill is too slow to be practical. But using the proper procedures, power units and a sharp ripping chain, a well-designed mill will move along at up to 10 sq. ft. a minute, cutting efficiently and well.

Most of the wood I have cut has been either from dead trees or trees that were going to be taken down for some other reason. People are willing to give away a dead tree rather than see it rot. Once the tree has been felled, I must decide where to crosscut it into logs. There is no set rule for this: it depends upon one's needs and interests. You may want to include the crotches, which a commercial mill would cut out and discard. Some of the most interesting patterns are hidden away inside the crotches, and they may be well worth keeping, if the wood is to be used for furniture or turning. The tree is then bucked up into separate logs, and the first one to be cut is rolled to a position that takes advantage of its features. For example, if the log is oval in cross section, placing the long

Author, right, and Edgar Anderson (page 11) mill lumber in woods. Two-man chain-saw mill cuts up to a 36-in. wide board from 1/4 to 15 in. thick. Four horizontal rollers can be adjusted up and down.

Distance between cutting bar and rollers shows on scale on vertical rod. Mill with two chain-saw engines weighs about 75 lbs.; ear protection is essential.

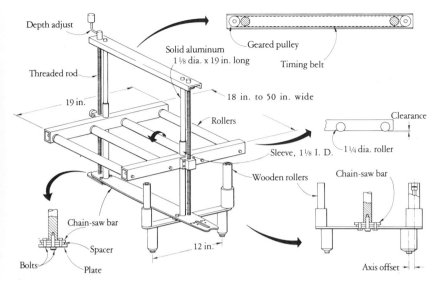

Depth adjust

Threaded rod

19 in.

Chain-saw bar

Bolts

Plate

Spacer

Solid aluminum
1⅛ dia. x 19 in. long

Geared pulley

Timing belt

18 in. to 50 in. wide

Rollers

Clearance

Sleeve, 1⅛ I. D.

Wooden rollers

Chain-saw bar

1¼ dia. roller

12 in.

Axis offset

Diagram at left shows principal parts of Sperber's mill. Diagram below shows how home-built slabbing rail guides first cut. Emery-faced vee blocks, detail photo above, are nailed near ends of log, then clamped to rail. Cross-braces are set below rail's surface so clamps don't interfere with rollers.

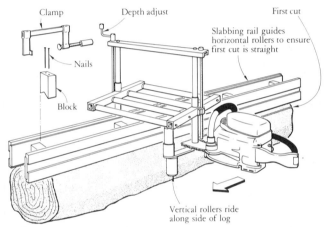

Clamp

Depth adjust

First cut

Nails

Block

Slabbing rail guides
horizontal rollers to ensure
first cut is straight

Vertical rollers ride
along side of log

diameter horizontally yields the widest boards. A knot or crotch in the horizontal plane results in a flame pattern on the board. To get the best pattern from the crotch, the cut should go through both centers on the same pass.

Since a log is irregular, a slabbing rail is used to guide the first cut. This rail, flat on its top edge, ensures that the cut will also be flat. The rail is placed on top of the log and secured by two wooden blocks nailed into the log at either end, with the nails going into the wood about 3/4 in. The rail is then clamped to the blocks with two adjustable clamps.

Next, the distance from the top of the rail to where the first cut is to be made is measured, and the mill is set to that dimension. One must be sure that this first cut will clear the nails holding the wooden blocks. The mill is then placed with its horizontal rollers resting on the rail and pulled through the log. It is very important on this first cut to keep the rollers flat on the rail and not allow them to tip to one side. This is not difficult, but some attention must be paid to it.

After the first cut, there is no need to use the slabbing rail, because the mill can roll directly on the flat top surface of the wood. The mill is now set and locked at the desired thickness. For the cabinetmaker 5/4, 6/4 and 8/4 are generally the most useful; for the turner, slabs four or five inches thick might be desirable. The carver might want slabs as thick as 10 inches.

Next the mill is placed on the log and pulled through. As the mill cuts, there is a tremendous amount of side force, which pulls the left-hand engine in toward the log. This pulls the vertical rollers firmly against the log but allows the mill to roll forward. With both front and rear vertical rollers firmly against the log, the mill sits at the slight angle at which it will cut best. As the mill moves along the log, the vertical rollers encounter bumps and depressions. By changing the angle, the side force can be shifted from the front to the back rollers, allowing the mill to move smoothly past these obstacles.

At the end of the log, the mill is pivoted around on the rear vertical roller to complete the cut. This keeps the front vertical roller from rolling off the end of the log, and also keeps the plank from falling onto the cutting bar until the very last second. At this point the bar is almost through the wood and cannot be trapped under the plank. Only when very thick planks are being cut is it necessary to drive a wedge into the kerf to support the plank as it is freed.

With slabbing rail (end view) in place, first cut is begun.

Chain-sawn lumber is stickered and sheltered to dry in air.

With ends of log resting on vee-cut blocks, Sperber makes bottom cut using one-engine chain-saw mill. Side force generated by engine pulls front and rear vertical rollers against the log. Mill advances at slight angle, at which it cuts best. At end of cut, mill pivots on rear roller as cutting bar swings free.

When making 2x4's or quartersawing, dividing cut stops a few inches short of log end. Then cut is wedged open and mill backed out, to permit 90° rotation of log for next series of cuts. For quartersawing, dividing cut is the first cut, and is made with slabbing rail.

After 90° rotation of log and first cut on top (with slabbing rail), log is square on three sides. Now groups of 2x4's can be sliced off, and separated later. By changing the mill settings, most construction lumber can be cut easily.

When the log has been cut down to a slab about 4 in. thick, it must be lifted up to prevent the lower vertical rollers from jamming into the ground. By the time a log is that small, it is light enough to lift and place a wooden block under each end. I use two 8-in. high blocks with a vee-cut in the top. Then the final cuts can be made.

Flatsawing is only one of the possible uses for the portable chain-saw mill. Sawing construction lumber is another. Anything from 2x4's to 15-in. x 15-in. beams can easily be cut. The length depends only on the length of the slabbing rail.

To square a beam or make 2x4's, the slabbing rail is set on the log, as in flatsawing, and the first cut is taken. Next a bottom cut is made (top photo). The log now has two parallel surfaces. If a squared beam is desired, no other cut will be made until the log has been rotated; or if it is to be cut into a number of smaller beams, it is divided into the desired dimensions (4 in., for 2x4's). These dividing cuts should stop about 2 in. short of the end of the log and, with the kerf wedged, the mill should then be backed out of the cut. This allows the log to stay in one piece so that the perpendicular cuts can be made. The log is now rotated 90° and the slabbing rail is once again set up and a top cut is made. Next the mill is set at 2 in. (for 2x4's) and pairs or groups of 2x4's are sliced off, to be separated later. When squaring a beam, once the log has been rotated 90°, a top cut is taken using the slabbing rail and a bottom cut is made to complete the beam.

To quartersaw a log, attach the slabbing rail and cut through the *center* of the log, stopping short of the end and backing out the mill, as in making dimension lumber. Then rotate the log 90°, reposition the slabbing rail and again cut through the center, this time all the way through. Place the halves of the log on the ground, curved side down, and make a top cut. Then split each half in two, leaving the log in quarters. Each quarter is propped up on blocks so that one flat face is horizontal and one vertical. Then make a cut, rotate the log 90° so the other flat face is horizontal, cut, rotate back 90°, cut, and so on. Because of all this manipulation, quartersawing is time-consuming. Unless you begin with a very large log, the boards will be so narrow that quartersawing will not be worthwhile.

The chain-saw mill is safer than the conventional chain saw. Since the chain is always engaged in the log, there is no kickback; if the chain breaks, it simply falls off the sprocket and is trapped in the log. A modern chain saw does not vibrate much, but milling is still a noisy and dusty operation. I always wear goggles and ear protection. I advise wearing a dust mask, particularly if you are working on the side of the mill where the rollers are. Pulling the mill through the log is relatively easy, but positioning the logs and hauling your lumber will wear you out. Chain-saw milling is hot, dusty work. At the end of the day you will be weary and grimy, but you will also have the satisfaction of beginning your woodworking where it should begin, with the tree. □

[Editor's note: The mills shown in this article were designed, built, and marketed by the author at Sperber Tool Works, Inc., Box 1224, West Caldwell, N.J. 07006. In 1977 the 36-in. mill attachment sold for about $500, and for about $1,300 complete with two chain-saw engines. The cost of the small mill was about $450 and $850, with and without engine. Portable chain-saw mills have also been made by Granberg Industries, Inc., 200 S. Garrard Blvd., Richmond, Calif. 94804 (pictures on page 16), by Haddon Tools, 4719 West Route 120, McHenry, Ill. 60050, and by Sears.]

Rip Chain

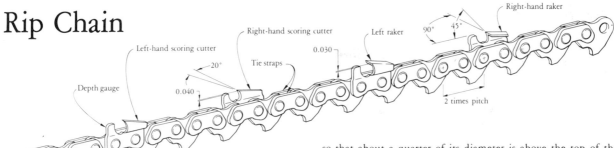

Ripping chain is the key to the chain-saw mill. The chain is designed to allow the fastest possible feed when cutting into end grain, parallel to the fibers of the tree. Chain-saw manufacturers don't make it—it is converted from crosscut chain by manufacturers of portable mills.

Logically, for fast cutting, one wants as many cutters in the wood as possible all the time. But the resistance of end grain is so great that too many cutters just overload the engine and the mill jams. The correct balance depends on the type of wood, size of log and power available. I use the Stihl 075 AV engine (6.7 cu. in., direct drive)—one engine in hardwood up to 12 in. diameter and softwood to 18 in., two engines in larger logs. If a portable mill is underpowered, the chain jams constantly and the work becomes slow and aggravating.

To reduce cutting resistance, skip chain is used. Two tie straps separate each cutter, rather than one tie strap as in ordinary chain. I use chain with .404 pitch, which is the distance between the center of one rivet and the rivet after next, divided by two. Furthermore, the chain consists of alternating pairs of right-hand and left-hand scoring cutters and pairs of raking cutters. As the chain speeds around the bar, a pair of narrow scoring cutters first severs the fibers by cutting a groove at the edges of the kerf. Then a pair of wide, chisel-style, flat-top rakers removes the bulk of the wood. This combination maintains highest chain speed, low vibration, and consequently a fast feed.

As in the diagram, the front edge of the scorers is ground at 20° from a line perpendicular to the face of the sawbar, while the rakers are ground square, at 0°. Rip chain is no more difficult to sharpen than ordinary crosscut chain. The most common mistake is waiting too long between sharpenings—I sharpen at least twice during a day of milling lumber. It's very important to sharpen the cutters uniformly. If one is a little too high it will be over-worked, the feed will be slow and the chain may break. It's easy to allow the cutters on one side of the chain to become longer than those on the other side. Then the chain will pull to that side and erode the groove in the sawbar. Soon the chain is traveling so loosely that it flops around as it cuts, leaving the wood rough. I guard against this by checking cutter length with a caliper. If the chain is properly maintained, the surface of the wood will be as smooth as that left by the best circular mill.

Using a sharpening jig ensures accurate cutter angles and lengths. When I am out in the field I use a hand file, but for no more than two sharpenings before using the jig again. The jig shown at right does a fine job without removing the chain from the bar; it costs about $18 (all 1977 prices). It can be fitted with an electric motor and a grinding stone instead of a file for about $42. The electric version is faster, more accurate and worth the extra money. With either method, the file or stone should be set

so that about a quarter of its diameter is above the top of the cutter. This imparts a front rake or cutting angle of about 45°.

Each tooth also carries a depth gauge to govern its cut, and the scorers must cut deeper than the rakers. I set the depth gauge on the scorers .040 in. below the cutting edge of the tooth, and on the rakers .030 in. below the edge. Sharpening jigs are supposed to file or grind the gauges to the proper setting, but I find that a flat file used freehand and checked with an auto ignition feeler gauge does the best job. Be sure the front edge of the depth gauge remains rounded so it can't grab in the wood.

If you are going to use a portable chain-saw mill, you must be able to sharpen the chain yourself. It is impractical to send the chain out from the woods two or three times a day for sharpening, at $10 each time. A hand or electric jig will do at least as good a job as a saw shop. Once you get the hang of it, a 9-ft. chain takes about 15 minutes to make razor sharp. —*R. S.*

Cutting angle of 45° is obtained by setting grinding stone so that one-quarter of its diameter is above cutter top.

Granberg's sharpening jig, about $18, files chain while on bar.

Tools and techniques for milling logs where they fall are ingenious and varied. Above left, Granberg's Mini-Mill chainsaw attachment for vertical cutting (about $50; all 1977 prices); right, Granberg's two-man Alaskan mill ($350 to $450, depending on size; chain saws not included). Left, Australian machine for cutting eucalyptus logs into railroad ties. The operator straddles the log and steers the whirling blade through the wood, with one wheel on either side of the log. Very few of these tie-cutters still exist; their use is now prohibited for obvious safety reasons. Below left, wedge-splitting slabs off a large chunk. Below right, pit sawing in Honduran forest: two-man team rips logs into boards to transport to market. Top man raises saw and follows cutting line; bottom man powers downward cut and gets face full of sawdust.

New Machines Turn Logs to Boards

by Paul Bertorelli

If you have a woodlot or can buy saw-logs from someone who does, you might want to make your own lumber. In the past, there were two ways to do it: you could haul the logs to a sawmill, if you could find one willing to do the work, or you could buy a chainsaw mill and cut the logs where they fell. High lumber prices and a growing interest in owner-built homes have produced a third choice for the do-it-yourself sawyer—portable bandsaw lumbermills.

In 1982, at the time this article was written, at least two companies were producing bandsaw mills that they claimed would turn logs to lumber faster, more accurately and with less waste than a chainsaw mill. The rigs are larger and costlier than chainsaw mills, but simpler and cheaper than circular sawmills of comparable capacity. Both bandmills are simply gasoline-powered horizontal bandsaws that ride on tracks, cutting into the stationary logs; both can be trailered or skidded through the woods. A third company planned to market its own smaller, less expensive bandmill. Others will probably become available.

Warren Ross of West Hempstead, N.H., made a 1,230-lb. rig that consists of a bandsaw mounted on a carriage that rides on a track of heavy channel iron. It's powered by a 5-HP industrial gasoline engine. To mill logs, the operator peaveys the timber onto the machine's 20-ft. track, dogs it down and pulls the bandsaw through the cut by hand, or—if the track is sloped slightly—lets it feed by gravity. Logs up to 17½ in. in diameter can be sawn on the Ross mill.

The Wood-Mizer lumbermill (Dupli-Carver, 4004 W. 10th St., Indianapolis, Ind. 46222) operates on the same principle but the saw is cantilevered over the log and is fed by a chain-and-crank system instead of being pushed or pulled by hand. As the cutting progresses, the log stays put while the saw carriage is moved up and down with another chain-and-crank mechanism. The Wood-Mizer, powered by a 14-HP rope-start gasoline engine, costs $4,421. The optional trailer with winch runs an additional $1,016 (all 1982 prices).

For the money, say Ross and Dupli-Carver president Don Laskowski, buyers of bandmills get more versatility than circular sawmills or chainsaw setups offer. With a ¹⁄₁₆-in. instead of a ³⁄₈-in. kerf, bandmills produce more lumber from a given log and less waste. The narrower kerf and fine adjustments make slabs as thin as ¼ in. possible. Both machines can resaw.

Laskowski says his bandmill can realistically saw 1,000 bd. ft. in a day, depending on the species and size of the logs. Ross makes similar claims for his mill. These machines are not intended for commercial lumbermaking but for property owners with timber holdings, for woodworkers, and for people interested in building their own homes.

Belsaw Machinery Co. (PO Box 593, Kansas City, Mo. 64141) sells a 40-in. circular sawmill for the same market, for about $3,000 (1982). It can saw logs up to 18 in. in diameter and 14 ft. long. Delta International (400 Lexington Ave., Pittsburgh, Pa. 15208; the former Rockwell International) also introduced a portable bandmill, for less than $2,000 (1982). □

Paul Bertorelli is editor of Fine Woodworking. *Chris Becksvoort, a cabinetmaker and writer in New Gloucester, Maine, contributed to this report.*

Inventor Warren Ross says his bandmill, which consists of a horizontal bandsaw mounted on a carriage that rolls on a channel-iron track, can cut up to 1,000 bd. ft. of lumber a day.

Don Laskowski, president of Dupli-Carver, uses his bandmill to square a log for timber. The machine can mill boards from logs up to 16½ ft. long.

Chainsaw Lumbermaking
Good-bye to vibration and fumes

by Will Malloff

Anyone can make lumber. All you need is a chainsaw attached to a mill, a straight board, a hammer and three nails. The board, positioned and nailed to a log, is a guide for the mill, which is adjusted to the depth of cut plus board thickness. The mill is pushed along the board and the sawbar pivoted out of the log at the end of the cut. That's all there is to it. But for efficient lumbermaking and the best results, there are a number of other considerations. Over the years I've developed and refined milling equipment and techniques, and now I feel I have the most effective, simplest system for ecological lumber production. To my surprise, a lot of people agree with me.

With a chainsaw, the logger decides what to harvest—trees that are mature, damaged or crowding other trees. A tree is felled and milled where it falls. Only usable lumber is removed, leaving the by-products to feed the land. Once you

EDITOR'S NOTE: This article is adapted from Will Malloff's *Chainsaw Lumbermaking* (The Taunton Press, Box 355, Newtown, Conn. 06470; 224 pp.). Malloff, of Alert Bay, B.C., is a professional logger and lumbermaker. Besides describing and illustrating the milling process in great detail, Malloff's book explains how to choose and modify ripping chains and mills, and how to make milling gear for timber joinery, natural boat knees, and more.

start to make your own lumber, you begin to notice usable wood everywhere you go. You're not restricted to milling only standing trees and you're not limited to working with the sizes and species available at the lumberyard.

Ripping chain—The most important factor in successful lumbermaking is properly prepared and maintained saw chain. Although you can use standard crosscutting chain, this will result in inefficient milling. You really need ripping chain, which you can make by modifying crosscut chain, using either a grinder or a hand file (figure 1). It's better to modify regular chain than skip-tooth chain or safety chain. I use a Stihl 090 saw for most of my milling, and I usually start with Oregon square-edge chisel chain (model 52L) made by Omark (Oregon Saw Chain Division, 9701 S.E. McLoughlin Blvd., Portland, Ore. 97222).

You'll find that a good disc-wheel chain grinder will soon pay for itself by its accuracy and speed in modifying and sharpening ripping chain. And one properly shaped grinding stone will do the work of several dozen hand files.

Chain modification—I grind my ripping chain cutters straight across the fronts with the round-edged grinding stone

Minimum milling: a chainsaw mill, a plank to guide the first cut, and a few nails to hold the plank on the log. Malloff, a chainsaw logger by profession, has improved every aspect of this setup, developing the rig shown on the following pages.

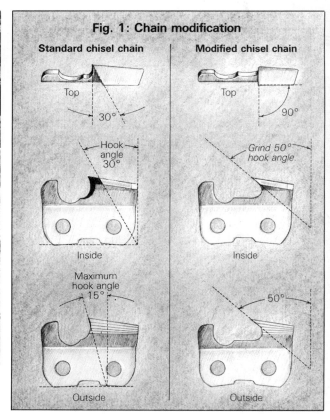

Fig. 1: Chain modification

Standard chisel chain

Top 30°

Hook angle 30°

Inside

Maximum hook angle 15°

Outside

Modified chisel chain

Top 90°

Grind 50° hook angle.

Inside

50°

Outside

Photos: Beth Erickson; drawings: Lee Hov

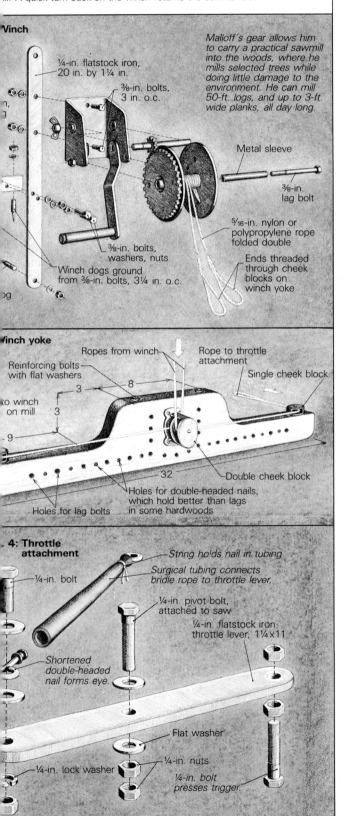

...he winch ropes, fig. 2, pass through the cheek blocks on the yoke, fig. 3.
...ne rope hooks to the nosebar end of the mill, the other to a short bridle
...pe, attached between the saw itself and the surgical tubing on the throt-
...e attachment, fig. 4. As the winch ropes tighten, the attachment pivots,
...nd the ¼-in. bolt on the end of the lever depresses the chainsaw's trigger
...witch to bring the saw to full throttle before forward pull is applied to the
...ill. A quick turn back on the winch returns the saw to idle.

Winch

¼-in. flatstock iron,
20 in. by 1¼ in.

⅜-in. bolts,
3 in. o.c.

Malloff's gear allows him
to carry a practical sawmill
into the woods, where he
mills selected trees while
doing little damage to the
environment. He can mill
50-ft. logs, and up to 3-ft.
wide planks, all day long.

Metal sleeve

⅜-in.
lag bolt

⁵⁄₁₆-in. nylon or
polypropylene rope
folded double

Ends threaded
through cheek
blocks on
winch yoke

⅜-in. bolts,
washers, nuts

Winch dogs ground
from ⅜-in. bolts, 3¼ in. o.c.

Winch yoke

Ropes from winch

Rope to throttle
attachment

Reinforcing bolts
with flat washers

Single cheek block

to winch
on mill

Double cheek block

Holes for double-headed nails,
which hold better than lags
in some hardwoods

Holes for lag bolts

**4: Throttle
attachment**

¼-in. bolt

String holds nail in tubing.

Surgical tubing connects
bridle rope to throttle lever.

¼-in. pivot bolt,
attached to saw

¼-in. flatstock iron
throttle lever, 1¼×11

Shortened
double-headed
nail forms eye.

Flat washer

¼-in. lock washer

¼-in. nuts

¼-in. bolt
presses trigger.

adjusted 50° from vertical (40° from horizontal). Commercial sawmills grind their blades for circular saws, gangsaws and bandsaws this way for a smooth, fast cut. Adjust the grinder so the stone is 90° to the chain, then tilt the stone to a 50° hook angle. Mount your chain in the chain track and adjust the stone to grind off the entire angled edge of the cutter—no more and no less. It is critical that the teeth be the same length and that the depth gauges be filed evenly.

Hand-filing—Chain modification with a file guide and round file is essentially the same as with a grinder; but file a 45° hook angle on each cutter instead of a 50° hook. The round file leaves a hollow-ground edge; if the hook were filed to 50°, the cutting edge would be weakened. Because guides are normally set by the factory to cut a 5° hook angle, you have to shim the file under both clamps to lower it so it will make the 45° hook. Start off with the file diameter recommended for your chain, but switch to the next smaller size (¹⁄₃₂ in. less) when the chain's cutters are about half-worn.

Keep filing until the hook angle on the side of the cutter is 45° and the top plate is 90° across. The bottom of the cutter gullet should be just above the top of the drive link. At least two files will usually be necessary to modify one chain.

The winch and yoke—In lumbermaking, you normally have to push the mill and roaring chainsaw through a cut, breathing exhaust fumes and spitting out sawdust all the while. But with my setup (photo, next page), you can stand back from the noise and vibration, and move the saw through the cut with minimum labor—all you have to do is crank a winch handle. Besides the winch, you'll need a remote throttle attachment for your saw, winch buttons to hold the ropes, and a winch yoke to pull the mill straight. The yoke also helps keep the guide rails of the mill level on the top plank.

I use a small boat-trailer winch as the base mechanism (figure 2). Make winch dogs (spikes that attach the winch unit to the log) by tapering ⅜-in. bolts. Hold each bolt in the chuck of an electric hand drill and, with the drill switched on, grind the taper on a bench grinder.

Assemble the winch and mount the winch rope. Cut a length of ¼-in. or ⁵⁄₁₆-in. nylon or polypropylene rope a little longer than double the length of the log you'll be milling, then splice or tie an eye to each end. Fold the rope in half and attach the fold to the winch drum. Later you'll thread the rope ends through the cheek blocks on the winch yoke (figure 3).

Throttle attachment—Because the operator is at one end of the log and the saw at the other when milling with my system, you need to build a remote throttle attachment to work the saw trigger (figure 4). This one is designed for a Stihl 090, so if you're using a different engine, you might have to adapt a little. The surgical tubing should be long enough (about 6 in. to 8 in.) to provide proper tension in both the open-throttle and closed-throttle positions. Through the saw handle, drill and tap a ¼-in. thread and mount the attachment by screwing the bolt into the hole and locking it with a nut and washer. I'll explain how to use this remote throttle attachment when we get to setting up.

Saw bridle button—I use a modified Granberg Mark III mill, but any mill should work. The winching rope is attached at one end to the mill and at the other end to the

Careful layout is the route to precision milling. Above, Malloff checks the height of the lag bolts that will support the guide plank. The end boards have been carefully aligned with vertical and horizontal layout lines drawn on both ends of the log. In this case, he's milling directly through the heart center of the log. If the heart were off center, he might mill to the average center instead.

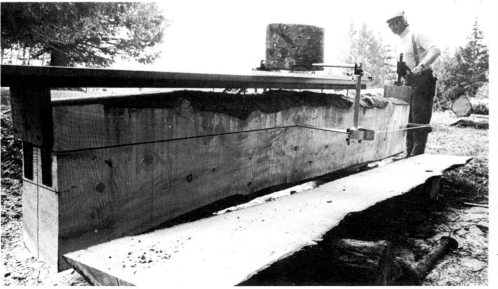

A yoke, fastened just below the line of cut, keeps the cut straight as Malloff cranks the winch, above. One rope is attached to the modified Granberg mill; the other rope is connected, by means of an adjustable bridle rope, to the saw itself and to a lever that controls its throttle. The mill, with its log-section counterweight, will be pulled to the end of the guide plank. Then the plank will be slid forward on the supporting lag bolts until it rests on the end board. The winch is attached to the plank itself, and the cut continues. Subsequent cuts don't require the plank and lags because the mill can ride directly on the flat-cut surface of the log. At left, with steel end dogs in place to control twisting, milling is well under way.

middle of a length of rope I call the bridle rope. One end of the bridle rope goes to the remote throttle attachment; the other end must attach to the saw. But since there's no place on the saw to accept a rope, you have to make a holding button. I call this the bridle button. On the Stihl 090, I substitute a $\frac{5}{16}$-in. by $1\frac{1}{2}$-in. bolt for the original shorter metric bolt in the handle to make this bridle button. This is the logical place for it, as the bolt is in a strong position on the saw and in the line of pull when winching through a cut.

End dogs—The inner tensions that have grown into a tree often make boards twist or bend while they're being sawn. This distortion can throw off a properly aligned milling system. So I've designed end dogs to help keep boards straight until the cut is complete—the dogs tack the board and log together, so the board can't deform during the cut (bottom photo, facing page).

The best end dogs can be forged from short pieces of automobile leaf spring, though other hardened steel would probably do as well. To make them, first round the ends of the spring stock. Then heat and bend the ends so that they are at right angles to the flat stock. Reheat the dog to a dull red, and allow it to cool slowly in the air. Grind the upturned ends from the outside to a sharp edge and then grind the edge straight across so that it is about $\frac{1}{32}$ in. to $\frac{1}{16}$ in. wide. End dogs with edges that are too sharp eventually deform and become difficult to drive.

I insert wooden kerf wedges every few feet in the cut. The wedges support the piece being milled and keep the kerf open, allowing the bar to travel freely. I also insert wedges behind the saw just before the end of the cut. This allows the mill to exit easily and eliminates end run-off. Six or eight wedges are enough for most jobs.

Setting up—Before you can begin to mill any lumber, you must establish a level surface on each log to guide the first cut. My system consists of a straight guide plank resting on end boards and pairs of leveled lag bolts placed along the length of the log. The wider the plank, the more support for the mill. The plank should also be thick enough to support the weight of the mill with minimum help from the lag bolts. The guide plank needn't be as long as the log, because you can mill in stages by sliding the plank off the end board and along the lag bolts as you go.

To stiffen the plank and help keep it straight, and to allow the plank to slide along the lag bolts without damage, attach two $\frac{3}{16}$-in., $1\frac{1}{2}$-in. by $1\frac{1}{2}$-in. angle irons to the plank edges, using countersunk screws about every 12 in.

The guide plank is supported at both ends of the log by end boards nailed or lag-bolted into the log end. The top edges of the end boards must be the same distance above horizontal index lines, reference points drawn on the ends of the logs, from which you calculate your milling patterns (upper left photo, facing page). I usually make pairs of end boards from common, 2-in. thick, dressed lumber. Heights of 4 in., 6 in., 8 in. and 10 in., cut to the width of the guide plank being used, cover most milling situations.

Measure and mark the log for the supporting lag bolts. When using a 10-ft. guide plank, I usually place a pair of lags every 4 ft. Remember to make sure the lags don't go so deep that they're in the path of the cut.

Position the guide plank, looking under it to make sure the angle irons rest securely on the lags and end boards. You'll need an overhang of at least 12 in. to support the mill as it begins the cut, so pull the plank out that far.

If you're milling with a winch, you'll need a weight to counterbalance the saw engine and to hold the guide rails of the mill flat on the plank. Make this from a block of log that is slightly larger in diameter than the space between the mill guide rails. Notch the log to fit over the mill handle.

The first cut—Determine how high to set the mill for the first cut by measuring on a vertical index line drawn on the end of the log. Mount the mill on the guide plank. Keep the thrust skid against the log and begin the cut with the nose end of the sawbar. Come to full throttle and cut until the back guide rail of the mill just passes the end board. Pause, and drive in both end dogs, spacing them as far apart as possible without splitting the slab.

Now position the winch yoke. Center it on the butt end of the log so that the outside pulleys are 1 in. or 2 in. below the mark on the vertical index line, and thread the winch ropes through the cheek blocks. Now slip one end of the bridle rope over the bridle button on the saw engine, and hook the other end of the bridle rope to the eye on the remote throttle attachment's surgical tubing. Gently take up the slack in the winch rope, and thread it through the bridle rope so that it will pull the throttle wide open before it begins to pull the mill forward.

When the winch is set up, start the saw engine and position the counterweight. As you start cranking the winch, the engine should open up to full throttle. To stop milling, or if the saw sticks in the cut, quickly crank the winch handle several turns backward. This will stop the pull and allow the engine to return to idle. Keep an eye on the guide rails of the mill to be sure they remain flat on the guide plank, and mill up to the last set of lag bolts. Crank the winch backward quickly to stop milling, allow the engine to idle and then turn the engine off. Leave the mill in the cut.

Pull the guide plank forward to the next cutting position. In the last position, the plank will just cover the end board. So set the winch dogs into the end of the guide plank and continue milling, adding kerf wedges as necessary. When the mill comes close to the end of the cut, remove the counterweight, winch ropes and yoke. Pull the guide plank forward so it projects beyond the end board to support the mill as it finishes the cut. Complete the cut by hand, keeping a firm downward as well as forward pressure on the mill.

You can mill a board or two off the top slab if you invert it in place on top of the log. Estimate the center of weight of the slab and drive a wedge on either side to provide a pivot. Absolute balance is not necessary, but the closer you guess, the easier it will be to move the slab. Swing the slab with a peavey, so that it crosses the log. Use a peavey or jack to flip the slab over. Swing the slab back into place, then lift it to near level and block it with wedges.

I don't normally use the winch yoke on shallow cuts. I attach the winch rope to the bridle rope at the engine end as when using the yoke, but attach the nose-end rope by slipping the loop over the mill's riser post. Once the counterweight is in position, you can start milling. The winch system is more complicated than hand-milling, but certainly less tedious. I often hand-mill short and narrow cuts, but find a day's work much easier with a winch. □

Woodlot Management
Thinning and pruning for more valuable trees

by Irwin and Diane Post

Growing trees is, in many ways, akin to raising vegetables in a backyard plot. Just as a rich harvest rewards the gardener's weeding and watering efforts, so too can labor in the woodlot produce dramatic, if slower, results. And woodlot management holds a special value for the woodworker—the pleasure of working wood he or she has helped to grow.

Forest management need not be complex nor does it have to be practiced on boundless tracts of land. The techniques we've outlined in this article can be used by anyone, on woodlots as small as an acre or less. Most management work consists of cutting and pruning trees following a thoughtful evaluation of the woodlot. From some woodlot work, you will have to wait for results, but other benefits come quickly. We've begun to manage only a small portion of our 50-acre woodlot in Vermont and we already have 3,000 board feet of hardwood plus 50 cords of firewood to show for our work.

Our management plans are aimed at meeting our future needs for lumber and firewood for ourselves and for sale, and at growing a healthy forest. You can shape your plan to suit your needs, and the climate, soil and type of trees that grow best in your area. You can design your own management plan, or seek help and advice from county, state or consulting foresters in your area.

Where is the woodlot? How big is it?—It's amazing how many people don't know their property boundaries. The first step in woodlot management is to find and mark the boundaries. The penalties for cutting someone else's trees are high in terms of good, neighborly relations, and even higher in possible legal costs and damages. Sometimes the boundaries are marked with stone walls, fences or blazes left by a neighbor or previous owner. Other times it will be necessary to hire a surveyor. In any event, be certain of the boundary before marking it—few things are more troublesome than a boundary mark that's in the wrong place.

It's also important to know the real size of your woodlot. The size determines the value of the land and the property tax on it, and it is the basis for estimating your wood harvest. Until the advent of electronic calculators, finding the area of an irregular parcel was tedious and fraught with error. As a result many parcels were guesstimated and recorded as, say, 25 ± acres, with no limits on the plus or minus. We recently helped a neighbor resurvey a parcel that was recorded as 150 ± acres; it turned out to be only 120 acres. If you are buying a woodlot, we suggest requiring the seller to have a survey map prepared as a condition of sale.

The traditional way to mark forest boundaries is with painted blazes on unmarketable trees on, or nearly on, the boundary line. A blaze is made by chopping several square inches of bark off the tree at about chest height, then paint-ing the wound a bright color. If you wait a few weeks before painting the wound, the paint will stick better. The blazed trees should never be harvested and they should be close enough together for the boundary to be easily followed. Repaint the blazes every few years.

A blaze is a wound, and a potential doorway for disease. If you want to avoid this risk, you can nail colored plastic to the trunk at eye level. Use brass or copper nails to avoid damage to sawblades if the tree is ever harvested, and plan to replace the plastic every couple of years.

Evaluating the woodlot—Once the boundaries are established, you can begin learning the characteristics of your land and of its trees. A forester "cruises" the woodlot by recording observations on a map and making field notes while walking through the woods.

A site index is a shorthand method of indicating the quality of the land and its ability to grow trees. The site index is a number indicating the average height of a tree species at a given age, usually 50 years. Thus a site index of 80 for white pine means that a 50-year-old white pine tree can be expected to be 80 feet tall. The site index reflects soil quality, topography, water availability and drainage. It does not depend on the number, health or size of the trees currently growing. A woodlot with a site index of 80 for white pine will still have a site index of 80 even after it has been clearcut.

You can figure site index by determining the ages and heights of representative trees of each species on your woodlot. These figures are then matched with a published table to find the index numbers. You can get site-index tables, comparative indexes, and help in evaluating your data from a state, county, or consulting forester.

The age of your trees can be found with an increment borer, an auger-like tool that removes a small core of wood from the tree trunk. Counting the annual growth rings from the pith to the bark gives the age of the tree, although you should add several years to account for the time it took the tree to reach the height of the bore. If you don't have an increment borer, you will have to figure age by felling trees and counting the annual rings. Cutting only a few trees will give enough data for figuring the site index.

Tree height can be measured with a variety of instruments including relascopes, clinometers and optical altimeters. But the simplest and cheapest instrument is a log and tree scale stick. This tool, resembling a truncated yardstick, is available from forestry supply houses and has a scale for determining tree height based on a simple sighting method.

Other qualities of the stand that should be noted during the cruise include tree diameters, rate of diameter growth, basal area, tree quality and species composition.

Tree diameter is usually measured at 4½ ft. above ground and is given as "DBH" or "diameter at breast height." Diam-

---

Irwin and Diane Post are forest engineers living in Barnard, Vt.

From *Fine Woodworking* magazine (March 1982) 33:82-87

Short of felling trees and counting the annual rings, an increment borer, left, is the best way to tell the age of trees. The tool removes a small, fragile cylinder of wood, right. The rings aren't as easy to see as in a cut tree, and must be counted carefully.

eter growth rates can be gauged from the increment core: widely spaced annual rings indicate vigorous growth while close rings show slow growth. Slow-growing stands usually need thinning.

Basal area is a relative measure of how dense a stand is and it helps you decide if thinning is needed. To understand basal area, imagine one acre of your woodlot with all the trees cut at breast height. Measure the cross-sectional area in square feet of all the stumps and add them up to arrive at basal area in square feet per acre. The more crowded the stand, the higher the basal area. Management plans often specify thinning to a certain basal area, taking into account site index and management objectives. In New England, for example, we generally recommend that hardwood stands be thinned to 50 to 70 square feet per acre and softwood stands to 70 to 80 square feet. Foresters measure basal area by "point sampling"

with a prism or tools such as a Cruz-All or Cruise-Angle. The forester stands at a randomly selected point in each forest type and makes a 360° sweep while looking through the instrument's sight. Each instrument comes with instructions on which trees should be counted for determining basal area.

Tree quality, unlike the measurements described thus far, is almost entirely subjective. It includes such factors as straightness of the trunk, limbiness, evidence of rot, and size and health of the crown. Tree quality is a predictor of log quality, so we want to remove trees of low quality, thereby "releasing" nearby high-quality trees from competition.

Ground conditions should also be noted during the cruise because they will affect access to the timber at harvest. Steepness of slope, stoniness and location of bogs and watercourses should all be recorded on the woodlot map.

Woodlots, no matter how small, are seldom uniform. There are usually differences in species, tree size and site index from place to place. Homogeneous areas are known as forest types. The management plan treats each forest type separately, with specific recommendations for each type.

The management plan—The management plan consists of a statement of the overall management objective, the forest-type map, the description of each forest type and the management recommendations for each forest type. Most woodlot owners want several benefits, so conflicting objectives have to be weighed. It's important to have a good picture of how different management strategies will change the appearance of the woodlot and it is useful to examine managed woodlots nearby and to talk with their owners. As you set your goals, remember that your needs may not align with those of the commercial lumber producer. Burls or spalted lumber, for example, are highly valued by some craftsmen but are virtually useless to a professional logger.

There are two general management strategies: even-age and uneven-age. In even-age management all the trees on a given parcel are the same age and they will mature and be cut at the same time. After the harvest, a new stand will be established through planting or natural regeneration. Uneven-age management is not so orderly. There are trees of every age from seedlings to sawlogs and the stand will be harvested and

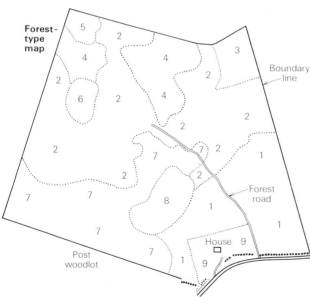

The completed forest management plan should include a detailed map of the woodlot. The numbers represent forest types. Area 2, for example, is a 19-acre tract with sugar maple, ash and beech as the predominant species. Each forest type on the map has a specific management objective and a list of recommendations to reach the objective.

thinned every 10 to 15 years. The best management for your woodlot depends on what trees you already have and their ages, the species you hope to regenerate, and aesthetics. For example, some species, such as the birches and oaks, require nearly full sunlight to the forest floor for good regeneration, while other species like sugar maple and beech regenerate well under the shade of standing trees.

Management recommendations also tell what products can be expected in the near term such as firewood, pulpwood or sawlogs and what equipment is necessary for harvest. The duration of a management plan is usually ten to twenty years, after which it should be updated.

The management plan prescribes the harvesting, thinning or pruning for each forest type in the woodlot. How do you decide which trees to cut and which to leave? Generally, the higher-value species that grow well on the site should be favored over short-lived species that don't reach sawlog size, species that don't do well on the site, diseased or poorly-formed trees and weed species. For example, on our woodlot, sugar maple, white ash, yellow birch and white birch do very well. Black cherry does less well but we favor the healthy cherries because we prize their wood for cabinetwork. Gray birch is a short-lived species that rarely attains sawlog size, so we cut it for firewood. We cut our beech trees also, because they have contracted scale disease. Striped maple is a weed species that can blanket the forest and prevent regeneration of the species we want. We cut all the striped maple we find.

A management plan can also benefit wildlife. We have a small deer yard on our land, an area of dense coniferous growth where deer find shelter in winter. From a wood production viewpoint this deer yard should be thinned, but we prefer to leave this stand uncut for the deer.

If you plan to do the management work yourself or if you have a large woodlot, it may not be possible to do all the work in one year. You should set work priorities, thinning first the areas with good site indexes and with forest types that will benefit most from attention. Schedule the work carefully. If you plan to sell your wood, your timetable should be flexible enough to suit market fluctuations. For instance, it has not been possible to sell pulpwood in our area for the past year, so we aren't cutting it now.

It's easy to underestimate how much work managing a woodlot is—particularly during the first treatment of previously unmanaged forest. It can be very discouraging to fall far short of your goals, and it's no fun when every spare moment must be spent in the woodlot. Most people would find a goal of treating about one acre a year of previously unmanaged woodlot about right. A first thinning in a typical New England forest would mean coping with between 5 and 15 cords of wood per acre.

Picking trees to cut—In an old field that grows up naturally into forest, many thousands of seedlings may sprout, but as they compete for sunlight, water and nutrients, most will die. By the time they reach 18-in. DBH, perhaps only 75 trees per acre will survive. Nature, however, does not always select the same trees that we would select. We want straight, clear, sound logs of the species we value. By judiciously lowering the competition among pole-size trees with good prospects of becoming quality sawlog trees, we can improve the quality of our future harvests.

The total amount of wood grown on an acre of land will be the same whether we manage it or not. Thus, by reducing the competition among the best stems through careful cutting, we don't reduce total growth but concentrate it in the best stems. These trees increase in diameter faster and attain sawlog size sooner than if we let nature run its course. Vigorous, fast growing trees are also healthier than slow growing trees, and are less susceptible to disease and insect damage.

Given the object of producing high quality sawlogs, we can readily decide which trees to cut and which to leave for future growth. For illustrative purposes, think of an uneven-age hardwood stand with everything from seedlings to sawlog trees. Large trees that are obviously hollow or very poorly formed should be cut, unless you wish to leave a few as den trees for wildlife. These trees may not yield a single sawlog despite their large diameter. Sawlog trees that have a lot of dead branches in the crown should also be harvested. Such trees are overmature and growing very slowly. Certain other mature trees may have taken over more of the forest than they deserve, with too many branches and too large a crown. These "wolf trees" cut off sunlight from large areas of the forest floor, distressing and weakening surrounding trees. Healthy sawlog trees should be cut only if you need the wood or if they are overcrowded. The pole-size trees, 4-in. to 10-in. DBH, will dramatically respond to thinning by increasing their rate of diameter growth. Trees of good form of the desired species should be favored by releasing them from competition on at least two sides. Trees with a strong lean should be cut because they usually contain large amounts of reaction wood, a source of trouble for the woodworker. Pole-size trees cut during a thinning make good firewood and rarely need splitting. It is generally not worth thinning saplings and seedlings because tight young stands encourage these trees to grow straight and to self-prune their lower branches.

Picking which trees to thin and which to save is easier to do from an armchair than in the woodlot, but it can be learned with practice. We mark the trees we want to cut, but you can just as easily mark the crop trees you want to save. *Two cardinal rules of marking a stand are to look up and to look at all sides of a tree before deciding to favor it.* Many straight trunks are topped by dead or nearly dead crowns. A trunk that looks sound on one side may be hollow or cracked when viewed from another angle. Special marking paints can be used, but any bright-colored paint will work. We walk in parallel strips 50 feet wide looking for high quality trees of the species we want to keep. Diseased or low quality trees are marked for removal. We then look closely at the remaining trees (see the box on p. 26) and decide which should be cut to give space on at least two sides of a good tree's crown. We next examine trees of desired species but of only intermediate quality, and those of high quality but of less desirable species. We cut any of these trees whose removal will give space on two sides of the favored trees' crowns.

Ideally, our crop trees will be evenly spaced. However, we don't hesitate to leave two good trees closely spaced if there are poor trees around them that will be cut. In hardwood stands where there are no potential sawlogs, poor quality trees may be left standing. These trees provide future firewood and shade that favors regeneration of desired trees. Removal of all shade encourages brambles and short-lived pioneer species. We leave an occasional (one to four per acre) old but healthy tree with a good crown. These trees have little lumber value but offer food for wildlife, and nest sites in hollow branches.

Pruning is an often overlooked route to producing high quality logs. Post uses a standard 17-ft. saw to prune a white pine stem.

Pruning future sawlogs—Pruning is one of the most overlooked ways of improving sawlog quality and it's the route to the clear boards we so prize in our woodworking. Pruning is simply cutting off the lower branches of trees very close to the trunk with a polesaw. The tool is available from forestry supply houses for about $25 (1982). Trees are usually pruned to a height of 17 ft., producing one "standard" 16-ft. sawlog with an ample allowance for stump waste. Pruning any higher with a polesaw is difficult and is generally not done.

To reduce the risk of infection, the cut should be made immediately outside the branch collar—where the trunk swells at the branch's base. Vigorously growing trees soon heal over the wound and grow clear wood. All of the dead branches and a few of the lower live branches can be pruned without hurting the tree. Don't leave stubs when you prune—the tree can't heal over them. As a stub rots, it provides entry for moisture, fungi and insects into the heart of the tree.

The branches of pole-size trees are small, and pruning wounds heal quickly. However, large diameter trees have thicker branches that heal over slowly, making it likely that they will be harvested before pruning does them much good.

Since there are many more pole-size trees to the acre than there are future sawlog trees, only the trees with the best potential should be pruned. Since there is little point in pruning firewood, it is sensible for pruning to follow thinning.

Harvesting and regeneration—Harvesting your own timber can be very satisfying. Through harvesting, you change the character and appearance of your woodlot, as well as obtain valuable wood. With patience and care, you can leave your woodlot in better condition than most loggers would.

On the other hand, it takes heavy and expensive equipment as well as a lot of time and skill to harvest sawlogs. And it is dangerous work. Many woodlot owners find that they are better off selling the stumpage rights to a logger. We strongly recommend that every such timber sale be supervised by a consulting forester. In most cases, the forester marks the trees that will be harvested (and those the logger should remove as culls), prepares a notice of the timber sale, shows the woodlot to loggers, takes bids and helps the landowner decide which bid to accept. The forester draws a contract, oversees the harvest and holds a damage deposit from the logger to pay for any damages. The forester has the authority to shut down the logging operation in adverse weather, when heavy equipment might damage the forest floor, or if excessive damage is done by the logger. The forester's fee is more than made up by the advantages of competitive bidding and of having a third party decide questions of safety and damage. Many states have regulations that the logger must satisfy before he finishes, such as cutting evergreen slash (the tops and other debris) to a low height to reduce the risk of fire, and taking steps to reduce erosion. If you have special concern for the condition the roads are left in, possible erosion problems, or trees you don't want cut, the forester will specifically include these in your contract.

When the harvest is over, attention must be given to growing new trees in the woodlot. Planting seedlings or spreading seed is sometimes necessary, but usually natural regeneration will do the job.

Artificial regeneration is usually limited to conifers in woodlots that have been clearcut or to new plantations on former agricultural land. Hardwoods, with the exception of prized species like walnut, are rarely planted for future saw-logs. Whenever trees are planted or seeded, it is important that they be suitable for the local soil, climate and water conditions. It is wise to plant species that are in reasonable demand. Thousands of acres of red pine were planted in the past, but there is currently so little demand that nobody knows what to do with them now. If you plan to start a tree plantation, remember that plantations need thinning just as often as natural stands.

Trees regenerate naturally in two ways: by germinating from seeds and by sprouting from stumps. Most hardwood species send up stump sprouts after a tree is cut. Some species are more prolific sprouters than others, and small-diameter stumps sprout more than do stumps of large diameter. Stump sprouts start life with a large root system and they often grow more than 5 ft. the first year. The problem with such sprouts is that there are often too many of them, and a stump may sprout double, triple and quadruple-stemmed trees. Cutting all but the best sprout from each stump may solve this.

In a given location, trees of a given species tend to have years of good seed production and years of poor seed production. It is often possible to affect the species composition of naturally regenerated forest stands by timing harvesting to follow an abundant seed crop of the species you wish to favor.

Although our efforts at harvesting and regeneration parallel those of the gardener, we do not have the gardener's ability to change crops from year to year. Our actions in the woodlot shape the forest for generations to come and that alone should give us pause to think twice about which trees we cut and which we encourage to grow. Few of us will live long enough to harvest sawlogs from seedlings we plant, but our children and grandchildren will benefit from our foresight if we decide wisely. ☐

For more information...

State, county and consulting foresters have lots of information on basic woodlot management, and much of it is free. Government foresters are often able to visit woodlots and offer advice, also free of charge. Some government foresters offer services at a nominal charge or they may charge for work that requires more than one day to complete. Check the white pages of your phone directory under the county and state listings to find the local government forester. If none are listed, ask the county agricultural extension agency for advice.

Consulting foresters are independent professionals, who must be licensed in some states. They can be contacted through the yellow pages, but it's better to check with the local government forester. Consultation fees vary, so discuss price before hiring a forester. Local foresters should also have information about tax advantages offered by some states to encourage woodlot management. Vermont's program, for example, reduces by 80% the taxes on our woodlot.

The tools described in this article, if unavailable locally, can be ordered from the following suppliers: Forestry Suppliers Inc., 205 Rankin St., P.O. Box 8397, Jackson, Miss. 39204; Ben Meadows Co., 3589 Broad St., Atlanta, Ga. 30366, and T.S.I., P.O. Box 151, 25 Ironia Rd., Flanders, N.J. 07836.

The American Forestry Association (1319 18th St. N.W., Washington, D.C. 20036) publishes a monthly magazine called *American Forests*. Useful books include: *Essentials of Forestry Practice* by Charles H. Stoddard, Ronald Press Co., New York, N.Y. and *Handbook for Eastern Timber Harvesting* (stock number 001-001-00443-0) by Fred C. Simmons, from the U.S. Government Printing Office, Washington, D.C. 20402. A booklet, *Woodlot Management*, is available from Garden Way Publishing, Charlotte, Vt. 05445.

Tree quality: the good, the bad and the firewood

It doesn't take a trained eye to spot a perfect sawlog: it rises arrow-straight and branchless for 15 ft. or 20 ft., large enough to yield clear boards and showing no signs of wounds, fungus or insect damage. Deciding which of the many less than ideal trees in the woodlot will yield good quality lumber and which to consign to the cordwood pile is more difficult. Here are a few tips to help you make these decisions as you thin and harvest your woodlot.

Crooks: An abrupt zig-zag in the trunk caused by the tree's changing growth direction as it seeks better light. Small crooks can be sawed but larger ones make handling the log difficult.

Curves and bows: Sweeping form in the trunk common in trees growing on hills. Curves occur, like crooks, because the tree wants better light. Trunks with curves usually contain reaction wood, which is difficult to saw, dry and use (see "Abnormal Wood," pp. 58-61).

Crook

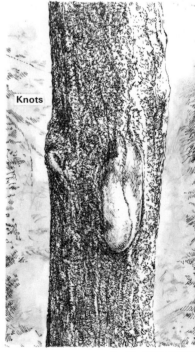

Knots

Drawings: Christopher Clapp

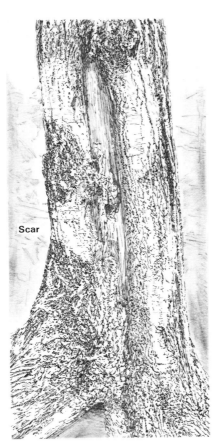

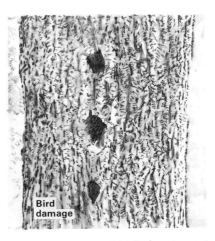

Knots: A common feature in nearly all logs, knots occur where branches grow out of the trunk. If the branch is alive when the tree is cut, the knot will probably be sound. If the branch is dead, particularly if it is large, the knot in the finished lumber may be loose.

Stem forks: Two stems on one trunk occur when the "leader" stem dies or stops growing. A second stem then forms and becomes the new leader. Stems that occur very low on the trunk reduce the lumber value of the logs.

Major dead branches: These occur when a tree is under stress and near death. If there are no good reasons to leave the tree standing, it should be removed for lumber or firewood.

Scars: Called "catfaces," scars are the signs of damage caused by fire or by previous logging operations. The wounds go through the bark to bare wood. If the tree survives, the wood above and below the scars may be sound.

Dead crowns: A healthy crown tops a healthy tree and those with dead or skeletal crowns are usually under stress. When the leaves have fallen check the crown's major branches for smaller branches; if these are numerous, the crown is probably healthy.

Cracks: Vertical cracks or seams caused by extremely cold weather or lightning can be several feet long and ¼ in. or so wide. The cracks heal over on the surface, but they can ruin a good log.

Insect and bird damage: Worm holes and loose bark can indicate significant insect damage. Bird damage is more apparent and sometimes the two are related because some birds feed on insects infesting trees.

Epicormic branching: Previously shaded trunks exposed to sunlight can grow small branches which cause minute blemishes in lumber cut from the logs. Care should be taken when thinning to keep trunks of potential sawlog trees at least partially shaded.

Overmature trees: Old trees with large, short trunks and heavy upper branches are often survivors from when the forest was an open field. Their lumber value is low but they do serve as wildlife shelters and are sometimes left standing for that reason alone.

Wind or ring shakes: Shakes are rarely detectable by reading a tree's bark but they will turn up as a defect in the lumber. They are caused by wind-created mechanical stresses that separate the tree's annual rings. —*I.P., D.P.*

Wind shakes in a maple log.

Mounted on the side of the diesel power unit is the mill's 4-cylinder starting engine, itself started by pull rope. On the conveyor is the dog board from a 12-ft. walnut log. Deck at feed end (inset) can hold 10,000 ft. of timber, enough to keep two men busy for several days.

Sawmilling
How one small mill works

by Dwight G. Gorrell

My father Gordon and I operate our own sawmill on our farm outside of Centerville, Kansas. I've been sawyer on this mill for over ten years, sawing logs harvested from our own stands. Most people don't think of Kansas as having trees, but eastern Kansas is about 40% woodland, with sycamore, cottonwood, ash and walnut predominating, along with hackberry, oak and our native evergreen, aromatic red cedar. The reward of having your own sawmill is that you can use timber that usually just gets wasted. Since 1963 when we first got the mill running, we have sawed mainly damaged, culled and thinned trees, having more than enough lumber for our shop and some specialty sales, all the while improving the timber stands on our land.

Our sawmill is located on a gentle slope, which makes it easy to roll logs toward it and provides good drainage. It's different from other mills mainly because we built several of its

major components from scrap iron and parts from highway vehicles and old farm machinery. We bought the blade, mandrel bearings and pulley, husk, dogs, setworks, headblocks, sawguides and part of the feedworks from an old sawyer. For the rest we learned to be make-do millwrights. Foresters and millwrights who have seen our mill tell us it compares well with others. When well tuned it does an excellent job.

The forerunner of the sawmill is the pit saw, powered by human muscle. The first true sawmill in the United States was the sash or up-and-down saw, powered by waterwheel. Then came steam power and the circular saw. Band headsaws next appeared, and at some large mills today double-cut band headsaws, with teeth on both edges of the blade, have increased production. Portable sawmills, both circular-headsaw-carriage and chain-saw types, are also available and useful where transporting logs is a problem.

Photos: Staff; Illustrations: Christopher Clapp

We use a single, circular headsaw, a 52-in. 8-gauge (⁵⁄₃₂-in.), 38-tooth, right-hand blade hammered for 600 RPM. The power unit is a Waukesha Hesselman multi-fuel spark diesel engine, 6 cylinders with 7-in. bore and 8½-in. stroke, whose governed speed is 950 RPM, loaded. It has a 4-cylinder starting engine. The carriage is 18 ft. long and has two movable headblocks, one movable bolster, and a stationary tail bolster with dog. A plate-feedworks provides variable speed, forward and reverse.

The saw will clean a 23-in. cant face, and we have sawed stock 25 ft. long, but it is rather difficult. We don't like to saw logs larger than 33 in. in diameter. Some sawmills have a smaller circular blade, positioned in the same plane above and slightly ahead of the headsaw. This topsaw is activated by a clutch and is used when the headsaw will not reach through a log. To square up a large log on our mill, however, we have to saw with the saw buried, which necessitates slow carriage speed and caution. A chain saw finishes the cut.

Except for an electric winch to turn large logs, we do all turning by hand. Small logs may be turned on the carriage against the knees, but large cants must be turned on the deck by rolling them off the carriage onto the face most recently cut, then sliding them back onto the carriage. This prevents damaging the headblocks and carriage.

Two men can get along quite well on a mill like ours. The sawyer and off-bearer (tail sawyer) are busy all the time, but under ideal conditions can saw several thousand board feet in a day. The sawyer makes decisions concerning actual sawing of logs, turns (or helps turn) the cant, controls carriage speed and direction, and operates setworks and dogs. Removing slabs and lumber, and helping to turn cants are the major responsibilities of the off-bearer.

In most large sawmills, the functions of dogging, setting and turning are automated. In older mills, before these jobs gave way to mechanization, they were done by men. One of them, called the setterman (setter), was responsible for operating the setworks. The setterman usually rode right on the carriage with the log, taking directions from the head sawyer through a system of hand and finger signals. Noise levels and distance made oral communication impractical. This sawmill sign language enabled the setterman and sawyer to make lumber and sawdust all day long without speaking a single word to each other.

Sawmilling actually begins in the timber. Trees must be properly felled to avoid splitting. When the trees are cut and bucked into logs, they should be cleaned as much as possible. Limbs, protruding knots, slivers, etc., should be removed flush with the surface of the log. Each end of the log should be a single, flat surface, cut square across. If the log has a large butt, this should be reduced. Final cleanup can be done at the mill, but it adds to the waste-disposal problem, which can be considerable because in mills like ours, bark, slab and sawdust are not burned for power. We do burn as firewood what waste we can, and bed livestock with the sawdust.

We avoid skidding logs through mud, gravel or rocks. These materials become embedded in the bark and wreak

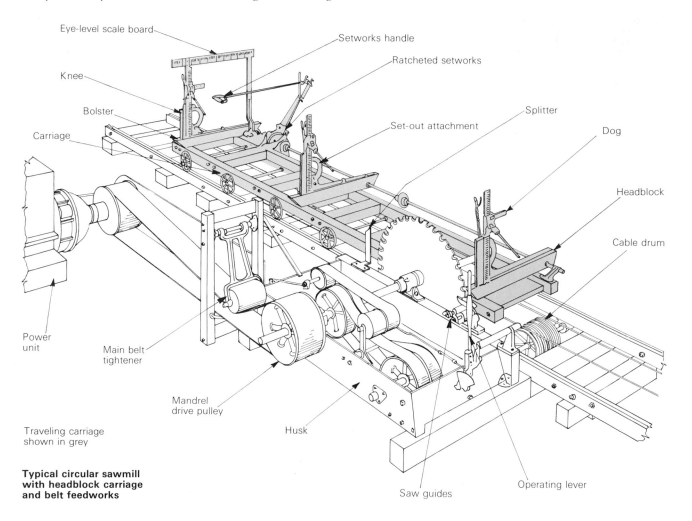

Typical circular sawmill with headblock carriage and belt feedworks

Glossary of terms

Bolster—Base of headblock on which log rests.
Buck—To cut log into shorter lengths.
Butt—Log end that grew nearest stump.
Cant—Log that has been slabbed on one or more sides.
Carriage—Movable frame plus headblocks and setworks that carries logs into sawblade.
Deck—Holding platform for logs before they go onto carriage.
Dog—Adjustable device for holding log firmly onto carriage.
Dog board—Last board in the cant, which dogs bit into.
Feedworks—Mechanism that moves carriage past headsaw, consisting of drive train and clutch.
Flitch—Lengthwise slice of log with wane.
Gig—To run carriage back after cut.
Gullet—Open space or cavity between two adjacent sawteeth.
Gumming—The deepening of the gullet, usually by grinding, to lengthen sawteeth that have been shortened by repeated sharpenings. Only solid-tooth, not inserted-tooth, blades require gumming.
Headblock—Upper part of carriage, consisting of bolster and knees.
Headsaw—Main or primary saw.
Holder (shank)—Holds sawtooth in recess of inserted-tooth blade.
Husk—Frame that supports mandrel and other working parts of sawmill.
Jointing—Bringing points of teeth on a circular saw into the same cutting circle.
Knee—Vertical extension of headblock that supports outside of log or cant; with setworks, it moves stock into sawline.

Lead—Slight misalignment of saw plate and carriage to keep cant away from trailing edge of blade.
Leveling—Hammering of saw plate to remove high spots and kinks when tensioning.
Mandrel (arbor)—Shaft that sawblade is mounted on.
Saw guides—Two wooden pins positioned one on each side of blade, ½ in. behind gullet, to restrain saw from being forced off line.
Sawing on the shares—Form of custom sawing in which the sawmiller keeps a share of the lumber as payment.
Setworks—Ratcheted mechanism that moves log out into sawline and regulates thickness of cut.
Slab—Outside chunk that comes off log when squaring up; there can be four slab cuts.
Slash—Parts of a tree remaining after log has been cut out (limbs and tops).
Splitter—Bladelike bar at trailing edge of blade to open kerf and keep boards and pieces away from saw.
Swage—*n*, Die or stamp for shaping metal by hammering; *v*, To spread the tips of sawteeth and provide clearance in the cut.
Tensioning—Creating internal stress in a sawblade by hammering.
Topsaw—Auxiliary saw that permits wider logs to be sawed.
Turning—Rotating log on its long axis for further sawing.
Wane—Bark or lack of wood at edges of a piece of stock.
Wind shake—Separation of annual rings within a tree, caused by twisting force of winds. (Wind is the largest single cause of timber damage in our area.)

---

havoc on the headsaw. One of the advantages of a mill pond, which unfortunately we do not have, is that logs may be floated. This not only makes work easier and soaks off dirt, but prevents checking and worm and insect infestation too.

Trees should be inspected for obvious signs of hardware, which is the bane of the sawmiller. It's a good plan to mark logs that come out of fence rows, yards and other localities where hardware can have grown into the tree. Even so, wire, nails, insulators, rocks, gate latches and once in a while Indian arrowheads find themselves in the path of the headsaw. We commonly hit bullets, but the nonjacketed ones don't cause any damage. When we hit hardware, we shut down, swage and file the damaged teeth (or replace them), cut or pull the hardware out of the log, and then it's back to work. We have a system that reduces the incidence of such delays. We yard all logs suspected of containing hardware—a metal detector helps in the determination—and saw these logs when the teeth are well used. It saves damaging new teeth.

Another hazard is wind-shaken logs and logs that have internal stress (reaction wood). They're not much good for lumber anyway. It is difficult to determine the extent of wind shake until after the log has been opened up on the mill. Logs with reaction wood, such as hackberry, will warp and twist while being sawed. In extreme cases, it is not worthwhile to finish sawing the log—and it can be dangerous.

Knowing where to buck a crooked or a severely tapered tree comes from experience and common sense. Species of wood,

size of logs and handling equipment determine whether logs are transported tree-length or bucked to their final length at the stump. The less cutting is done in the woods, the fewer pieces there are to handle and the more footage can be hauled per load. Smaller trees are usually easier to measure and buck in the mill yard or even on the deck than in a slash pile.

With the log on the deck, butt toward the front, we make a final cleanup, removing mud, gravel and loose bark with a garden hoe. Then we roll the log onto the carriage.

The opening face of a log affects the grade, grain pattern and yield of stock. Sawing for a particular grain pattern requires the opening face to be oriented just right, especially for crotch cuts. Knowing where to make the BOF (best opening face) requires observation, experience and luck. The two objectives of a sawyer are to obtain maximum-grade lumber and good volume production per hour. The principal objective in specialty sawing is to achieve maximum exposure of desirable figure, which militates against sawing for volume. It is not possible to succeed by any one method. Either the frequent turning required to recover the maximum-grade values reduces volume, or the minimum turning necessary to get high production sacrifices grade. Turning procedure must be varied in accordance with log qualities, sizes and headsaw capacity. In specialty sawing, each log must be sawed on an individual basis. During a typical day of sawing, a sawyer makes many quick, irreversible decisions.

Having decided on the opening face, the front dog is set and the log moved over into the sawline by the setworks, a ratcheted crank at the front of the carriage. If the log is appreciably tapered, I set out the small end so that a uniform face can be cut from end to end. Because our headblocks do not have set-out attachments, I block out with a wooden wedge between knee and log, and then set the tail dog. I'm now ready to feed the carriage past the saw for the first cut.

Dog bites log.

The feedworks of our mill deserves some explanation; it is unlike any other I have seen. It consists of a drive plate on a horizontal axis in contact with a friction wheel on a vertical axis. Plate and wheel are controlled by two levers: The right moves the drive plate to and fro; the left moves the friction wheel up and down. Together, through a system of cables and pulleys, they control both the speed and direction of the carriage. To move the carriage forward for the cut, the right-hand lever is pushed to the left. This moves the drive plate into contact with the friction wheel, gradually, much like the clutch of a car engages. To increase the speed of the carriage, the left-hand lever is pushed down, which raises the friction wheel on the drive plate, increasing the circumference in contact, and thus the speed. To reverse carriage direction, the right-hand lever is eased back, and the left-hand lever is raised. This lowers the friction wheel below center, where the drive plate rotates it in the opposite direction. The higher the handle (or the lower), the closer to the edge of the drive plate is the friction wheel, and the faster it moves. At any point, up or down, the drive plate can be withdrawn from contact with

The plate-feedworks, above, is the ideal transmission. Right-hand lever moves feed plate in and out to start and stop carriage; left-hand lever moves friction wheel up and down to control carriage speed and direction.

Sawyer and off-bearer are a team. Here board is held away from contact with trailing edge of blade and pulled down as carriage is gigged.

the friction wheel, thus stopping the carriage. The beauty of this arrangement is in the subtle control of speed and direction it affords. It gives me the control to slow up as I see a knot approaching the blade, and to back off if the blade begins to hog into or dodge out of the log. By controlling the load on the saw I can maintain optimum blade speed, critical for clean sawing and long blade life.

Sawing is a matter of attending with all your senses. I watch the teeth as they enter the log, wary for any deviation from the sawline. I listen to the blade. When it's cutting well, it's quiet; if it grows loud, something's wrong: the teeth are dull, the saw guides not properly set, the tension off or the speed wrong. And the two feedworks levers, whose solid brass handles warm to brilliance after a day's sawing, are my connection with the mill.

With the opening cut made, the carriage is gigged, the cant turned, the face positioned on the bottom side, resting squarely on the bolsters, and the same procedure makes the second cut, blocking out if necessary. Cuts one and two are the only cuts that can be blocked out. Most of the time I square the cant on all four sides before sawing it, taking just enough off each face to give a flat surface so the cant will rest firmly on all bolsters. By opening all four faces on the cant, I can choose the high and low-grade faces and saw accordingly.

With the cant squared up, it is now ready to be sawed into boards. Pulling the handle on the setworks moves the log across the sawline a regulated distance. This distance, minus the kerf, equals the thickness of stock that will be ripped off. Shrinkage rates of green material must be considered when sawing within close tolerances; no sawmill produces lumber without some variation among boards.

There are a few general principles that can be applied when sawing logs. Highest lumber grades (clearest boards) are most often found immediately under the bark. The procedure for grade-sawing lumber should be first to take high-grade material from the better faces by taper sawing (sawing parallel to the bark) and then to turn to a different face as the grade drops below that offered by adjoining faces. Low-grade faces can be sawed by the most convenient method. Knots should be near the center of a board instead of along the edge and cut across rather than with their grain—round knots are better than spike knots. Thin stock should be taken from the outside of the log, while larger pieces should be taken from near the center. Sawing around the log, or "boxing the heart," produces a single, large timber containing the pith of the log in its center. Production sawing requires that a sawyer be familiar with the lumber grades and grading methods established by the various lumber inspection associations.

After sawing, the headsaw edges flitches and rips wide boards. Stack the flitches onto the carriage with bark edges clearing sawline. Make the cut, gig the carriage, turn the flitches over, placing sawed edges against knees, and saw off the other bark edge. To rip boards, measure over from the best edge at leading end and mark. Line up saw and cut.

Sawmilling like this involves lots of hard work, but I never tire of watching that big blade make cut after cut. It's a pleasure to see and hear a well-tuned saw whisper through a log, and to savor the aroma of freshly sawed wood. The thrill and anticipation of what the next cut will bring is even greater when visions of fine furniture that the log could be crafted into fill my mind.

Sawmill technology — The nucleus of any sawmill is the headsaw itself. Like any woodworking tool, in order to perform well, it should be understood, used properly and maintained. Headsaws are designed to do a specific job under widely varying conditions, including hardness of wood, size of logs, knots, pitch or sap content, grain variation, feed rate, ambient air temperature and angle of tooth attack through the log. Blade diameters range from 32 in. to 72 in., with 48 in. to 52 in. most common. Blade gauge, the thickness of the blade at the rim, ranges on the Birmingham scale from 10 (⅛ in.) on thinner saws to 5 (⁷⁄₃₂ in.) on heavy blades, common gauges being 7, 8 and 9. Most sawmill blades are thicker at the center than at the rim by one or more gauges.

Teeth are almost exclusively the swage-set, inserted type;

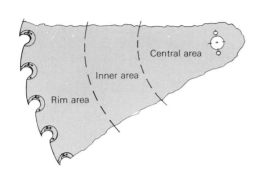

The three areas of a saw plate.
Detail shows parts of an inserted sawtooth.

Central area

Inner area

Rim area

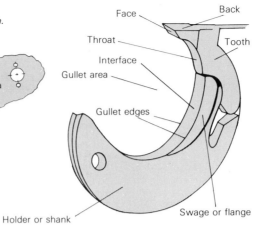

Face

Back

Throat

Tooth

Interface

Gullet area

Gullet edges

Swage or flange

Holder or shank

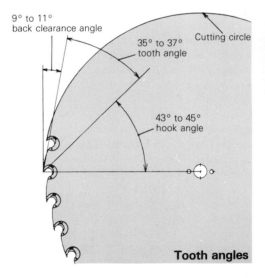

Tooth wrench (left) removes and installs teeth and holders. Swage (above) has two slots: convex-faced for forming points and flat-faced for shaping cutting edge. It is struck (right) with short, sharp blows.

After swaging, sharpen the tooth by first dressing the sides with a bastard file supported by the plate (left). Then file straight across the face of the tooth (above) at the correct angle (right). One light stroke on the back of the tooth removes any burr.

9° to 11°
back clearance angle

35° to 37°
tooth angle

Cutting circle

43° to 45°
hook angle

Tooth angles

hardly any spring-set or solid-tooth blades are used anymore. Carbide-tipped teeth are available for inserted-tooth blades. Special tooth styles are made for sawing frozen timber. The parts of an inserted-tooth blade include the plate, the teeth (bits) and the holders (shanks). The plate is a large, circular piece of high-grade steel, at the center of which is the mandrel (arbor) hole, or eye, usually flanked by two smaller holes for lug pins to keep the mandrel from slipping in the saw. At the periphery of the plate are circular recesses (sockets) to accept the teeth and holders. A *V*-groove in the outer edge of the holder fits over a way in each socket on the plate. Com-

pression of the holder against the socket keeps the tooth and holder tightly in place. The most obvious advantage of an inserted-tooth blade is that, as teeth become worn-out or damaged, they can easily be replaced. Also, this type of blade does not require gumming or jointing. There are several styles of teeth for headsaws and the number of teeth in blades of the same diameter may vary considerably.

Proper maintenance of the headsaw is by far the most important single task involved in efficient sawmill operation. Maintaining the saw includes keeping a close check on the condition of the plate and keeping the teeth sharp and in shape. Sawteeth should be sharpened correctly at least once a day or more often as necessary. When sawing large, dry hardwood, it is not unusual to sharpen up after each log. When a saw does not cut easily, it is usually dull or has lost its swage or set. Experienced sawyers can tell when the saw is getting dull by the sound it makes.

There is nothing really difficult about swaging and sharpening the teeth. As sawteeth wear or become damaged, they need swaging to restore the cutting edge to its original width. Swaging is spreading the point of a tooth to provide clearance for the saw plate while in the kerf. There are two types of swages available, the lever type (rolling swage) and the upset swage (hammer swage); the upset swage is the handier. In the working end of the upset swage there are two slots (dies). One slot has convex faces: It forms the tooth points; the other slot has flat faces: It shapes the cutting edge. The swage is struck with short, sharp blows using a 1-lb. hammer. It is recommended that the tooth first be shaped with a file, which is okay for routine swaging, but for reshaping a tooth that has hit hardware, it is not practical.

When the tooth is properly swaged, it is ready to be filed. Use an 8-in. mill bastard file with two round edges, and dress the sides to bring each tooth down to its final cutting width. This is done by allowing the point of the file to ride lightly on the saw plate while filing the corners of the tooth. File both corners evenly until the cutting edge of the tooth is the correct width and centered with the plate. You can make a small gauge to check finished tooth angles and dimensions, or use a new tooth for comparison.

The cutting edge is now ready to be sharpened. This is accomplished by filing the face of the bit in a single plane, parallel to the original face. Grasp the file securely, gripping the tang with one hand and the point with the other. To keep it from chattering, steady the sawblade by pressing against it with your body. Push the file full length straight from the shoulder without dropping your elbows. The file should move straight across the tooth. Avoid notching the throat. (This is the reason for using a file with round edges.) Keep the throat rounded as the tooth is sharpened back. Do not try to sharpen a tooth by filing on the back of it. It is important to keep the cutting edges of the teeth as far from the center of the saw as possible. Sawteeth should be uniform in length so that cutting edges travel in the same cutting circle. After side dressing and sharpening, a light stroke on the back of the tooth will remove the burr.

Holders require maintenance also. Besides holding teeth in place, they trap and remove sawdust from the cut. They are manufactured with a flange, or swage, about 1½ to 2 gauges thicker than the saw plate to reduce the amount of sawdust slipping out of the gullet and to reduce contact with the wood. Holders with worn flanges and rounded edges will allow sawdust to leak out of the gullet, which hastens wear on the gullet edges and saw plate, and causes the rim area to heat. Holders with rounded edges but in otherwise good condition can be restored to their original condition by sharpening straight across the interface. Loose holders can be tightened by peening, but it is best to replace badly worn or loose holders with new ones. They are removed and installed using a special inserting (tooth) wrench. Holes in the shank allow pins in the tooth wrench to engage the shank and the shank is rotated into or out of the socket.

Sawmill blades are not symmetrical in section, but crowned on one side. Thus blades are identified as right or left-hand to indicate on which side the log runs. The shape allows for a thicker center section to sustain the high torque of the mandrel, and a flat face to run on the log side. But to maintain this flat face at operating speed, a sawblade must be properly tensioned. The inner area between the center and the rim must be hammered into concavity, prestretched or made to "fall away" from plane to compensate for the centrifugal force and friction-caused heat at the tooth zone that expands the rim more than the adjacent inner metal. If the stress in these two areas is not equal at operating speed, the saw tends to buckle and weave and will neither stand up straight nor cut a straight line. But the tension of a properly maintained sawblade can remain correct for years. The secret is in keeping the teeth sharp. Dull teeth and worn holders cause the blade to heat up, warp and lose tension. But these problems can produce the symptoms of lost tension before tension is actually lost. Only after checking all mill adjustments and making sure that teeth are properly shaped and sharpened and that holders are not defective can it be assumed that a blade that continues to cut unevenly is in need of retensioning. Specialists must attend to tensioning along with leveling (the hammering free of high spots, kinks or twists)—most mills do not retension their own blades.

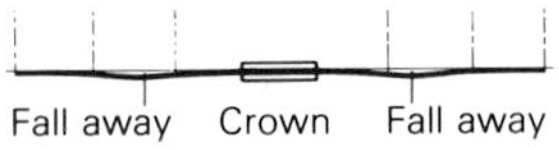

Cross section of a sawmill blade: Fall away varies from 1/75 in. to 1/12 in., depending on diameter, gauge, saw speed, number of teeth, kind of wood sawed, horsepower available, carriage speed.

When mounted on the sawmill mandrel, the blade needs to be plumb and have the correct amount of "lead" before it will operate satisfactorily. Lead refers to the slightly nonparallel alignment of the guide track and saw plate, the leading edge of the headsaw being slightly closer to the carriage than the trailing edge. Lead counteracts the natural tendency for the saw to run out of the log, especially on the slab cut, and also provides clearance for the trailing edge of the saw, preventing contact with the cant while sawing. Standard lead for most headsaws is 1/32 in. to 1/16 in. Lead is adjusted by shifting the mandrel bearings and should not be forced into the saw by sharpening the teeth with a high side or by adjusting the saw guide to one side.

Saw speed and carriage speed must be in the proper relationship for a mill to operate correctly; this is largely a matter of seeing and hearing and feeling what the saw is doing. For each sawmill blade there is an optimum speed, which should be maintained while in the cut, regardless of variable sawing conditions encountered. A common speed for headsaws is 600 RPM (8,000 ft. to 9,000 ft. per minute at the rim). Carriage speed, on the other hand, varies from log to log, depending upon the hardness of the wood and cant-face width. A faster carriage speed can be used to saw a small basswood log, for example, than can be used for a large burr oak.

Bite is the distance the log or cant advances into the saw between successive teeth. Interaction of the saw speed and carriage speed determines the bite. In order to calculate horsepower requirements for sawmills, bite must have an established value. Sawtooth manufacturers have advocated standardizing a bite of 1/8 in. for softwoods and 1/10 in. for hardwoods. A standard bite value of 1/9 (.11) in., halfway between, has been adopted by some people. Under actual sawing conditions bite fluctuates, but good saw performance requires that bite be held as nearly as possible between 1/8 in. and

¹⁄₁₀ in. Maintaining the standard bite of .11 in. with a 40-tooth blade at 600 RPM, it should take approximately four seconds to produce a 12-ft. flitch.

It is important to have plenty of steady, dependable power to turn the headsaw. Because sawmill blades are tensioned to turn at a constant speed, the speed of the power unit should be fairly constant under widely fluctuating loads, producing high torque at low shaft speeds. Large-bore, long-stroke, industrial diesel engines and large electric motors make ideal power units for sawmills. A few mills still use steam engines. As late as 1904, 10% of U.S. sawmills were powered by waterwheels, some reaching the colossal diameter of 35 ft. Some mills produced as much as 20,000 board feet per day using water power.

Dealing with a sawmill — Buying lumber directly from a sawmill can be quite different from preconceived notions that woodworkers may have. Unawareness on the part of the buyer as to what is involved in logging and lumbering, or in producing a specialty product, often causes misunderstanding, especially in pricing. By examining what brings a board from the stump to the consumer, the woodworker can better appreciate the wood and how its price is arrived at.

Availability and desirability determine lumber pricing. Mill-run lumber is usually less expensive than lumber the buyer picks through and selects. When we do specialty sawing, each piece is evaluated and priced individually. Width of stock is probably the single most important factor, followed closely by species, unusual figure or grain, then thickness, length and dryness. Customers who want a certain size piece of a particular species are often unable to find what they need. Their next thought is to have it sawed out. Most of the time this can be done, but having a large, special piece cut out of a log can be expensive because it often requires sacrificing the rest of the log.

An example of a sawmill product that is quite special, largely because of the species that it is cut from, is the osage orange bow stave, from which the English long bow is made. Because the osage orange tree is short and bushy, it is difficult to find a tree that will produce any staves at all. Staves, which are about 1½ in. square by 6 ft. long, must have straight grain and no defects. Some bowyers even specify the desired curvature and orientation of the annual rings in each stave. Even from a good tree, most potential staves are rejected because of the exacting requirements of the bowyer.

We used to do custom sawing, sawing logs to the owner's specifications. There are two ways that a sawyer can charge on a custom-sawing job: by the board foot or by an hourly rate. Determining which payment method to use is the privilege of the sawyer, because he judges if the logs are good, poor, large or small. When charged by the board foot, the customer pays according to the amount sawed. The content of irregularly shaped and waned pieces must be averaged. Usually, only those jobs that have good-quality, average-size logs are paid for by the board foot. If the logs are small, or of low yield, a sawmiller may charge on an hourly basis. It costs just as much to operate a sawmill for a small log as it does for a large one, though the yield is less. The same applies to sawing logs that are rotten, hollow, wind shaken or otherwise defective. Some people, upon finding out the log they brought in was not good, think they shouldn't have to pay for having the log sawed. The sawyer is forced to explain that it costs as much to saw a bad log as it does to saw a good one.

During our custom sawing days, it was not uncommon to have customers bring in logs with large, protruding knots, limb stubs that were too long, logs that were too crooked, logs that were too long for the amount of taper and logs with jagged or uneven ends. Whenever the sawmiller must do chainsawing or cleanup work on these logs, there is usually a cleanup fee added to the bill.

Some sawyers charge a flat fee for each piece of hardware or foreign material that is struck and causes damage to the saw teeth. This is to cover shut-down time of the mill and cost of repairs. If the logs have been skidded through mud or gravel, an additional charge may be assessed to compensate for the more frequently required saw sharpenings.

Once in a while, a wood enthusiast will come to our mill, bubbling with excitement about getting a big this-or-that kind of tree sawed into lumber. "It must be at least this big around!" he exclaims, gesturing to indicate a tree that would be much too large for our mill. Although there are ways to saw oversize logs, we have learned that most of the time it's not worth doing. It is time-consuming, wasteful and risky. Even though these monarchs contain unusual figure, they will often be defective—hollow, rotten in the center or shaken.

A sawmiller likes (as do most people) to be paid when the job is completed. Besides, fresh-sawed lumber should be properly stacked and stickered as promptly as possible.

We have done custom sawing "on the shares" and the lumber was divided according to who did what. Usually, if we cut the trees, loaded and hauled the logs and sawed the lumber, the owner received one quarter and we kept three quarters. If the owner cut the logs and hauled them to the mill, the lumber was divided half-and-half. Actual division of the lumber can be accomplished by separating it into four equivalent piles and allowing the tree owner first choice. This system has been used for a long time and seems to work well.

Once in a while, people will ask if they can help saw their logs or just help around the mill. Statistics show that sawmilling is a hazardous occupation. More than once, though not at our mill, an off-bearer has inadvertently placed a board in contact with the trailing edge of the headsaw, which promptly fired it through the mill-house wall like a giant arrow. Unless they are experienced, we strongly discourage people from helping around the mill. □

Loading walnut planks.

Dwight Gorrell and his father, Gordon, operate their home-built sawmill and a woodworking shop on the family farm near Centerville, Kansas.

The State of the Forests
Where our wood comes from and where it's going

by Eugene Wengert

An understanding of the prospects for this country's hard-wood use must begin with an inventory of its sawtimber. The United States has approximately 75% as much forest land today as when Columbus landed. This amounts to 737 million acres, or about one-third of the country's land area. Of this, about 255 million acres are used for parks, wilderness and recreation areas, or are unsuitable for growing commercial timber. On these non-commercial areas, equal to the combined land area of California, Oregon, Washington and most of Idaho, timber harvesting and in some cases even timber management is prohibited.

The remaining 482 million acres are our commercial forest land. This does not mean all the wood on it is available for commercial harvest; it means this land is capable of growing wood at the rate of at least 20 cubic feet per acre per year, and that the land hasn't been legally withdrawn from commercial use. The 482 million acres include golf courses, windbreaks around farm houses as well as slopes too steep to log. Only about half of our commercial forests are in production for timber. In all, they contain 2,569 billion board feet of sawtimber—softwood trees 9 in. in diameter or larger at breast height (dbh), and hardwood trees 11 in. dbh or larger. The geographical distribution is shown in figure 1.

Wood use—From our forests comes a wide range of products—paper, lumber, boards, chemicals, fuel etc. In 1977, the total U.S. consumption of wood products, including 10% that was imported, was 13.2 billion cu. ft., several billion cubic feet more than in the 1960s. Most of the growth has been in softwoods, and we're now cutting more softwood sawtimber than is growing to replace it (figure 2). Hardwood consumption has remained fairly constant since the late 1950s.

For convenience, wood use (both softwoods and hardwoods) can be divided into six product classes, as shown in figure 3. The raw material requirements of these products would seem not to be in conflict. Pulp and paper uses logging and mill residues for almost half of its material needs. The remainder can be logs of small diameter or logs otherwise unsuitable for sawmilling. Softwoods are preferred, as they make stronger paper. In the lumber category, profitable sawmilling of hardwoods requires straight logs 10 in. in diameter or larger; many softwood mills can profitably saw smaller logs. Wood fuel is primarily residue-based and does not require the larger logs suitable for sawing. Plywood demand is almost all softwood; logs should be straight and greater than 15 in. in diameter. Particleboard is residue-based, except waferboard, in order to keep the cost competitive with plywood and lumber alternatives. Most miscellaneous uses have special requirements; utility poles, for instance, must be 30 ft. long and at least 6 in. in diameter.

In reality, when figuring the impact of these various demands on the raw material supply, the overriding considera-

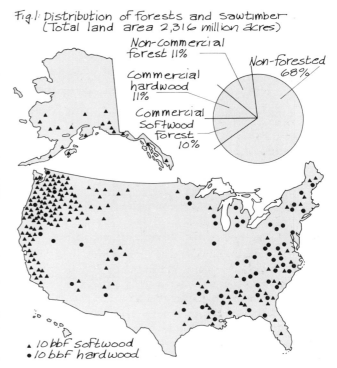

Fig. 1: Distribution of forests and sawtimber (Total land area 2,316 million acres)

Non-commercial forest 11%
Non-forested 68%
Commercial hardwood 11%
Commercial softwood forest 10%

▲ 10 bbf softwood
● 10 bbf hardwood

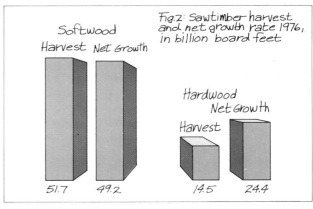

Fig. 2: Sawtimber harvest and net growth rate 1976, in billion board feet

Softwood
Harvest   Net Growth
51.7   49.2

Hardwood
Net Growth
Harvest
14.5   24.4

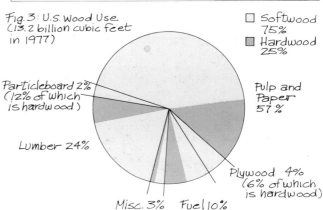

Fig. 3: U.S. Wood Use (13.2 billion cubic feet in 1977)

☐ Softwood 75%
■ Hardwood 25%

Particleboard 2% (12% of which is hardwood)
Lumber 24%
Pulp and Paper 57%
Plywood 4% (6% of which is hardwood)
Misc. 3%   Fuel 10%

Drawings: Claudia W. Underhill

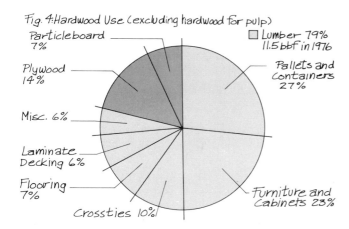

Fig. 4: Hardwood Use (excluding hardwood for pulp)

Particleboard 7%
Plywood 14%
Misc. 6%
Laminate Decking 6%
Flooring 7%
Crossties 10%

☐ Lumber 79%
11.5 bbf in 1976

Pallets and Containers 27%
Furniture and Cabinets 23%

Fig. 5: Only ¼ of the wood felled in the forest becomes lumber.

½ is left in the woods...

½ gets lost to edge trimming, end trimming and sawdust at the sawmills.

tion is the capital investment in the manufacturing facility. A multi-million dollar pulp, plywood or particleboard plant cannot afford to shut down for lack of raw materials. A small sawmill (and 90% of them are small) cannot compete, so timber that is best suited for lumber may, when supplies are short, get eaten in making other products.

Figure 4 shows how we use our hardwoods. (Exports, about 100 million bd. ft., much of it high-quality veneer logs, are not included). The largest portion goes to pallets and containers—almost 300 million wooden pallets, averaging 25 bd. ft. of lumber each, are made per year. Laminate decking, furniture and face and back veneers for plywood demand the best logs. However, because only about one-fourth of the lumber sawn from a good log is No. 1 Common and better, it is important that economic uses exist for smaller saw logs. Pallets and cross-ties are such products. With these two products potentially using three-fourths of the lumber from a log, it is common that a mill's entire production goes to them, with no sorting for the higher grades of lumber. Even high-yield logs are often sawn for low-value products, because it may be uneconomical for sawmill owners to do otherwise. The furniture and cabinet industries can try to combat this practice by paying more for high-grade lumber, or by learning to use low-grade lumber.

Future wood use—The amount of wood used in the U.S. will continue to increase during the next several decades with a doubling occurring before the year 2030. Much of the increase in supplies will come from hardwoods, as we are now cutting softwoods at a rate greater than their growth rate. U.S. Forest Service projections indicate a doubling of hardwood usage before 2010.

In addition to cutting more trees, improved use of the tree will provide more fiber. Presently, approximately one-half of the tree is left in the woods—some of that material could be sawn, some chipped and some used for fuel. Additionally, of the one-half of the tree that does go to the sawmill today, only one-half is converted to dry lumber (figure 5). Improved efficiency in milling will increase supplies. The same benefit is possible in the secondary processing plant when lumber is converted to cabinets or furniture.

With the many advantages of wood over other products (low energy to produce, environmentally clean, etc.), the future will bring increased demand for lumber, plywood and particleboard. Wood will be too valuable to burn at locations very far from the production sites, so wood-fuel use will decrease in total percentage. Likewise, the use of wood for pulp will show a slight percentage decrease in overall usage.

The big unknown in the future of wood is the potential for using wood for chemicals. Already, laboratory research has made animal feed, urethane-based chemicals, adhesives, gasoline and much more. When this breakdown of wood can be done economically, a tremendous new market will develop.

Regarding hardwoods specifically, increased mechanization in material handling promises increasing needs for wooden pallets and containers. The growth of this industry is tremendous, having doubled in less than 10 years. The production of furniture, cabinets and millwork will grow as the population matures and disposable income increases. The railroad beds in the U.S. are in need of extensive repair, so the demand for cross-ties is expected to increase. As the preferred species for both pallets and cross-ties is oak, there will be increasing pressure on furniture oak supplies, and it is likely that other species will be used more in furniture.

One unknown in predicting hardwood demand is the use of yellow poplar for construction lumber, which the U.S. Forest Service and others are seeking to develop. To be competitive with the pine 2x4, yellow-poplar construction lumber will be relatively inexpensive compared to furniture stock.

Robert Phelps, a chief economist in the U.S. Forest Service, sees a continuing loss of quality in our hardwood log supplies and, therefore, a decrease in the yield of higher grades of lumber per log. Although supplies of hardwoods seem plentiful, unless the forests are well managed, their quality will not be as high as possible. As improved management now will not benefit lumber production for at least two decades, the furniture and cabinet industries must, in the interim, learn to use a lower average grade of lumber.

Hardwood ownership—Who owns our hardwood timberlands is one of the critical considerations for the lumber producer because the owner determines whether the timber is available for harvest and to some degree the quality and growth of the timber. About three-fourths of the commercial hardwood forest land in the United States is classed as nonindustrial, private forest (NIPF), mainly in the eastern United States. Neither the wood-using industry nor government agencies control enough good hardwood acreage to have a large impact on future timber supplies. Therefore, in considering the present and the future of timber supply, it is necessary to look at the NIPF owners, four million of them.

The primary concern for a large (although unknown) number of NIPF owners is not the production of trees for harvest. They consider wildlife, recreation and other objectives to be more important, even though harvesting can be one of the most useful ways to realize other land-management objectives or benefits. They consider (erroneously, most of the time) that timber harvesting cannot complement these other objec-

From *Fine Woodworking* magazine (March 1981) 27:87-89

tives. In one survey in the East, 41% of the NIPF owners were consistently against harvest. In addition, the NIPF owner usually does not manage the forest for optimum or even good timber growth, thinning out diseased or poorly formed trees, for example. As a result, much of the NIPF is producing wood volumes and quality below the land's capacity.

Why is this picture so bleak? If there is one common reason, it is that managing land for timber is uneconomical. Thinning and other management is expensive, especially as most NIPFs are in small acreages. Taxes, including capital gains, are high. Hardwood timber returns are often not realized for 75 years. And hardwood stumpage prices are low. To add to the unattractiveness of this situation, the NIPF owner is being underpriced by the federal government: 40% of the timber sold off federal land on the board-foot basis (excluding pulp) has been priced below $80/mbf. More than 21% is sold at below-cost prices. The NIPF owner must pay for forest management, cost of roads, sale preparation, reforestation, and then taxes to support his competitor.

To ensure our future hardwood supplies, we had better be interested in the private-forest landowner and his problems; poor incentives to produce timber for harvest and poor knowledge of the benefits (economic, ecological, scenic and so on) of good management practices should be every hardwood user's concern. (For more, see *Timber Supply—Issues and Options* (Publ. No. P-79-24, Forest Products Research Society, 2801 Marshall Ct., Madison, Wis. 53705.)

Future hardwood ownership—The 1980 ownership pattern of private (75%), public (13%), and industry (12%) will change very little over the next decades. The most significant changes will be as follows:
—Increasing withdrawal of hardwood forests on public lands from commercial timber harvesting into wilderness and other "reserved" lands and resultant increased importance of NIPF.
—Increased incentives and benefits for better forest management on NIPF.
—Increased economic advantages (decreased capital-gains tax) in selling timber on NIPF.
—Increased dependence of the hardwood lumber users on the NIPF for their raw material.

Federal leadership should make reforestation of hardwood sites more attractive, ensuring wood supplies far into the 21st century. Improvements in harvesting will also make the economy of small-tract harvesting more attractive, as necessary to provide the quality and quantity of wood required for our growing needs.

Harvesting—There are many different techniques used to harvest our hardwood forests, from horse logging to helicopter logging, from very selective cutting to clear cutting, and from wasteful cutting to very wise cutting. The basic harvest procedures are determined by economics. Usually, it's more feasible to remove all the mature, salable trees at one time in a small patch than to cut only a few trees every several years. This patch cutting usually aids in reforestation. (In past years we have removed only the good trees in our hardwood forests, leaving the poorer trees to mature and produce seeds for genetically inferior trees in the future.) Also, it is common today that only the merchantable part of a tree (beginning at the decay-free butt and moving upwards in 4-ft. increments until just before a 6-in. diameter is reached) is removed from

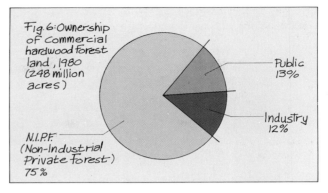

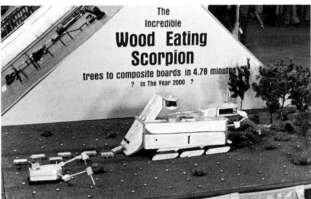

A part of the exhibit that accompanied Wengert's seminar on future hardwood use, this partly science-fiction monster incorporates extant technology in one unit to produce dry, defect-free, dimensioned composite boards from whole trees cut and swallowed at the front end. The smaller unit at left is busily replanting.

the woods and taken to the mill—about one-half of the tree is left in the woods (figure 5).

Present logging practices are, from a material standpoint, wasteful. From an economic standpoint, they are acceptable. A recent Forest Service (Princeton, W.Va.) study of a hardwood logging site found almost 70 tons of residue per acre, of which nearly one-quarter was sawable and three-quarters was chippable. If these residues can be used for fuel, pallets and particleboard (and maybe even furniture parts), this certainly will help the hardwood-supply picture.

Harvesting in the future will be more mechanized with more of the tree (more fiber) removed from the forest. The grapnel skidder will shear the tree close to the ground and carry it to the landing where large branches may be removed and perhaps some of the tops. These residues will be baled (like a hay bale) and then sold for fuel or other residue use. Merchandizing of the long, tree-length logs will take place at the mill. Clear cutting in small patches will continue.   □

Gene Wengert is professor of wood technology at Virginia Tech in Blacksburg, Va. This article is adapted from his contribution to a report, prepared with Mark White and Fred Lamb, that was presented in seminar at the Louisville furniture manufacturers' fair, September 1980. The report, entitled "The Lumber Complex of the Future," goes on to describe present-day sawmilling and lumber-processing techniques as compared with what they will probably be in the year 2000. It was published in summary form in installments through 1981 in the trade magazine, Furniture Design and Manufacturing *(400 N. Michigan Ave., Chicago, Ill. 60611).*

Logging with a Horse

by F. Jack Hurley

Big John and Rex Harral.

S kid logs with a horse? Nobody works with a horse anymore. Why would anyone want to? That pretty well sums up the attitude of most of us. Yet there are people who still use draft horses for a variety of chores including hauling timber. Not long ago I ran into an expert on the subject.

Rex Harral is a man of the country, born and raised in the foothills of the Arkansas Ozarks. He is slow of speech and deliberate in his movements. On first impression, he seems a romantic rustic, a figure from the past. Get to know him, however, and these preconceptions break down. In the first place, he is not a romantic at all; the term pragmatist would probably fit him better. In the second place, he is not particularly isolated, for he reads widely and voraciously, especially technical farming publications and craft journals. He is an effective small farmer who supplements his income by making and selling hardwood bowls and traditional furniture. He is also an excellent blacksmith whose woodcarving tools are recognized and sought after throughout the region for their beauty and edge-holding ability.

At sixty, Harral is well past the age when there would be any need to prove his toughness and endurance. His object is to get a job done with a minimum of fuss, so he does use a tractor for certain jobs. On the other hand, if a horse can do a job better, Rex will use a horse. He has always kept a few draft animals. They cost very little to keep, given the fact that pasture is available and that horses burn no gasoline.

Harral insists on using horse power for getting logs out of his woods, 100 acres of mixed pine and hardwood in north-central Arkansas. Harral bought the land nearly 40 years ago and has taken timber off it ever since. Depending on what was ready for the sawmill, and also on his reading of market conditions, Harral has sold from 2,000 to 6,000 bd. ft. of timber every year. This might not sound impressive to a Weyerhaeuser executive, but that timber has played a major role in paying for the land, and has often meant the difference between profit and loss at year's end. In addition, the woodlot has provided all the material for Harral's woodcraft and has heated his home for the past 37 years.

Today the woodlot is in beautiful condition. The trees have grown tall and straight. There is a good variety in size, with roughly 5% of the timber ready for the mill each year. By careful selection and thinning, Harral has made the land far more productive than it was in the early days.

He considers draft horses important in his timber management program. Why use a horse? The photo (far right) of a log being pulled by Harral's best timber snaker, a horse known as Big John, illustrates one reason. Properly hitched together, with the singletree pulling evenly on the tug lines from the horse's shoulders, draft animal and log are hardly more than 2 ft. wide. They move between the young trees, doing them minimal damage. There will be the occasional scuffed bark or bent sapling, but that is all. Contrast this with the tractor or, worse yet, Caterpillar. In either case the woods are likely to be left a tortured mess, carved and crosshatched with temporary roads. Harral's woodlot has only one road and it runs right through the middle. The trees are felled and limbed in place with a chain saw. When all the logs marked for harvest each year are down and ready, Big John drags the timbers out of the woods to gathering points along the road, to be picked up by the log trucks.

A second reason to use draft horses is safety. A good-sized saw log, improperly handled, can kill a man. Using long, cotton lines (roughly analogous to the riding horse's reins) Harral can walk well behind or to the side of the action while still maintaining excellent control of the horse. On a long pull where precise control is not necessary he may even drop the lines and simply control the horse by voice. Harral uses commands that go back to the dawn of western civilization. GiUp! or HiUp! gets the horse moving. Whoa! calls for a stop. Gee! means bear to the right, while Haw! moves the horse to the left. Obviously this sort of response requires training, but that's not as difficult as one might imagine. In fact, many people use large logs when training draft horses to pull. Most draft horses are not as nervous as riding horses, and a few days work with one person leading at the horse's head while another works the lines from behind will generally get things started. From there it is a matter of always accompanying the tug on the lines with the voice commands, until they come to mean the same thing to the horse.

Harral and Big John have worked together for 16 years, since the horse was two years old. Big John is still a strapping, healthy horse with probably a good six to eight years of work left. Man and horse are a well-coordinated team, their movements and interactions honed by practice. "Back up, John," Rex calls, and John immediately takes a couple of steps backward, loosening the tug lines so that the skidding tongs (bottom photo) can be set into a log. "HiUp," comes the command and the big horse moves off at a fast walk, a 10-ft. long, 22-in. log skidding easily behind him. With tugs on the lines accompanied by Gees! and Haws! they reach the logging road. When they get to the gathering point it's "Whoa, John, back up, John." The tongs are released and then man and animal disappear into the woods to repeat the process. No one is overworked. No one appears to be hurrying. Yet at the end of the day there are three or four truckloads of logs at the loading point.

This brings up the final point in defense of horsepower. According to Harral, working in the timber with a well-trained draft horse is actually easier—and more efficient—than working by yourself with a tractor or Caterpillar. "If I used one of those things, I'd be totally wore out with climbing on it to back up a few feet, then off to set the tongs, then back on to skid, then back off to release the tongs. I swear, I don't see how folks do it," he says. As it is, Harral and Big John are tired at the end of the day, but they are not exhausted, and if necessary they can both get up and go at it again tomorrow. ☐

F. Jack Hurley, woodworker and history professor, lives in Memphis, Tenn. For more about using horses to drag timber, see the quarterly magazine Draft Horse Journal *or the* Draft Horse Primer *by Maurice Telleen (hardcover). Both are available from* Draft Horse Journal, *Box 670, Waverly, Iowa 50677 (write for current prices).*

From *Fine Woodworking* magazine (September 1981) 30:98-99

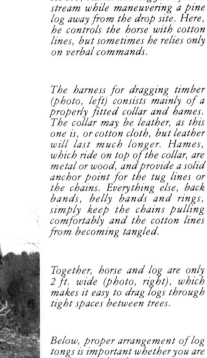

Above, Harral and Big John ford a stream while maneuvering a pine log away from the drop site. Here, he controls the horse with cotton lines, but sometimes he relies only on verbal commands.

The harness for dragging timber (photo, left) consists mainly of a properly fitted collar and hames. The collar may be leather, as this one is, or cotton cloth, but leather will last much longer. Hames, which ride on top of the collar, are metal or wood, and provide a solid anchor point for the tug lines or the chains. Everything else, back bands, belly bands and rings, simply keep the chains pulling comfortably and the cotton lines from becoming tangled.

Together, horse and log are only 2 ft. wide (photo, right), which makes it easy to drag logs through tight spaces between trees.

Below, proper arrangement of log tongs is important whether you are working with a horse or a tractor. The tongs must be placed far enough forward so that the hinge point of the tongs clears the front of the log and does not ride on top. Otherwise, the tongs will be damaged and the log will dig into the ground and not pull smoothly.

Dockside at Hamburg, a jumble of cranes, rigging and sheds, is one of many stops for exotic woods on their way to market.

The Trade in Exotic Hardwoods
How wood gets from the tropics to your shop

by Irving Sloane

History records that the demand for exotic hardwoods has always been brisk and, occasionally, voracious. The ebony forests of Mauritius were cut down by the Dutch in the 17th century, and West Indian mahogany (*Swietenia mahagoni*) was so heavily cut for Spanish shipbuilders and 18th-century furnituremakers that by the mid-19th century it had disappeared from commerce. A measure of the ancient esteem for rare woods is the name Brazil, taken from brazilwood (*Caesalpinia echinata*), an important item in the European trade of the Middle Ages, centuries before Brazil was discovered. Originally, brazilwood came from Sri Lanka, but it also grows in Brazil. It was used for dye extraction before being sought for violin bow making. It is more commonly known today as pernambuco.

Working with exotic woods—rosewood, ebony, boxwood—is one of the great pleasures of being a musical instrument maker. My search for such woods has led me and many other musical instrument makers to Theodor Nagel & Co., of Hamburg, West Germany. A family-owned firm established in 1837, Nagel is the world's foremost timber trader special-

izing in exotic hardwoods. An order for 200,000 ebony fretboards is not unusual, but neither is an order for just one.

Home base for Nagel is a ten-acre tract in the industrial Billbrook section of Hamburg. The firm's timber-sawing and grading operations, dry-kilns and storage sheds spread along both sides of the Billstrasse, the district's main road. Here trucks deposit logs and square-edged timbers from all over the world, brought from dockside at the ports of Hamburg and Bremen. The wood is resawn into boards, and custom-sized billets or scantlings for grading, the ends are waxed to retard checking, and finally it is shipped. Nagel employs almost 100 people here in Hamburg and another 500 world-wide, with sawmills in Brazil, Indonesia, India, Sri Lanka, Africa, Mexico, the United States and Austria. Their Indian sawmills in Kerala and Mysore cut and shape rosewood and ebony into parts for violins and guitars. The firm's customers include the world's major manufacturers of guitars, pianos, organs, harpsichords, violins and woodwinds. Nagel also supplies furniture manufacturers in Europe and Scandinavia.

The export manager in charge of sales to the musical in-

From *Fine Woodworking* magazine (January 1983) 38:78-81

strument trade is Peter Wiese, a wiry, intense native of Hamburg with almost 30 years of experience in the timber business. Buying and selling rare woods in the international market requires shrewd judgments about world supply and demand, a profound knowledge of these woods and large amounts of capital. Wiese works hard at his job—buying wood and seeing customers—all the while preoccupied with shipping costs, fluctuating exchange rates, and customers trying to preserve liquidity by shrinking their wood inventories. His sales domain is the world except for France, Scandinavia and the Iron Curtain countries. At 7:15 each morning he is in his office, reading telexes from distant places. He is a born trader, forthright and voluble.

"It's tough today, and very competitive," Wiese says. "We're buying and selling a product which is gradually growing scarcer in a world market where economic conditions are changing every day." He explains that dealers used to ship logs to Europe for sawing, but in recent years many developing countries have embargoed the shipment of logs. In such countries as India, Sri Lanka and Brazil, logs must be sawn into dimensioned lumber before export, the idea being to create local jobs. This trend has changed the import business. "Some of our big saws here are closed down," Wiese says, "although we still handle many logs from Africa, Burma and North America. But today you cannot export a board from Brazil thicker than three inches."

This saddens Wiese; cutting open a log felled in some wilderness outpost and freighted halfway around the world is part of the romance of the timber trade.

The stiffest competition Nagel faces these days comes from the ubiquitous Japanese. Their buyers will spend as long as three months in one area buying wood. Nagel, though, requires buyers to return home after a maximum of three weeks—by which time a buyer's aggressiveness, sharpness and resistance to bad deals will start wearing down. Life at the company's tropical sawmills is difficult, Wiese says. "Often we send a person out, and after a few months he starts going bush. His attitudes change, he sleeps late, he drinks, and when he comes home to report we can see that he is changed. It's definitely not for people who are upset by insects and lizards. I myself have been sick twice with malaria."

Still, Wiese declares, "I am a timber man. Timber is a business you have to have a certain feeling for—a gift, you might say. I wouldn't trade my job for any other."

Wiese joined Nagel in 1960. His first overseas assignment was to comb the backwoods of Florida, Georgia and the Carolinas to find hickory logs for European ski makers. It was a hard lesson in how money can be lost in the timber business: "Finally I had accumulated a load dockside in Jacksonville for shipment to Hamburg. That same day the Teamsters went on strike and nobody would move my logs. Day by day I watched them split under that baking sun, and I had to get rid of them for half their value."

He chuckles over the memory while leading me into the yard, a complex of sheds dominated by a large kiln. A corner of one shed is used as a sales display for offcuts of a variety of rare woods. These are stacked on shelves and sold by weight to craftspeople for a nominal price.

We pause in front of one of many big storage sheds piled high with logs: "That balsa lumber from Ecuador and Venezuela will go to the model-making trade. The teak will go mainly for furniture and flooring. This is lignum vitae from Mexico and Central America, one of the heaviest woods." Lignum (*Guaiacum spp.*) contains a natural lubricating oil, guyacan, which makes it suitable for lining ship propeller shaft tubes and for other mechanical applications. The lignum logs are short, 3 ft. to 4 ft., with yellow sapwood and greenish heart. I suggest that this species is also used for the soles of fine wooden planes, but Wiese says no, that's vera wood (*Bulnesia arborea*) from South America. It's not as oily as lignum and a bit lighter in color, but it has the same hardness and weight.

Wiese feels strongly that woods should be sold by their correct names so people know exactly what they are buying. "There are many close substitutes for different woods. Take mahogany—even experts are at a loss sometimes to explain what can be considered a genuine—*Swietenia*—mahogany. Another example is rosewood. The Brazilians call rosewood—*Dalbergia nigra*—jacaranda. The English cutlery makers call it Bahia wood. In India, rosewood—*Dalbergia latifolia*—is called palisander. In Germany it is known by both names regardless of where it comes from, and some Germans have translated the English word rosewood into *rosenholz*. But this is wrong because *rosenholz* is actually tulipwood—*Dalbergia variabilis*." Wiese has a diploma from Hamburg University's School of Forestry and Wood Research; botanical Latin comes easily to him.

Brazilian rosewood is a favorite of mine, so I pursue discussion of its availability with Wiese and his associate, Belsemeyer, who has just returned from Brazil. "All gone," Wiese says, explaining that only veneer cutters can afford to buy the few logs still reaching market. I wonder whether undiscovered rosewood might grow deep in the jungle, but Belsemeyer replies, "Rosewood doesn't grow in the jungle, it grows in the central coastal regions," where it's often planted as shade for cocoa trees. Unfortunately, fertilizer for cocoa spoils the wood. So does prolonged storage of the logs. Unwilling to give up, I ask if logs are ever smuggled out in defiance of the government embargo. Belsemeyer doubts it: "The customs people wouldn't jeopardize their jobs for one log or even for a large bribe. It just wouldn't be worth it to them."

In some countries, India for example, logs are gathered at government depots, then auctioned in parcels of up to fifteen logs each. Half the annual supply of East Indian rosewood is auctioned during September in Mysore, with bidding conducted through native go-betweens. Wiese himself usually attends. "You have to go there many days in advance to study the parcels, make notes, and decide how much you will be willing to pay. Bidding is done in Hindi, but you quickly learn what is one, two, three and so on."

Burmese teak (*Tectona grandis*) is also sold at central depots, but at prices fixed by the government. The Burmese, like the Indians, use elephants for dragging logs because they can work in narrow places where tractors won't fit. In inaccessible areas, teak trees are girdled and left to dry for a couple of years before felling. Then they can be floated downstream; green teak is so heavy it sinks.

We are walking through the yard and a big zebrano log from Africa catches Wiese's eye. He's brought along his timberman's gouge, with which he takes a short, glancing swipe at the end grain, leaving a shallow groove. "When logs stand in storage they get covered over with a coating that hides the true color and grain," Wiese explains. "Here where I've made the cut you can see the color and grain, which look very good

Peter Wiese, above, uses a timber gouge to inspect a bubinga log. Scooping into the log's end grain reveals the wood's color and texture. Behind him is lumber 'sawn in the boule.' Wood is more commonly sawn in this manner in Europe and is stacked in the order it comes from the log, thus preserving the relationship of color and figure from board to board. Theodor Nagel & Co. is a principal supplier of musical instrument woods and provides its customers with custom-sized blanks and billets. At right, a worker dips the end grain of billets in wax to guard against checking during drying and shipping.

on this log. When I go to buy logs, I take the gouge so I can see what I'm buying." Near the edge of the log he points to a dark stain, a resinous suffusion which probably goes right through the wood and will have to be cut away.

Nearby a stack of bubinga logs have just come in, 109 tons Wiese recently bought. On one of them he shows me another defect that can diminish the lumber yield: a large, circular split in the annual rings. "This is bad, a ring shake that may run through the entire log." He hurries to the other end of the log to check. "No, it doesn't show on this end. We can determine approximately where the shake ends by tapping the log with a hammer. You go along tapping, with your ear close to the log, listening carefully to the sound. It will change when you reach the shake. We have to know so that we can cut the log in the right place."

We pass to another shed where a 10-ft. log provokes a cry of pleasure: "This is the finest grenadilla log I have ever seen—East African blackwood. In the size, the grain, the color, an incredible log. It's in the rosewood family, *Dalbergia melanoxylon,* and will be used for making woodwinds and bagpipes. I wish they were all like this one—on some logs we're lucky to get out 20% of usable wood."

Wiese interrupts our yard tour to chew out a man for improperly stickering a log sawn through-and-through. "It really gets me to see that sort of thing," he says. "You bring a log 5,000 miles and then they sticker it the wrong way. Nobody does it, but ideally the end sticks should protrude a bit so they shade the end grain of the board underneath."

There are many woods of great beauty that never find their way to the sawmill. "It's the old story of supply and demand. We sometimes try to introduce new woods, but people who buy wood are very conservative, especially musical instrument

makers, who don't like to experiment." As substitutes for Brazilian rosewood, Nagel now sells amazonas and Santos palisander (*Machaerium scleroxylum*), "a beautiful wood but with the same drawback that cocobolo has, it may cause skin irritation in some people. Gaining acceptance for these woods is going to take time."

Another problem with introducing rare species, says Wiese, is that "they have to have a certain diameter or else there is no profit in it. Many are too small, and others—the top-quality logs of large diameter—will be bought by veneer cutters who will pay big prices." Then there is ocean freight: "I could buy woods in South America for very little, but the freight will cost $200 a ton. I can bring logs into Europe from Africa for $150 a ton including the price of the logs."

Some woods are disappearing from the market not because they no longer can be found in the forest, but because demand is just too low. Satinwood (*Chloroxylon swietenia*), for example, once was sought for making hairbrush handles, but now they're made of plastic. Cocus (*Brya ebenus*) from Jamaica is a beautiful brown wood, but likewise in limited demand and difficult to get out, so there's no incentive to go after it. Pernambuco, the Brazilian wood used for violin bows, is also increasingly hard to find. Snakewood or letterwood (*Piratinera guianensis*), a hard South American wood used for canes, umbrella handles and flutes, has almost disappeared from the market—Wiese estimates the entire annual demand at not more than three tons. "Even if you were willing to pay $3,000 a ton for it you would still buy only $10,000 or $15,000 worth, small stuff for an established timber trader. Labor is expensive today. When people were hunting for bucks, you found men who would go into the forest, cut the trees and carry them out. Nobody seems interested in doing this kind of work today."

On the other hand, boxwood (*Buxus sempervirens*), a favorite of wind instrument makers, is still valuable enough for Nagel to send men into the mountains of France or Turkey to cut it from the high, rocky places where it grows. Ebony is another species that normally grows as isolated trees, the best of it (*Diospyros ebenum*) coming from Sri Lanka. The wood is so heavy that it's usually cut into manageable chunks on the spot, then packed out.

The world's finest ebony was supposed to have come from Mauritius, but Wiese says he has seen a small piece only recently, for the first time. "The best African ebony (*Diospyros crassiflora*) is from Gaboon but very difficult to get. Cameroon is where most African ebony comes from. Gaboon is harder and blacker. Quality can vary greatly in ebony even within a two-mile area, depending on soil conditions. The best stuff grows in the mountains."

We pass a man loading the trunk of a Mercedes with bags of wood. "Those are offcuts of grenadilla," Wiese says. "We bag and sell it for firewood. It makes a fine fire, long-burning, good heat, and slight, pleasant smell. Lignum vitae is even better—it burns with a green flame." As if sensing some concern of mine for the depletion of the earth's forests, he notes that "90% of world wood consumption is for firewood and burning down forests to clear land for agriculture."

·   ·   ·

In the future, it's clear that technological advances, labor and freight costs, and political upheaval will have more to do with the availability of rare hardwoods than the extinction of individual species. Timber traders are drawn to countries where conditions favor investment: political stability, abundant supply of desirable species, a minimum of red tape. Volatile politics in South and Central America, parts of Africa and the West Indies have wiped out some traders.

If the price of a rare hardwood rises above what buyers are willing to pay, they will turn to substitutes—cheaper woods, plywood or plastics. And as demand dwindles, timber traders will drop those species in favor of the ones that sell well. Many manufacturers have switched to plastics for their labor-saving benefits, or to improve product performance. Composition bowling balls, for example, are far superior to their forerunners which were turned from lignum vitae. Woods from which dyes were extracted have been supplanted by chemical dyestuffs.

For the professional woodworker using rare hardwoods, the future looks expensive rather than bleak. Amateurs may have to switch to domestic hardwoods unless they can afford the escalating prices due to rising labor and shipping costs. For Americans, some of these costs are offset by the dollar's current high exchange rate. Shops using large quantities of rare woods might even find it worthwhile to import their own wood, rather than buying it on the domestic market. □

Irving Sloane is a musical instrument maker and an author of books, including Making Musical Instruments, *published by E.P. Dutton, 2 Park Ave., New York, N.Y. 10016. He lives in Brussels, Belgium. Theodor Nagel G.M.B.H. accepts mail orders for wood and has no minimum price or weight restrictions. Small orders are shipped via parcel post; orders in excess of 50 lb. are shipped by sea freight. Nagel's address is Postfach 28 02 66, D2 Hamburg 28, Germany. Photos by the author.*

Whither Rosewood?
A supply outlook for exotics

by Paul McClure

As conditions in the world market shift, woodworkers who enjoy exotic hardwoods need to know the current status of the different species. Why are some, such as teak and rosewood, becoming difficult to obtain? Are these shortages temporary, or are they harbingers of disappearance? Are available substitutes worth considering? Are new woods emerging in attractive supply?

Some woodworkers feel that we should not import wood from Third World countries, in order to protect our own economy and to not participate in the depletion of the tropical rain forests. But I feel that these are isolationist views which ignore the interdependence of the world economy, and which forget the fact that most land clearing has been done for agriculture, not timber. In fact, increased demand for wood is likely to lead to sound forestry policies in developing countries that don't yet know the value of their forests.

These days, the supply of exotic woods is primarily influenced by political decisions in Third World countries. For instance, most of the teak (*Tectonia grandis*) that is sold on the export market originates in Thailand, India, Sri Lanka, Indonesia, Burma and China. Only the last three are presently exporting teak in log form. Thailand, India and Sri Lanka have banned the export of logs and roughsawn lumber. Their economists believe that the teak stands have been overcut, and that there's more money in milling and exporting small pieces of dimensioned lumber. Consequently, teak exports from these countries have fallen off, because such pieces are of less value to the average cabinetmaker and boatbuilder. Burma, China and Indonesia have picked up supplying the world's demand for larger pieces. The export of ebony (*Diospyros spp.*) and satinwood (*Chloroxylon swietenia*) is similarly constrained because these woods also originate in India and Sri Lanka.

Shortages are not new in the business of importing and exporting wood. They are cyclical and have recurred for as long as records have been kept. Most woods whose availability is now restricted politically, geographically or economically will probably return to the marketplace in two or three years. At present, most woods reaching the American market come from Central and South America. Wood export from the Orient has dramatically decreased and the supply from Africa has become unpredictable.

Brazilian rosewood (*Dalbergia nigra*), however, a prize South American wood, is liable to remain scarce. The tree is peculiar in that it has to be quite old (around 200 years) to be of value. The wood's beautiful figure and fragrance are the result of the tree's gradual deterioration from the center out. Young trees have drab brown heartwood and no scent. There are few saleable rosewood trees left, hence the Brazilian government no longer allows rosewood to be cut and exported in log or lumber form.

Cocobolo (*Dalbergia retusa*), which is yellow, red, brown,

violet and black when freshly cut, darkens with age to reds and blacks that resemble Brazilian rosewood, for which it's been a popular substitute. Unfortunately, many of the areas where cocobolo grows are in political turmoil, and it can now be purchased only sporadically from a government-approved agent or party. Most of the best cocobolo comes from Nicaragua, but since the ouster of President Somoza, wood has been hard to get. Currency problems in Costa Rica have had a similar effect on supplies from that country. Panama, where cocobolo was first exploited in 1911, has had continuing production problems. With the United States decreasing its involvement in Panama, the situation is not likely to improve. Southern Mexico and Guatemala remain the only dependable sources, but they can supply merely half of what we once received, and then only sporadically.

Paldao (*Dracontemelum dao*), which grows in the Philippines, is a beautiful, light-brown wood, variegated by black streaks. It is in limited supply because the Philippine government stipulates that it can be cut only when it impedes construction. This wood was quite abundant on the market until the 1970s, but concern about its overexploitation led to the current severe limitation on cutting.

Zebrawood (*Brachystegia leonensis*), from western and equatorial Africa, is also becoming hard to get. With the decolonization of Africa, and subsequent withdrawal of European technicians, the newly independent countries are having difficulty with their production methods. Wood buyers can no longer be assured that zebrawood logs will be quartersawn, a procedure essential for proper kiln-drying, and are consequently reluctant to commit their company's funds. Thus zebrawood has doubled in price in the past year.

On the other hand, Brazilian kingwood or violetwood (*Dalbergia cearensis*), which had disappeared for about 20 years, is again available in limited quantities. This wood has a fine violet-and-black color and is truly a wood for the

connoisseur of fine cabinets. Kingwood is a small tree, however, 3 in. to 8 in. in diameter, and prone to considerable degrade. The yield is therefore minimal.

Tulipwood (*Dalbergia frutescens*), beautiful with its red and yellow variegations, is presently available from Brazil in limited quantities. The log is small, the yield minimal, and the piece usually contains the pith of the tree, which results in some checking.

Pernambuco (*Guilandina echinata*), the violin-bow wood, is native to Brazil, but it grows only in the states of Bahia and Pernambuco. This wood is scarce mainly because of its remote geographic location, not because of overexploitation or government embargo.

The supply of some long-popular exotics has been more reliable. Padauk (*Pterocarpus soyaxii*) is a bright orange color when freshly cut, turning to rich maroon when exposed to sunlight. This wood comes from western Africa and is one of the most stable, durable woods available. It makes excellent flooring in high-traffic areas, and it is also good for exterior use. African padauk is quite abundant, and no shortages are foreseen in the near future. Another member of the genus, Andaman padauk (*P. dalbergoides*), also known as vermilion, comes from the Bay of Bengal's Andaman Islands, where it is logged by convict labor. These stands have been exploited since the mid-1800s, so now very little vermilion is available for import into this country. Andaman padauk is pink to red and maintains its color well. A third member of the padauk genus, narra (*P. indicus*), known as amboyna when in burl form, is indigenous to the South Pacific islands and is either red or yellow, depending on growth conditions. This species has been logged since the early 1700s and exported to Europe from the Philippines. There's currently a moratorium on cutting these trees where we have been used to getting them; however, stands of narra have been discovered in Papua New Guinea, and are being marketed as PNG rosewood, though narra is not related to the rosewoods.

Obeche (*Triplochiton scleroxylon*), from western Africa, and ramin (*Gonystylus spp.*), from Malaysia and Indonesia, have been abundant for many years and are in great demand in Europe and Japan, respectively. Both woods are relatively bland, good for carving and molding. Obeche is cream-colored, lightweight and soft (too soft for most furniture), and must be worked with very sharp tools. Ramin is straw-colored, heavier and easier to machine.

What of new woods and substitutes? First, the word "substitute" is inappropriate. No wood will be exactly like another wood. Each is unique, and though one wood will be similar in some respects to another, it will never perfectly replace it. Each wood should be recognized for its own characteristics and used accordingly. On the other hand, many jobs can be done by any of several woods.

The extent to which species are interchangeable can be illustrated with the mahoganies. During the 18th century, true mahogany was highly esteemed—dark reddish-brown in color, it was stable, easy to work and beautiful when polished. This was Cuban mahogany (*Swietenia mahagoni*), procured from the Caribbean islands. Around 1920, as supplies of this wood diminished, inroads were being made into Honduras. This country and its neighbors are the source for Honduras mahogany (*Swietenia macrophylla*), the wood that most cabinetmakers have been using to make fine furniture for decades. It is close in color and figure to the Cuban species, but

From *Fine Woodworking* magazine (January 1983) 38:81-83

coarser. Recent political turmoil, currency instability and over-grazing of livestock in Central America have decreased the supply of Honduras mahogany, so a number of other woods are being sold as substitutes. Brazilian mahogany (*Cariniana legalis*) is not related to the *Swietenia* genus but is similar in appearance, and it is becoming more competitive in price and availability. It is lighter in color than the true mahoganies. Another stand-in is African mahogany (*Khaya ivorensis*), whose color varies from light brown to deep reddish-brown and whose texture is coarser than that of the South American mahoganies. This wood was quite popular during the 1960s, but higher prices now make it less attractive. Lauan (*Shorea spp.*), known as Philippine mahogany, has been marketed since the early 1920s as a mahogany substitute, although lauan varies considerably in weight and color, and its texture is coarse and difficult to finish. Lauan is popular in public-school industrial arts programs, as it is relatively inexpensive. Much of it is also made into plywood in Japan.

Caviuna (*Machaerium actufolium*), native to Bolivia, looks like Indian rosewood, but is richer in grain and color, does not have the fragrance and is usually cut on the quarter. It sands and polishes very well and comes in medium sizes. Flat cut, it has a most impressive figure of intermingled browns and purples. It costs less than Indian rosewood, and therefore could replace it in the marketplace. As with rose-wood, however, some people develop a skin rash from handling it.

Goncalo alves (*Astronium graveolens*) is a beautiful wood that can be used in many furniture applications. It is golden in color, aging to dark red, with broad black stripes. Unlike most foreign woods, it comes in wide widths and long lengths. It grows in Brazil, and is plentiful at present.

Putumuju or arariba (*Centrolobium robustum*), also from Brazil, is a newly available, moderately priced wood. It is yellow, red and black, with some tinges of green. It seems to be abundant.

Purpleheart (*Peltogyne densiflora*), another Brazilian wood, is still quite abundant, compared with other exotics. The tree is usually large and yields wide, long, clear lumber. Purpleheart has a large amount of silica-oxide, as does teak, and the two woods are of similar density. The silica rapidly dulls cutting tools. Purpleheart is used mostly for accents (inlays and borders), rather than in large pieces, because of its weight and brilliant purple color.

Bocote (*Cordia spp.*) is the color of tobacco and has irregular dark brown or blackish streaks. It is hard and waxy in texture and comes from a tree that reaches heights of 100 ft. Bocote grows in Central America and Mexico, and still can be obtained with relative ease at a moderate price. It makes beautiful turnings and small cabinets.

These and other woods, mainly from South America, are filling the need for exotic woods in contemporary woodworking. While some historically popular species are now hard to get, other less familiar species are becoming available. And while the general quality of wood, both domestic and imported, seems to be declining, a sharp eye can still find choice stock, whether in the forest or at the lumberyard. □

Paul McClure is a wood technologist who has worked in the lumber trade for 12 years. He has recently opened a hardwood retail outlet, a branch of Wood World, in Tempe, Ariz.

Storing precious scraps

by Tom Dewey

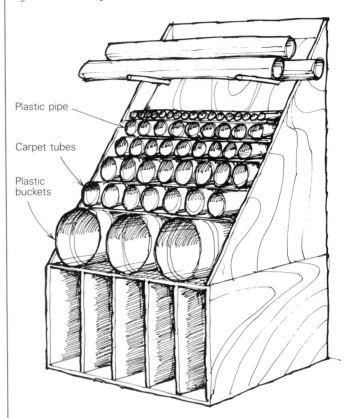

Plastic pipe

Carpet tubes

Plastic buckets

...And then there was the deceased frugal widow who, friends found, had very carefully labeled shoe boxes "pieces of string too short to save" and had, of course, just as carefully stowed them away. Like her, I had a scrap box into which I tossed little pieces of wood I didn't really need but couldn't bring myself to burn. I'd paw through the jumble, wasting time trying to locate that dandy piece of ebony I remembered being there. Most of the time I ended up cutting a new piece anyway, creating yet more scrap and an even thicker clutter.

It finally came to the point where it was either me or the scrap, and I was forced to deal with the problem. My solution occupies no more floor space than the original scrap box, holds a lot more, and keeps wood out where it sort of winks at me as I pass by.

I turned the original box on its side, made a sloping rack out of plywood and nailed this to the wall. I fashioned bins from 5-gal. paint buckets, sections of plastic drain pipe, carpet tubes and, for small pieces of wood, lengths of 1½-in. plastic pipe. Two broomstick braces—inserted through the rack into holes in the studs behind—hold more carpet tubes across the top of the main rack. I store longer pieces of molding, splines and shim stock in these. Plywood, wider boards, and odds and ends go in the bottom.

The rack has turned out to be so accessible that I find myself storing cutoffs as I work, instead of letting them pile up until I'm done. When I'm looking for a small turning square, I can invariably find just what I need. □

Tom Dewey makes custom cabinetry in Coudersport, Pa.

Wood Identification at FPL

Sharp eyes and lots of experience get it right

by Paul Bertorelli

As a material, wood has a lot of things going for it—not the least being its enormous variety. There are more than 20,000 different kinds of trees growing in the forests of the world. So many of these woods are favored by man for his shelter, furniture and objects that just telling them apart is nearly a full-time job for a handful of laboratories in the U.S. and abroad.

One of these places is the U.S. Department of Agriculture's Forest Products Laboratory, located in Madison, Wis. There, a staff of three wood scientists divide their time studying wood anatomy and identifying thousands of samples sent in each year. To aid their research and to compare knowns with unknowns, the FPL scientists have the world's largest wood research collection—some 100,000 cigarette-pack-size blocks stored in banks of indexed drawers. The collection grows by 200 to 300 specimens each year.

About half of the lab's identification work is done for the wood industry. The rest of the samples to be tested come from the general public or various government agencies and museums, and more than a few bar bets have been settled by the lab, according to Regis Miller, who supervises it. Miller says the lab likes to guarantee satisfaction but can promise only to identify a particular wood's family and genus—picking the species is usually not possible.

Miller begins the task of identifying a strange wood by slicing a small chunk off the specimen's end grain. Next he wets the cut surface so the wood's characteristics can be scrutinized through a 14-power hand lens. If the wood happens to be a distinctive domestic species, Miller can usually identify it just by looking through the lens. At this stage, he can sometimes use color, odor and density for a quick identification.

More frequently, though, he must take thin slices off the sample, making sure to get radial and tangential sections. These match-head-size shavings are then placed on a glass slide with a solution of half glycerine and half alcohol, and boiled on a hotplate. This process drives out air bubbles that can obscure the wood's inner structure.

Peering through a lighted microscope at the thin slices, Miller begins what can be a complicated mental juggling act by asking himself if he has seen this cellular pattern before. "There's no substitute for experience . . . you've got to know what you're looking for, and the only way to know is to have seen it before," he says. With more of the wood's inner structure revealed, Miller can sometimes call up the proper mental image to identify the wood, or he can at least get close enough to root out a sample with which to compare it.

If the wood's identity still isn't apparent, the real work begins. Miller falls back on his knowledge of wood anatomy to pick out the sample's dozens of individual characteristics. He then pages through hefty books called dichotomous keys, which list thousands of wood samples by anatomical detail, an arrangement that permits a methodical narrowing of possibilities. Notes kept on index cards help Miller supplement information printed in the keys. Eventually, this process of elimination points to a small number of wood families.

Wood anatomists at the U.S. Forest Products Laboratory in Madison, Wis., have nearly 100,000 specimens of wood for research and identification. Here, Regis Miller, the lab's supervisor, searches for a sample.

Woods from temperate climates, particularly North America, are the easiest to identify because they are few in kind, and Miller has seen many of them before. There are, however, thousands of tropical species, some of which have never been identified at all. And tropical woods have a way of passing in and out of commercial importance, a fact that diverts a fairly steady stream of tough-to-pick unknowns into the lab. Computers can make wood identification faster, and FPL researchers are designing computer-assisted identification systems for domestic and tropical species.

Miller estimates that only 1% of all the samples examined can't be identified, either because they don't appear in the keys or his notes, or because he can't find a sample in the collection with which to compare them. "You get to a point where you've worked on a sample for two or three days and you've gotten nowhere. We have other work and we just have to move on," Miller says.

Because of limited time and staff, the lab requests that samples be sent only by people with a clear need for identification, and in limited numbers. Samples should be at least 1 in. by 3 in. by 6 in., though smaller pieces can also be identified. Place of origin and local popular name, if they are known, will help. Specimens should be sent to the Center for Wood Anatomy Research, U.S. Forest Products Laboratory, PO Box 5130, Madison, Wis. 53705. There is no charge for the identification service. □

Paul Bertorelli, editor of Fine Woodworking *magazine, visited the Forest Products Laboratory facilities in the spring of 1982. For more information on the world's huge variety of woods, contact the International Wood Collectors Society, c/o Bruce Forness, Drawer B, Main St., Chaumont, N.Y. 13622. The IWCS, formed in 1947, is dedicated to the advancement of knowledge about wood. The Society sponsors wood identification workshops, regional and national conventions and an annual wood auction, and it publishes a monthly newsletter. Its members frequently swap wood samples.*

Hardwood Lumber Grades

There's a method to the madness

by David Sloan

I've bluffed my way through many a lumberyard. I learned young. When I was a kid, I wanted a big hunk of maple to make a rifle stock. At the lumberyard, the man in charge pointed to a pile of thick maple planks. "Come and get me when you've found what you want," he said. I did, and for years afterward, that's the way I bought wood. Whenever I'd hear lumberyard lingo like "FAS or number one common, sir?", I'd put on my poker face, giving a knowing nod, and say, "Sure. Uh, do you mind if I look through the boards?" I didn't have the slightest idea what lumber grades like FAS or No. 1 common meant, but I knew a nice board when I saw one.

My bluff worked fine until I bought wood for a big job. I didn't have time to pick through a hundred oak boards, so I went with a grade called No. 2 common because it was cheap. Much to my dismay, there was a short, narrow, knotty board for every nice one that came off the truck. I suggested that the knots added character, but my customer didn't agree. I had to order more oak, and ultimately lost money on the job.

That lesson motivated me to learn about lumber grades. I picked up the basics from books. Recently I rounded out my education by attending a three-day log-, lumber- and tree-grading workshop in Indiana, where I even got to do a little grading myself. Purdue University and the Indiana Hardwood Lumberman's Association sponsor several of these workshops each year. Attending one is a good way to learn about hardwood grading. (For information, write to Daniel Cassens, Dept. of Forestry and Natural Resources, Purdue University, West Lafayette, Ind. 47907.)

Grades provide the basis for determining lumber quality and price. The *concept* of hardwood grading is simple: a high-grade board must have more clear, defect-free surface area than a low-grade board. The grading system provides standards for defects and board size, and equations for calculating clear surface area.

The standard grades of hardwood lumber are (from best to worst) firsts and seconds (FAS), selects, No. 1 common, No. 2 common, and No. 3 common. There are special grades for certain species, but in general the standard grades are what you'll find. The chart on p. 48 describes the top four standard grades. No. 3 common boards aren't suitable for furniture, and usually end up as pallets or shipping crates. Familiarity with the top four grades will get you through most situations, although lumberyards rarely stock all four. Some yards will have only FAS and No. 1 common; some will sell a mix of the top two grades and call it "selects and better"—it varies from yard to yard. Increasingly popular is a non-standard grade called "FAS one face" (abbreviated F1F). In this grade, one board face will

To choose the grading face, grader Wally Cole flips a red-oak board with his steel-tipped lumber rule. Cole marks a grade with his crayon-tipped wand and records the surface measure and grade in the logbook in his left hand.

Calculations make the grade

The drawing below shows how a grader visualizes clear face cuttings on the board's worst face. To make the grade, the cuttings must exceed minimum size and contain enough cutting units to meet minimum requirements based on board surface measure (SM). One cutting unit = 12 sq. in. (i.e., 1 in. x 12 in., or 2 in. x 6 in.). Both boards shown have an SM of 8 (SM = [width in in. x length in ft.] ÷ 12; drop fractions under ½). The chart gives the minimum cutting sizes and maximum number of cuttings permitted. To determine minimum number of cutting units required, multiply SM by a conversion factor (10 for FAS and selects, 8 for No. 1 common, 6 for No. 2 common).

Minimum standards for hardwood grades

Standard grade	Minimum board size* (width x length)	Minimum size of clear face cuttings* (width x length)	Minimum % of clear surface area on graded face	Maximum number of cuttings permitted:	
				SM	Cuts
Firsts and seconds or FAS (two separate grades combined and sold as one)	6 in. x 8 ft.	4 in. x 5 ft. or 3 in. x 7 ft.	Firsts: 91⅔% Seconds: 83⅓%	4 to 7 8 to 11 12 to 15 16 and over	1 2 3 4
Selects (graded on best face)	4 in. x 6 ft.	4 in. x 5 ft. or 3 in. x 7 ft.	91⅔%	2 to 7 8 to 11 12 to 15 16 and over	1 2 3 4
No. 1 common	3 in. x 4 ft.	4 in. x 2 ft. or 3 in. x 3 ft.	66⅔%	1 2 to 4 5 to 7 8 to 10 11 to 13 14 and over	clear 1 2 3 4 5
No. 2 common	3 in. x 4 ft.	3 in. x 2 ft.	50%	1 to 3 4 and 5 6 and 7 8 and 9 10 and 11 12 and 13 14 and over	1 2 3 4 5 6 7

*May vary for some species.

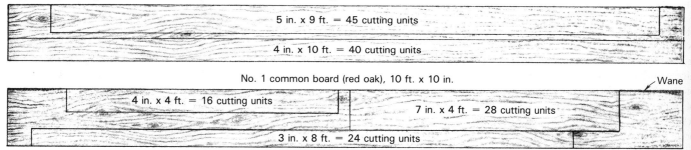

Clear face cuttings

FAS board (red oak), 10 ft. x 10 in.

5 in. x 9 ft. = 45 cutting units
4 in. x 10 ft. = 40 cutting units

No. 1 common board (red oak), 10 ft. x 10 in.

4 in. x 4 ft. = 16 cutting units
7 in. x 4 ft. = 28 cutting units
3 in. x 8 ft. = 24 cutting units

Wane

grade FAS, and the other face No. 1 common or better.

Here's how grading works. Boards aren't graded by their overall appearance, as you might think. The system is based on the assumption that a hardwood board will be cut into smaller pieces to make furniture parts, flooring, etc. Boards are graded by overall length and width, and by the size and number of imaginary "clear face cuttings" (the furniture parts) that the lumber grader visualizes (no actual cutting is involved) in between knots and other defects on the board's *worst* face. One grade, selects, is graded on the best face; F1F is graded on both faces. No unsound defects, such as large holes, loose knots or wane, are allowed on the reverse side of the imaginary cutting. The higher the grade, the wider and longer the clear cuttings have to be, as shown in the drawing above.

In addition to the size of these clear cuttings, the grading rules also specify the number of cuttings a board must contain to make a grade. That's not all. When the surface area of all the clear cuttings in a board is added up, the total must exceed a specified minimum requirement. The surface area of the cuttings is measured in cutting units. One cutting unit equals 12 sq. in. of board surface. (To find the number of cutting units in a cutting, multiply width in inches times length in feet.) The total

number of cutting units required varies for each grade and also within each grade, depending on the board's overall surface area. Two boards that are exactly the same size with the same number of defects and the same amount of defect-free surface area could end up as different grades—the *location* of the defects could prevent a board from having large enough clear cuttings to make the higher grade.

The defects in between the clear cuttings can vary drastically from board to board within a grade. They could be tiny knots, but are just as likely to be holes or large knots. There are size limitations for knots and holes, but in general the grading system isn't concerned much with the defects, only the clear wood in between.

The actual rules for determining grade are ridiculously complex, but they work. To make things even more complicated, grading rules differ somewhat depending on the species. For example, in cherry the "clear cuttings" may contain tiny knots. The National Hardwood Lumber Association's pocket-size rule book (PO Box 34518, Memphis, Tenn. 38184) gives all this information. It reads like the instructions for an IRS tax form, but it's worth having if you want to understand lumber grading. And if you buy lumber in quantity, it's essential.

After reading all this, you may conclude that the grading sysem has little relevance to small-scale woodworking—a valid point, perhaps. The system was designed to meet the needs of the lumber and wood-products industries, not the individual woodworker; without the rules, million-board-foot lumber transactions would be impossible. But if you understand it, the system will enable you to buy and sell boards in quantity, sight unseen. When you specify a grade, you don't have to examine the boards to know, very specifically, what you're getting in a shipment. If there's a dispute between buyer and seller, out comes the rule book. The grade can be verified by measuring the board in question and making a few calculations.

Every decision in the lumber business, from the felling and bucking of the tree to the sawing and edging of the boards, is made with one thought in mind: produce as many high-grade boards as possible. The more high-grade boards a log yields, the greater the profit for all concerned. A wide board that would make some woodworkers swoon with delight will be ripped in two if doing that will raise the grade.

So how can you tell which grade to buy? If you need only a few boards, or you're concerned with a board's overall appearance, you're better off using my old trick of picking out what you want. (Be considerate. Ask permission before you pick, and restack any boards you move.) The best boards will always be in the FAS pile, but if you want to save money, look in the No. 1 common pile first. You'll find a few nice boards. The difference in retail price between an FAS board and a No. 1 common board is roughly 40% (for red oak), but sometimes the difference in appearance isn't that great. A knot that was a defect in the grader's eyes may be pleasing to yours.

When you need a quantity, say, 50 bd. ft. or more, the law of averages starts to work and you can buy blind by grade alone. Not surprisingly, the NHLA rule book ignores aesthetics. In the real world, however, any large single-grade order will contain nice boards, ugly boards, and boards in between. The larger the order, the more likely it is that you'll have an even distribution of nice, ugly and in between (remember statistics in high school?). So when buying by grade, it's always a good idea to order a little more wood than you'll need, to allow for waste. The lower the grade, the more waste you should expect. You'll have minimal waste with FAS or selects, but you'll pay more.

Even if you want perfectly clear stock, you may not always need to buy FAS for every furniture project. The chart gives the minimum sizes for clear cuttings in each grade. These are the smallest clear pieces that you can expect to get out of a board. Consider what size pieces of clear stock your project requires and buy the lowest grade that will give you that size. If only one side of the board will show, buy selects (or F1F) instead of FAS. The cuttings are the same size as FAS, but selects cost a little less.

What if your project requires long, wide, pretty boards and you don't need a lot of little furniture parts? Pick if you can. On a big job you may have to buy blind. The chart gives you the minimum percentage of clear surface area you can expect on the graded face. If money's no object, play it safe and buy FAS or selects. In these grades you'll have wider boards and fewer defects. But if, like me, you don't mind a few knots in the middle of your pet project, or gluing up narrower boards, you can usually save money by ordering No. 1 common. You'll get a few ugly boards, and roughly 17% less clear wood than with FAS, but each board foot will cost about 40% less. And besides, those knots add character, remember? □

David Sloan is an associate editor at Fine Woodworking.

A grader in action

Grading requires a lot of measuring and a lot of math. When you're learning—juggling unfamiliar tools, rules and numbers—it seems to take forever to grade just one board. George Screpetis from Pineville, La., an instructor at the Purdue University grading workshop I attended, said that a pro spends only a few seconds with each board. Fumbling as I was at the time, that was hard to believe. It took me a few seconds just to get my grading rule book out of my back pocket. I decided to see for myself.

Wally Cole is a professional grader at Cole Bros. Lumber Co., a sawmill in Woodbury, Conn. He's an amiable young man, in his early thirties I'd guess. The afternoon that I stopped by, I found him standing on the grading platform armed with the tools of his trade: a lumber rule, a crayon-tipped wand and a logbook. As the newly sawn and edged red-oak boards shuttled along on the roller-chain conveyor that crossed the platform, he quickly eyeballed each board's length and measured its width with his lumber rule. A scale printed on the rule gave him the board's surface measure (surface area in square feet). Giving the board a quick flip with the steel-tipped rule and his boot, he chose the worst face for grading, mentally calculated the required number of cutting units and visually laid out the clear face cuttings. Then, with a flourish of his crayon-tipped wand, he marked the board with a grade symbol. As the graded board moved down the conveyor, he ticked off the grade and surface measure in his logbook. Two handlers working with him stacked the boards into piles by grade. The entire grading sequence took only a few seconds for each board, just as George Screpetis had said.

A good grader like Cole can grade as much as 10,000 bd. ft. in an 8-hr. shift. Graders often get paid by the board foot, so speed is just as important as accuracy. Sometimes Cole seemed to do nothing more than flip a board with his rule before he marked a grade. In fact, he was so fast that I couldn't wind, focus and shoot my camera fast enough to keep up with him. "The best boards grade themselves," he explained. A defect-free board takes only a glance, because if it's large enough to make FAS, no further scrutiny is needed. It's automatically FAS.

Cole was grading to fill an order. The customer had specified standard FAS, F1F, No. 1 common and No. 2 common. If a customer's specifications differ from the standard grading rules, Cole will grade to meet those specs.

I asked if some species were more difficult to grade. Cole said that red oak is one of the easiest woods to grade green because it doesn't have unusual characteristics. Yellow poplar, also being sawn the day I visited, is tougher to grade because it has tiny burls that look like knots at first glance. The burls aren't considered defects in poplar, but knots are, so the grader must check each board carefully to avoid confusing the two.

Hardwood boards are often graded twice: once green, and again after kiln-drying. Since the boards are already graded when they go into the kiln, the dry-grader regrades only boards that have drying-related defects that would cause a drop in grade. Boards more than 10 in. wide are usually picked out at the second grading and sold at a premium. —D.S.

Quartersawn Lumber
The quality's in the cutting

by Sam Talarico

A quartersawn board is special. Dimensionally stabler than a board sawn any other way, it won't cup as it dries, and as the seasons change, it won't move very much in width. This stability makes quartersawn boards ideal for drawer slides, tabletops, frame rails and stiles—wherever cross-grain movement or cupping could be a problem. Because their surfaces wear more evenly than those of plainsawn, or flatsawn, boards, quartersawn boards are often used for flooring. When quartersawn some hardwood species, such as the oaks, also reveal spectacular, shimmering flake figure scattered across the grain.

If quartersawn lumber is so attractive and well behaved, why saw any other way? Economics. Quartersawing yields fewer clear, knot-free boards than does plainsawing, and it isn't practical for small-diameter logs. For these reasons, most commercial sawmills don't do it. It's also a time-consuming and fairly wasteful way to cut up a log.

Quartersawn lumber owes both its dimensional stability and its subdued figure to the orientation of the annual rings. Figure 1 shows the difference between a plainsawn board and a quartersawn board. A plainsawn board is a tangential slice from a log. The board's face is more or less tangent to the annual rings, which form ellipses or parabolas on the surface. Theoretically, the ideal quartersawn board is a radial slice. The annual rings are perpendicular to the face, and their edges form parallel lines on the surface. (In commercial practice, any board with rings 60° to 90° to the surface is considered quartersawn.) Because wood moves roughly twice as much tangentially to the rings as it does radially (this ratio varies with the species), the plainsawn board moves more in width, the quartersawn more in thickness.

A tree's rays radiate from the heart like the spokes of a wheel. In quartersawing, the sawblade cuts roughly parallel to the rays. Severed rays show on the board's surface as the flake I described earlier, which is also called "ray fleck." In species where the rays are small, this may hardly be noticeable. Hardwood species with very large rays produce the best flake. Mahogany is good, but in Pennsylvania, where I live, white oak is the best, with red oak and sycamore close behind.

Alternative methods of quartersawing are shown in figure 2, along with the conventional method shown in figure 3. The log is first quartered, then the boards are sawn from the quarter. This method is a compromise. For each board to be the ideal—a true radial slice—the log quarter would have to be repositioned after each cut, which would be a slow and costly procedure. Boards quartersawn the conventional way are close to being true radial slices, and there's no need to turn the log after each cut. This system produces narrow boards with tapered edges, but the widest boards are the most perfectly quartered—the rings are closest to 90° to the surface.

Sawing "through and through," or flitchsawing, produces a few boards near the center of the log that contain the pith. On either side of the pith, the rings are almost 90° to the board's surface. If you rip one of these boards through the pith, you'll have two quartersawn boards. Even though they weren't sawn from a quartered log, these boards are radial slices and therefore quartersawn.

When the growth rings are cut at an angle too far off the radial, the boards are referred to as riftsawn. The rings are less than 60° but greater than 30° to the board's surface. The figure is still straight, but since the cut isn't parallel to the rays, the flake is less pronounced. Riftsawn flake is sometimes called "comb figure."

When you shop for quartersawn hardwood, don't expect to find a wide choice of species. Mostly you'll find red and white oak from about 4/4 to 8/4 in thickness. Widths of 4 in. to 6 in. are

This white-oak log shows a fine example of the cross-grain flake that quartersawing produces in species with large rays. The flake comes from slicing the rays longitudinally.

From *Fine Woodworking* magazine (September 1984) 48:50-51

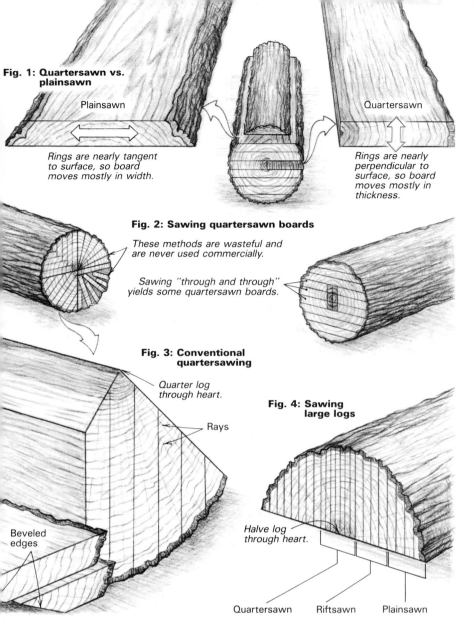

Fig. 1: Quartersawn vs. plainsawn

Plainsawn

Quartersawn

Rings are nearly tangent to surface, so board moves mostly in width.

Rings are nearly perpendicular to surface, so board moves mostly in thickness.

Fig. 2: Sawing quartersawn boards

These methods are wasteful and are never used commercially.

Sawing "through and through" yields some quartersawn boards.

Fig. 3: Conventional quartersawing

Quarter log through heart.

Rays

Beveled edges

Fig. 4: Sawing large logs

Halve log through heart.

Quartersawn   Riftsawn   Plainsawn

A large bandmill can handle bigger logs than can a circular sawmill. Even so, the buttress of this 46-in. dia. log had to be trimmed with a chainsaw to fit.

average. You'll also find that dealers' policies vary greatly. Many hardwood dealers sell quartersawn boards for 20% to 75% more than plainsawn boards of the same species. Sometimes the highly flaked boards are sorted out and sold at a premium. On the other hand, some sellers don't even offer quartersawn as a separate grade, and won't charge extra for the quartersawn boards mixed in with the plainsawn boards. (There usually are some in any pile. Look on the end of the board for rings at 60° to 90° to the faces.) Some dealers will let you pick out the boards you want, some won't; but don't expect anyone to move a ton of lumber so you can pick out one board. In my experience, some lumberyards' quartersawn grade is a mixture of about two-thirds riftsawn boards and one-third quartersawn. Quartersawn softwoods are more standardized. Most places you can ask for "vertical-grain" or "edge-grain" Douglas fir or southern yellow pine. Expect

to pay a lot more for this grade.

A few lumber businesses, like mine, specialize in quartersawn hardwood. I find that the biggest demand is for boards with lots of flake, so I saw primarily to get the best figure. I saw my best logs on the bandmill at C.F. Martin & Co. in Nazareth, Pa., shown in the photo above. The blade makes a narrow kerf, which allows me to cut thin boards without much waste. On the bandmill, I rarely quartersaw oak or sycamore thicker than 5/4— the more boards I get out of a log, the more surfaces there are to showcase the flake. When I'm using a circular mill, however, the ¼-in. to ⅜-in. kerf of the blade turns a lot of potential boards into sawdust. So instead of wasting all that wood sawing thin boards, I saw thick boards and resaw them later on a bandsaw to expose the flake.

If you want to have your own logs quartersawn at a local sawmill, there are a few things to consider before you talk to

the sawyer. Sawyers at small mills may not be familiar with quartersawing, so be prepared to explain what you want. Quartersawing small logs produces very narrow boards, so I recommend cutting only butt logs (from the bottom of the tree) with a minimum small-end diameter of 20 in. Butt logs contain the highest-quality boards and yield the best flake. Very large logs are unwieldy, though, and most sawmills aren't able to cut them. If I have a log that's too large for the mill, I rip it into manageable halves with a chainsaw, then saw it as in figure 4. Technically, this is not quartersawing, but like the "through and through" sawing method in figure 2, it produces quite a few quartersawn boards in addition to riftsawn and plainsawn boards. It saves the time (and expense) involved in quartering a very large log. When halving or quartering a log, always locate the heart on both ends, snap a line, then rip through the center of the heart.

Quartersawn lumber takes longer to dry than does plainsawn. Because of the orientation of the rings, moisture is released from the edges rather than from the face of the board. Before drying, I number the boards in the order in which they came off the log. This enables me to bookmatch boards to make a wider panel.

Because quartersawn lumber is more expensive, some people might consider it a luxury. True, you wouldn't buy it for building sawhorses. But, like a good wine, it's well worth the price for a special occasion. □

Sam Talarico is a lumber dealer, woodworker and winemaker in Mohnton, Pa. Photos by the author.

What Does "Grain" Really Mean?

Some seventy meanings clarified

by R. Bruce Hoadley

What we commonly call grain is the result of exposing the tree's annual rings on the surface of a board. With a ring-porous hard wood such as ash, the large earlywood cells are sliced lengthwise, resulting in bands of distinct lines.

Seldom can a discussion about wood get far without the use of the word "grain." Yet grain is such a versatile word that its many accepted meanings are often confusing, and sometimes even contradictory. A woodworker who says "I don't like the grain of that board" could be talking about any number of things. Most likely, he means the board's *figure,* the visual pattern on the board, but he could also be talking about the *slope of the grain* (too much slope weakens a board), or about the way the board grew in the tree—a luthier, for example, senses that an *edge-grained* piece of spruce is stiff enough for a guitar top, a *flat-grained* piece isn't.

Here are some seventy phrases involving specific meanings of the word grain. They are all the result of two variables: the way the tree grew and the way it was sawn.

Planes, surfaces and direction—"Grain," first and foremost, commonly designates the alignment of the longitudinal cells that comprise the bulk of wood tissue, as shown above. *Grain direction* is a better term when used in this sense. We speak of wood splitting *along the grain* or *with the grain,* meaning parallel to the fibers; *across the grain* means generally perpendicular to the fibers. Surfaces cut parallel to the grain direction are called *longitudinal grain* or simply *long grain,* as opposed to *end grain,* which is the surface perpendicular to the fiber direction.

Grain can also refer to the position of the growth rings with respect to both the plane of cut and the appearance produced. For example, a tangential surface—parallel to the growth rings— is said to have *tangential grain.* This term is also applied to boards whose widest surface has this orientation. Synonymous with tangential grain are *flat grain, plain grain* and *slash grain.* If the surface is perpendicular to the growth rings, it is said to have *radial grain,* that is, the wide face of the board was oriented on a radius of the tree stem. *Edge grain, vertical grain* and *quarter grain* are flexible terms, but they all represent grain that is more radial than tangential.

Obviously, boards can be cut with varying degrees of grain orientation. In commercial lumber, *flat grain* includes boards with growth rings oriented at angles of 0° to 45° to the wide face; *edge grain,* 45° to 90°. *Bastard grain* indicates that the growth-ring placement is clearly neither flat grain nor edge grain, but somewhere in the 30° to 60° range. *Mixed grain* refers to a quantity of lumber that includes assorted edge, flat and bastard grain in any combination. *Side grain,* as the opposite of end grain, can mean any of the above long-grain surfaces, and it sometimes indicates, confusingly, flat grain only. In boards or panels, the better of the two surfaces is sometimes referred to as *face grain.*

It is generally assumed and expected that the grain direction is parallel to the long axis in boards, dowels and turnings. Such pieces are said to be *straight-grained.* Deviation from this ideal is termed *cross grain.* The degree of cross grain is expressed as *slope-of-grain.* A slope-of-grain of 1 in 12 indicates that grain direction deviates 1 in. away from the board's axis for every 12 in. along the surface. Severe cross grain is called *steep grain,* and pronounced deviation from the surface plane, especially in veneer, is called *short grain.* When the axis of a board is not parallel to the growth rings, the result is called *diagonal grain.* *Dip grain* indicates an undulation in the grain direction, as typically occurs in the vicinity of a knot.

From *Fine Woodworking* magazine (May 1985) 52:58-59

A board may be cut straight along the axis of a tree, but grain direction in trees is not always straight up and down. For example, within a straight stem, the fibers may have a helical alignment, referred to as *spiral grain*. Any board sawn parallel to the stem (or log) axis will likewise have spiral grain. In some species the stemwood has spiral grain that alternates cyclically from right to left, producing *interlocked grain*.

Various other characteristic patterns of distortion in grain direction can develop in the tree. These result in distinctive patterns on machined surfaces. For example, *curly* or *wavy grain* produces a washboard surface when split radially, and the barred visual effect produced when the wood is machined smooth is also called curly or wavy grain. In maple it is sometimes called *tiger grain*, or *fiddleback grain* because of the traditional choice of such wood for the backs of violins.

Grain and figure—If we are speaking primarily of fiber orientation, as we have been, "grain" is the word to use; if we are referring to the wood's surface appearance, it is more meaningful to use the word "figure." The following grain patterns produce characteristic figures when the wood is surfaced.

Intergrown cell structure in the crotches of forked trees is called *crotch grain*. In certain species, such as black walnut, if the crotch is sawn down the middle into two Ys, the pattern is aptly called *feather grain*.

Bulged or bumpy growth layers are called *blister grain*, and produce blister figure when sawn tangentially. If the blisters grow elongated rather than round, the grain is called *quilted*. *Leaf grain* and *flame grain* are somewhat showy tangential cuts resembling their namesakes.

Sometimes wood grows in localized tight swirls and dimples. In maple, *bird's-eye grain* results. When a piece of bird's-eye maple is split tangentially, one surface will have numerous little peaks, and the other will have corresponding craters. When surfaced, the figure resembles lustrous, deep eyes. *Dimpled grain*, characteristic of lodgepole pine, splits similarly. Another spot-like figure occurs in burls, a result of dormant-bud proliferation.

Interlocked grain, surfaced radially, results in bands of light and dark that shift back and forth with changes in light direction. The resulting figure may be called *ribbon* or *stripe grain*. Roe figure is similar, and the grain, also interlocked, may be called *roey*.

More properly called "figure," some "grain" depends on the characteristic patterns produced by the rays when the tree is cut radially. When the ray flecks are conspicuous or particularly lustrous, the wood is called *silver grain*. *Rift grain*, occasionally called *needle-point grain*, is produced on a longitudinal surface oriented 30° to 45° to the rays, the term being used especially for white oak with its large rays; the term *comb grain* is used where the vessel lines are parallel to the board's edge and produce a uniform pencil stripe.

Grain and surfacing—When wood is being planed, it tends to split ahead of the cutting edge. On a board with cross grain, the splitting will follow the direction of the fibers, either running harmlessly up and away from the surface or running troublesomely into it. Thus we prefer to plane *with the grain* rather than *against the grain*. If we go wrong, *chipped* or *torn grain* results. In most wood with a pronounced figure, wood fibers are intergrown in various directions or at steep angles. This is why figured wood is more difficult to work.

When flat-grain surfaces at a high moisture content are machine-planed, or when knives are dull, denser latewood may rise above adjacent earlywood. This surface unevenness (which is most pronounced on the pith side of flatsawn boards of uneven-grained softwoods) is called *raised grain*. If the growth rings actually separate, *loosened* or *shelled grain* results. When we saw or plane wet wood, or hardwoods with reaction wood (tension wood), the fibers may not cut cleanly, and the frayed, fibrous surface that results is called *fuzzy* or *woolly grain*.

Earlywood and latewood—Visual contrast between earlywood and latewood is expressed as evenness of grain. Southern yellow pine and Douglas fir thus have *uneven grain* because of their distinct growth rings, while basswood has *even grain*, because its growth rings are barely discernible. In softwoods, visual contrast parallels workability—an uneven-grained carving block usually means jumpy cuts.

In describing growth-ring width (rate of growth), as in structural grading of lumber, narrow rings are termed *narrow grain, close grain, fine grain* or *dense grain*. Wide rings are described as *wide grain, open grain* or *coarse grain*. To add to the confusion, similar terms are often used to indicate relative cell size or permeability. We hear the terms "open-grained" and "coarse-grained" used to describe woods that have large cells and absorb finish readily, but the term "texture" is preferable in reference to relative cell size. Woods with large cells should be called *coarse-textured*; woods with small cells, *fine-textured*. Much of the confusion about grain can be avoided by using clarifying adjectives or by substituting a more appropriate term such as texture, figure, or growth-ring placement. For example, following popular usage, one might be tempted to describe a given piece of ash as being both close-grained (if growth rings were narrow) and open-grained (because of its large pores). It would be better to describe such wood as "slow-grown" and "coarse-textured."

Other miscellaneous uses of the word grain appear from time to time. Some are doubtless local in origin or use. *Short-in-the-grain*, for example, has been used in Britain to describe wood prone to brittle fractures. When an individual is lacking a specific term to describe a particular aspect of wood, the word grain is readily pressed into service to fit the situation at hand. An ambiguous term such as *tight grain* might be used by the cooper in reference to white oak (whose "water tightness" is due to tylosis-filled vessels), by the ébeniste in reference to maple (based on its fine texture), or by the violinmaker to describe fiddleback figure (where the bars are closely spaced). Various other uses seem to have been coined to fit the situation at hand—one reads of clear grain, wild grain, swirly grain, variegated grain, or grain character; these terms have little specific meaning to me. I've also heard people say, "The grain runs a bit," and "The grain is heavy." I'm not sure what these statements mean, either.

Getting to the end of my list, there is *graining*, which is the texturing or painting of surfaces to imitate natural texture or figure. At its best, graining is a fine art; on the other hand, the plastic cabinet on my TV set warns of "simulated wood-grain design," and I suppose this is part of the category, too. Other meanings of grain get us away from wood, and concern themselves with cereals, weight tables, and beaches. I suppose I've missed a few, but for now the thought of inventing any more uses for this overworked word sort of . . . well . . . goes against *my* grain. □

R. Bruce Hoadley is a contributing editor to Fine Woodworking. *An excellent pamphlet,* Figure in Wood: An Illustrated Review, *is available from Research Information, 101 Comer Hall, Auburn University, Ala. 36849 (write for current price).*

Spalted Wood

Rare jewels from death and decay

by Mark Lindquist

Lindquist amid treasure trove.

There is no official documentation of spalted wood that I have been able to find. Apparently nobody was crazy enough to consider using "rotten" wood in the past, or at least nobody would come out and show that he had used it, and accepted it. I'm sure one important reason it wasn't used was the lack of the kind of abrasives that are available today. Any turning done with spalted wood requires extensive sanding to get past all the pecks and chips that occur from working the brittle wood, even with the sharpest tools. Working with it is like working with torn end grain everywhere, but that's part of the challenge. In the end, the pain is forgotten as the piece comes to life.

Spalting is caused by water and fungus. If you've ever noticed a piece of sheetrock or plywood that accidentally got wet from the water on the floor or ceiling, you'll recall the edge where the water stain stopped, leaving an interesting pattern. The material soaked up the water like a sponge, and the water combined with chemicals in the wood or sheetrock, to leave a stain in a random, arbitrary pattern. Spalting is like this, but far more complex. Combine this staining with the fungus at work breaking the wood down, the mineral content of the soil that the tree grew in, the mineral content of the water trapped in the tree, the temperature and other climatic variables, the softer and harder parts of the wood in the tree, and countless other biological functions, and suddenly there is an incredibly complex system that results in spalting. I can't explain exactly how the process occurs; I can only speculate that the prominent black lines are caused by the accumulation of mineral deposits within the wood that separate the harder and softer areas as well as define the zones that have been attacked by fungus.

There is one thing so far that I have found consistently predictable: the absolute unpredictability and inconsistency of the wood and its structure, the spalting, and the patterns. Each piece is completely different from the next, even six inches down the same tree. That, too, is part of the challenge of the material. One tree may have good workable spalted wood, while the next, although appearing the same, will be useless. So working with the wood requires patience, faith, stamina, and above all, experience. With each piece of spalted wood comes a program of rules and problems that have to be worked out. Only by working the wood can one gain the knowledge, experience and understanding necessary to appreciate and succeed with the material.

Mark Lindquist, of Henniker, N.H., is a writer and a sculptor who earns his living by turning and carving spalted wood and burls.

Finding spalted wood at just the right point is crucial, because if the wood decays too long it will be really rotten, unworkable, and useless even as firewood. If the wood is found too early, it lacks character and seems bland like conventional wood, which, after one has once seen beautiful spalted wood, is plain to the eye. Spalted wood that is too soft will have very punky spots that are impossible to do anything with, which, in combination with harder spots, will not allow the piece to be turned. Spalted wood that is too hard will most likely check, because it's right in between and is really unstable. One beauty of spalted wood is that in a sense it has been allowed to age. It is no longer green, and needs only to dry out. For some reason, spalted wood caught in the right stage is stable enough to resist checking. I attribute this to the relaxation of tension within the wood that ordinarily causes splitting.

As far as I know, spalting occurs mainly in these woods: all birches, beeches and maples. It occurs in elm, but rarely in red and white oak. Apple spalts, but spalting is relatively unknown in walnut and butternut. Most of the white woods show good spalting. The process occurs at different rates for different trees, and of course depends on climate and enviornmental variables.

White, yellow and gray birch spalt very quickly after felling. White birch usually starts showing some figure within a year and a half; gray birch and yellow birch take a bit longer, but they spalt quickly nevertheless. Black birch spalts

[Editor's note: According to J. S. Boyce in *Forest Pathology* (McGraw Hill, 1948), "Narrow zone lines, usually black but sometimes dark brown, are a common phenomenon of many decays. They are frequently formed in the white rots, and they are more common in decayed wood of hardwoods than in conifers. At times black zone lines may be fantastic in pattern." Boyce goes on to identify the various fungi, bacteria and parasites responsible for each type of decay, and the characteristics and colors typical of each.

In essence, a fungus first invades the wood (incipient decay), establishes itself, and then breaks it down. The zone lines mark the intermittent progress of each type of fungus as it advances into the wood, or the point where the tiny filaments (mycelia) of two competing fungi clash for possession of the tree's tissues. Generally the wood is softer behind each zone line and harder ahead of it. Says Boyce, by way of example, "In aspen three stages of decay have been recognized. In the incipient stage the wood is faintly colored from light pink to straw-brown; in the intermediate stage it is colored from straw to chocolate-brown, but it is still hard and firm; and in the advanced stage is included all soft, punky wood irrespective of color. Wood in the incipient and intermediate stages is utilized for some purposes but in the advanced stage is always rejected."]

From *Fine Woodworking* magazine (Summer 1977) 7:50-53

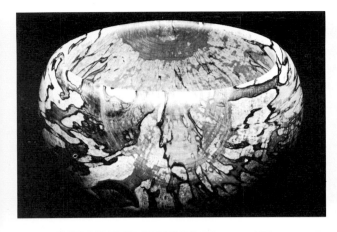

Spalted maple bowl with ladle, 10-in. dia., $375; spalted yellow birch fruit bowl, 12-in. dia., $250. Both were made and priced

for museum collections. Maple rosebud vase, right, 2-1/2 x 6 in., about $50 (1977), is by Melvin Lindquist, author's father.

the slowest of all the birches because it is the hardest; however, when it spalts it is very beautiful, and if caught at the right point will work easily and still remain hard. Birches tend to spalt regularly and predictably with the grain because of the straightness of the tree's normal growth.

Beeches also spalt predictably with the grain, but the wood is often unstable and checks easily. Spalting occurs after two years in most cases. Elm spalts rather quickly, also within two years. However, it frequently lacks character and often looks anemic. But if it's found at just the right time, and the wood has good figure in it, some beautiful pieces may result. Apple spalts, but oh boy does it crack! Oak may spalt, but it tends to rot from the outside in. Occasionally, though, oak will provide a splendid, magnificent piece of spalted wood.

But the best of all spalted woods are the maples, especially old New England sugar maples. Old sugar maples contain infinite grain configurations with fantastic and beautiful patterns. The old-time makers of fine furniture and musical instruments coveted the beautifully grained maple wood that someone's grandfather had stored for generations to come. There are names for the recurring grain configurations, although today it's difficult to get such wood, and the cost is unbelievable. There are tiger maple, fiddleback maple, bird's-eye maple, blister maple, curly maple and burly maple, to mention a few. Because of all these various grain patterns and because of the hardness of the wood, old sugar maple trees can contain remarkable patterns, designs, and even pictures of recognizable objects.

Soft maple will spalt in anywhere from two to four years.

Rock maple, or sugar maple, starts to spalt after two to five years, and once the process is working, there is a point at which it quickly speeds up and the tree goes rotten all the way. Just before that is the time to get it. I once found an old sugar maple, full of maple sugar taps, on the side of a dirt road, and I estimated the tree had begun to grow two hundred years ago. It was full of tiger, curly, and blister configurations, all magnificently spalted. The lines were so intricate that it looked as though an ancient Chinese calligrapher had deliberately penned his designs within the wood. The wood itself was still very hard; its texture was sensuously creamy, and the color of the aged wood was rich and golden. I was amazed at the beauty that was hidden within the old rotting hulk of a tree. The farmer must have thought I was crazy to touch it, but he didn't say anything for fear that he might scare me away and the blasted mess would stay there forever. There were maps of the world, animals, birds, fish, mountains, even a detailed "painting" of a rose, all done in fine lines like a pen and ink drawing. The most amazing thing was that the wood between the dark lines changed color from area to area, so that it seemed to be a carefully executed design of the most sophisticated combination of lamination and marquetry.

By far the most exquisite of spalted woods, and in my opinion better than the rarest exotic, is a piece of choice, aged, pictorial-figured, spalted sugar maple. The pictures within such wood seem to be a record of the tree's history: the storms, the sunny days, the cool moonlit nights, the wars that happened during its time, the sunsets, the pain and cold

Block cut from spalted maple log, above, shows fungal zone lines extending throughout the wood, a three-dimensional lattice. Dark area at center is completely decomposed. Downed rock maple tree, left, shows spalted end grain. Mushrooms growing on end of maple log, below, are reliable clue to spalting inside.

of the ever-changing New England weather. There is mystery locked inside, and infinite beauty—a worthless old tree making a last attempt to display its glory.

Think of the availability of the material: the cost is your time. Quality depends upon your perseverance and faith that the right piece is there, free for the taking. The process of working spalted wood begins with finding the material—in essence, found art. Finding spalted wood is very simple once you know what to look for. All I do is go out in the woods and look for fallen or dead standing trees. Maples are the best, because they take longer to spalt. Birches are often disappointing because the bark almost always looks intact, but the inside of the tree may be rotten to the point of mush. But no matter what you look for, you'll never know what's inside the log until you cut it. A lot of it is guesswork, a lot is based on experience and keys or signs to look for. The best source for exceptional spalted wood is the dead, fallen tree that has been lying around and looks as if it's not worth the powder to blow it to oblivion. Check the soil that the tree is resting on. If it is rich dark earth, or mossy, or covered with rotting leaves, that's a good sign. If the end or side of the log is covered with mushrooms it is a good bet that spalting will lie within. Many times you can see spalting on outer layers of the wood, where the bark has come off the tree. After a while you acquire X-ray vision and can guess what is going on inside the log. But there is no substitute for cutting into the wood to find out what's there. Most of the time, it's a surprise.

Normally I approach the end of the log that has been exposed to the weather, and cautiously crosscut off about three inches of the end. This usually takes out the end checks and the "mock spalting" that often occurs on the surface. Having exposed the face of the log at that point, I usually make a second cut about 16 inches down the log because I work with relatively small sections that are easy to carry out of the woods, and happen to be the length of the bar on my lightweight saw. If the figure or picture is good, I rip six-inch thick sections working around the center, cutting through any faults, cracks or spots that might check later. Stay away from the center or pith because it's a sure thing that it will check. The other possibility at this point is to take the log or butt to a mill (they may not saw it, fearing metal or doubting its worth) and have it cut into boards. It's difficult to work it this way because you never know what you'll run into.

Cutting spalted wood is theoretically similar to cutting gems and lapidary work. As in cutting picture jasper, the object is to get the greatest possible amount of picture from the piece at hand. The wood must be carefully studied and observed before cutting, to ensure the best picture within the chunk, relative to the bowl being turned. So this introduces the sculptural theory of the object being contained within the mass, which it is the artisan's function to release.

Spalting has characteristics too numerous to list, but among them are some that govern cutting methods to produce the best figures. The end grain of a log gives a clue to what is inside. The picture will often be very beautiful and full, if the log is well spalted, and it can be worked, providing the entire crosscut disc is not used (because it will definitely crack). So the best use of spalted wood, allowing the most control, is side grain or ripped stock. The lines forming the picture in the end grain will normally travel parallel, lengthwise with the log. So if the figure is double-lined, making swirly star-shaped patterns in the end grain, the log may be crosscut several times, like slicing ham. That same picture will occur several times, with slight variations, for a considerable distance until the pattern shifts because of a limb or irregular growth. The lines that make end-grain patterns also make side-grain patterns. Birches, which spalt more regularly, have fairly straight, predictable lines, sometimes close together, traveling the entire length of the log. The side-grain figure will resemble zebrawood, but the color will be far brighter. The end-grain picture will be a network of fine black lines.

If a good spalted log is found at just the right point, the markings may be consistent and predictable throughout, and thus easy to cut, because the broken-down, partially rotten wood is very soft and cuts nicely. Deciding where to cut is the real problem. You must learn to see the wood, the finished object, in your mind's eye, and then balance that against your observations of the log, its faults and patterns. In essence, you must flow and harmonize with the wood and the wonder of the graphics and design within. A wrong move will spoil the picture; the right move will unfold unbelievable beauty.

Here is an opportunity to cut the wood with the same care that later will make the object. The tree was carefully grown, and your object must be carefully made simply because of the nature of the material. So the harvesting or gathering of the wood must be equally special. It really is like a crop. The tree dies and begins to decay; when it spalts just right, harvest.

After the wood is cut, I usually paint the ends of my chunks with an inexpensive white glue and water solution, applied liberally, to keep the ends from drying too quickly. I use epoxy to seal the very best pieces, because they come only once in a lifetime. I see them as uncut diamonds, so the expense is worth it. After sealing I stack the wood in an open-air shed, making sure to sticker between the pieces for air circulation. I leave the blocks in the shed for a year, and then bring them into an indoor shed. The indoor shed is closed with less air circulation, but it freezes in the winter and heats up during the summer. I do not sticker the blocks indoors, but merely pile them on top of each other. After a few years, they are dry enough to turn. The thinner the block the quicker the drying. You may use the usual green bowl methods (turn unseasoned wood, dry it, turn it again), but you may run a large risk of splitting, depending on the piece. I'm three years ahead of myself on wood, so I let it age by itself. A climate-controlled room would be effective, but nature will do the job, given the chance.

Spalted wood has always been around; it might be right in your own back yard. Recognizing the potential, and the limitations of the material, anyone can have free access to wood so rich and alive with color and character that it transcends the nature of the wood it was before its metamorphosis. Realize the wood has made a transition, a long journey from one life to another, and catch it, discover it, at just the right moment. Your woodworking will enter a new phase unlike any other you've experienced. ☐

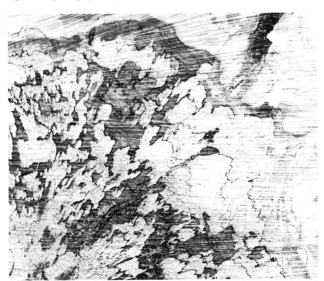

Fresh-cut end of spalted maple log shows advanced decay and highest degree of spalting in rainbow colors, a rare find. Covered

jar made of spalted tiger maple, 6-in. dia., is production work to retail in the $50 to $100 range (1977) in craft galleries.

Abnormal Wood
Dealing with knots and reaction wood

by R. Bruce Hoadley

While some irregularities in wood may increase value, as when a distinctive figure is produced, others decrease value. By tradition, any irregularities that decrease value are branded as defects. Although some of the features described below seem to be negative in woodworking, the woodworker is urged to reserve judgment on nature's irregularities. These were indeed defects when hand tools could not deal with them, but now many of these irregularities can be routinely machined using power tools.

Knots—The commercial hardwood lumber-grading system assumes that every knot is a defect and bases grade on the size and number of clear areas among the knots (and other blemishes). On the other hand, many beautiful works of craftsmanship and art have been produced using, or even featuring, knots. The woodworker should first of all understand what knots are and how their structure relates to the rest of the wood. Knots are simply the parts of limbs that are embedded in the main stem of the tree (figure 1).

As the tree grows, branching is initiated by lateral bud de-velopment from the twig. The lateral branch thus was originally connected to the pith of the main stem. Each successive growth ring or layer forms continuously over the stem and branches, although the growth ring is thicker on the stem than on the branches and the branch diameter increases more slowly than the trunk. As the girth of the trunk increases, a cone of branch wood—**the intergrown knot**—develops within the trunk. Such knots are also termed **tight knots** because they are intergrown with surrounding wood, or **red knots**, especially in conifers where they often have a distinct reddish tinge. At some point the limb may die, perhaps as a result of overshadowing by limbs higher up. The limb dies back to approximately the trunk surface, its dead cambium unable to add further girth. So subsequent growth rings added to the main stem simply surround the dead limb stub, which may begin to rot. A number of years of growth may be added to the main stem, surrounding the branch stub. The dead part of the stub becomes an **encased knot**. It is not intergrown and therefore is also called a **loose knot**, often with bark entrapped. Knotholes result when an encased or loose knot falls

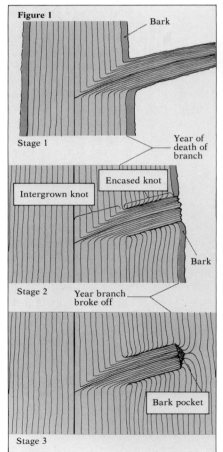

Figure 1

Bark

Stage 1

Year of death of branch

Intergrown knot

Encased knot

Bark

Stage 2

Year branch broke off

Bark pocket

Stage 3

Bruce Hoadley

Coniferous trees, left, are characterized by excurrent form, i.e., a dominant stem from which whorls of lateral branching occur at regular intervals, or nodes. The pattern is often present on plywood made from rotary-cut softwood veneer, right.

A knot is the basal portion of a branch whose structure becomes surrounded by the enlarging stem. Since branches begin with lateral buds, knots can always be traced back to the pith of the main stem.

From *Fine Woodworking* magazine (January 1981) 26:72-75

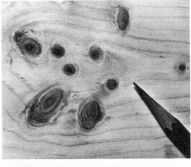
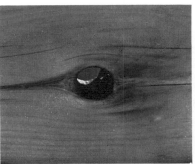

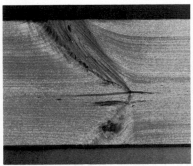
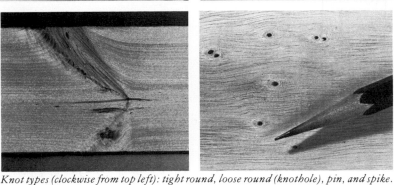

Knot types (clockwise from top left): tight round, loose round (knothole), pin, and spike.

A carving chunk may appear flawless at first glance (A in drawing below). Removing wood adjacent to the pith (B) will locate internal knots (C and photo above). Scars in the bark (at X) may be a sign of knots large enough to ruin the block for carving.

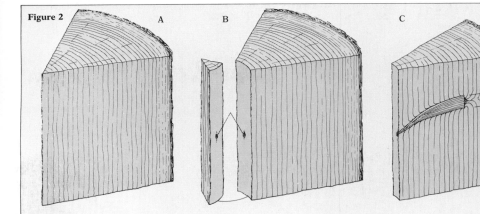

Figure 2

out of a board. Encased knots are also called **black knots** because they commonly are discolored by stain and decay. In time the stub may become weakened by decay and fall or be broken off, or it may be pruned back flush with the trunk. Further growth layers will enclose the stub, and eventually the cambium will form a continuous layer. From this point on, solid layers of wood and bark will be formed beyond the overgrown knot. But as the cambium moves outward, the knot-scarred bark layers persist for an amazing number of years, providing a clue to the buried blemish.

Knots may be classified by how they are cut from the tree. If they are split by radial sawing and extend across the face of the board they are termed **spike knots**. On flatsawn boards they usually appear round or oval and are called **round knots**. Knots smaller than ¼ in. in diameter are called **pin knots**.

Understanding knots can be useful to the woodworker. Nothing is more devastating to a carver than to work halfway through a block of wood only to uncover an interior knot flaw. Yet the trained eye can usually predict such a blemish. If a wedge is taken from a log and the first few growth rings near the pith are removed (figure 2), any branches will be seen at least as tiny knots. If none are present, there will be no knot-related defects in the piece. If any are located, the bark should be carefully examined for scars. Experience can tell much about the size and depth of such defects.

Since every knot originates at the pith, every knot that appears on the bark side of a flatsawn board will also appear on the pith side of that same board. On the other hand, some knots on the pith side may have ended and grown over before reaching the bark surface. Therefore, the bark side is often the clearer, higher-quality face.

There are a variety of reasons why knots commonly are considered defects. The wood of the knot itself is different in density (usually higher), and its grain orientation is more or less perpendicular to the surrounding wood. Because shrinkage is greater across the knot than in the surrounding wood, encased knots may loosen and drop out. Although intergrown knots remain tight, they may develop radial cracks. Encased knots are usually considered worse defects because of the discoloration and the entrapped bark associated with them. From the standpoints of strength and machining properties, the disorientation of grain direction is troublesome not only because of the knot itself but because the entire area is influenced by the knot. For example, a spike knot extending

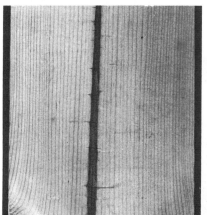

Reaction wood forms in trees that lean. The curving sweep of the tree at left, although picturesque, means that unpredictable compression wood will be found within. Right, pronounced reaction wood from leaning hemlock tree, shown in cross section.

Top, wide growth rings surrounding the pith are juvenile wood, which is lighter and weaker than narrow-ringed mature wood. Needle scars also indicate juvenile wood.

Abnormal appearance of earlywood and latewood on a flatsawn surface, left, indicates compression wood. Compression wood in white pine may appear as a dark streak on a flatsawn board, right.

across a board may cause it to break in half under small loads.

Knots may also be an asset, and have been valuable features of figure in many ways. Knotty pine is often thought to be characteristic of Colonial decor, though in reality, knots were mostly avoided, plugged or painted over by early cabinetmakers. Knotty pine as wall boarding seems to be a 20th-century invention to use the increasing stocks of common grades of lumber. Other species that exhibit knots with some degree of regularity, such as spruce, cedar and other western softwoods, have been successfully marketed to feature their knots. Individual pieces of wood with knots increasingly are fashioned into masterpieces of cabinetry and sculpture.

Juvenile and reaction wood—The first few growth rings added around the pith may not be typical of the mature wood formed by the tree. This core of atypical tissue is termed **juvenile wood**. It is prevalent among conifers, especially plantation-grown trees, which grow rapidly until crown closure, when competition with other trees slows growth to a more normal rate. Juvenile wood is characterized by wider growth rings of lower-density wood and less strength. It may also shrink abnormally, resulting in greater tendency to warp, especially by twisting. Pieces of wood including (or very near) the pith should be suspect. Some trees and species show little or no juvenile-wood abnormality.

Reaction wood is a term applied to abnormal wood formed in tree stems and limbs that are other than erect, that is, par-

allel to the pull of gravity. The principal concern to woodworkers is the occurrence of reaction wood in leaning trunks from which otherwise defect-free wood might be expected. Causes for leaning stems include partial uprooting by storms, severe bending under snow or ice, and tree growth toward sunlight available from only one direction. Reaction-wood formation seems to include a mechanism for redirecting stem growth to the vertical, resulting in a bowing of the stem. Therefore boards or pieces from a log with noticeable bow should be suspected of containing reaction wood and should be examined very closely for it.

Reaction wood has different traits in softwoods and hardwoods. In softwoods, reaction wood forms mainly toward the underside of the leaning stem. Because the pull of gravity presumably puts the lower side of the leaning trunk in compression, reaction wood in conifers is termed **compression wood**. The part of the growth ring containing reaction wood is usually wider than normal, resulting in an eccentrically shaped stem with the pith offset toward the upper side (photos, above). The abnormal tracheids usually appear to form wider than normal latewood. Even-grained woods, such as eastern white pine, therefore appear uneven-grained. However, in woods that are notably uneven-grained, such as southern yellow pine, the latewood is duller and more lifeless than normal and tends to even out the contrast.

The two main disadvantages of compression wood for the woodworker are its effects on strength and shrinkage. Since

Eccentric rings on cross-sectional surfaces of red oak log indicate tension wood.

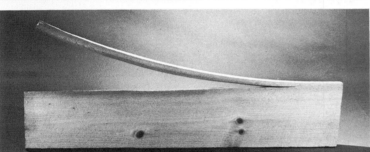

Strength and shrinkage of reaction wood are unpredictable. Brash failure, top left, can be disastrous. Abnormal shrinkage in compression wood, top right, is a frequent cause of warp. Above, reaction wood on edge of pine board has split and bent away.

The abnormal fibers of tension wood, containing a greater-than-normal amount of cellulose, left a woolly surface on this cottonwood board when it was sawn from the log.

reaction-wood tracheids are thick-walled, the wood is usually denser than normal. But because they contain less cellulose, and the cellulose chains are not parallel to the long direction of the cells, the wood is weaker than normal. The woodcarver is especially aware of the abnormally hard but brittle qualities of compression wood. In finishing, compression wood may not stain uniformly with normal wood. The carpenter notices the difficulty in driving nails and the greater tendency to split. For structural uses where load-bearing capability is vital, as in ladder rails, unknowing use of reaction wood has resulted in fatality, because the wood breaks suddenly when bent, and at lower-than-expected loads.

Abnormal longitudinal shrinkage is the second major problem. Normal wood shrinks so slightly along the grain that it is usually negligible. Compression wood shrinks up to 10 to 20 times the normal amount. What's more, because reaction-wood formation is non-uniform in a given board, the shrinkage is uneven. Drying of reaction wood, or changes in moisture content, creates uneven shrinkage stresses in the wood. This, along with juvenile wood, is a major cause of warp in framing lumber. Most distortions that develop in stud walls probably result from reaction wood. In woodworking, attempts to ripsaw pieces containing reaction wood may result in the wood's pinching against the saw or its splaying widely apart as the cut progresses, both potentially dangerous occurrences.

In hardwood trees, reaction wood forms predominantly toward the upper side of the leaning stem. Because gravity causes the upper side to be in tension, it is termed **tension wood**. In hardwoods, however, there is less tendency than in softwoods for the pith to be off-center in the stem, and tension wood may develop irregularly around the entire stem. Tension wood is often quite difficult to detect. Sometimes it looks silvery, other times dull and lifeless, and in some cases there is little if any visual difference. Indications of crookedness or sweep in the log are signals of possible tension wood. The abnormal fibers of tension wood actually contain a greater than normal amount of cellulose. This wood is commonly stronger than normal. Of concern to the woodworker is the way this wood machines. Fiber structure does not sever cleanly but leaves a fuzzy or woolly surface. Aside from the immediate problem of machining tension wood, seemingly successful efforts to smooth the wood leave a microscopic woolliness upon the surface. Upon finishing, stain is absorbed irregularly and the surface appears blotchy. As with compression wood, longitudinal shrinkage in tension wood is both irregular and greater than normal, resulting in warping and machining problems. □

R. Bruce Hoadley is a contributing editor to Fine Woodworking. This article is excerpted from the chapter "Figure in Wood" in his book, Understanding Wood: A Craftsman's Guide to Wood Technology (hardcover, 272 pp.), published by The Taunton Press, Box 355, Newtown, Conn. 06470.

Black Light Makes Some Woods Glow

Bright colors in fluorescent woods

by R. Bruce Hoadley

A rather unfamiliar property of wood—fluorescence under ultraviolet radiation (black light)—is a fascinating visual phenomenon well worth investigating. Certain woods viewed under black light appear to emit a mysterious glow or fluorescence, which is almost sure to inspire ideas in woodcraft.

Fluorescence is the absorption of invisible light energy by a material capable of transforming it and emitting it at wavelengths visible to the eye. The human eye can see light over the spectrum of wavelengths varying from about 8000 (red) down to about 3800 (violet). (Wavelengths are measured in Angstrom units, which equal about 4 billionths of an inch.) Above 8000 is invisible infrared light; below 3800 is invisible ultraviolet light. The black light commonly used for visual effects is in the 3800 to 3200 range and is referred to as long wave or near ultraviolet light. It won't harm the eyes. Light in the 3200 to 2900 range includes sun-tanning and burning rays. Below 2900 is shortwave or far ultraviolet, which is used to kill bacteria and is very dangerous to the eyes. Sterilization units or other sources of shortwave ultraviolet should never be used to view fluorescent materials.

Commercial long-wave or black-light lamps emit light averaging about 3700, although the light may range from as low as 3200 to about 4500, well into the visible range. We therefore often see a purple glow, although most of the light emitted is invisible. Chemicals in a fluorescent material absorb this invisible light and transform the energy so that the light emitted from the material is visible in a particular color.

Many domestic species of wood exhibit fluorescence. The table at right lists the principal species, although there are doubtless others. The colors listed are typical, but both hue and brilliance will vary among individual samples. Countless other species from around the world also show fluorescence, but our native species are as attractive as those found anywhere in the world.

Yellow is the predominant color, and also the most brilliant, as in black locust, honeylocust, Kentucky coffeetree and acacia. Barberry, a lemon-yellow wood under normal light, is also among the most brilliant yellows, but since it is a shrub it is difficult to locate pieces large enough for anything but jewelry, inlay or other small items.

Perhaps the most interesting is staghorn sumac. Its sapwood has a pale lavender-blue fluorescence. In the heartwood, each growth ring repeats a yellow, yellow-green, lavender-blue sequence. Yucca and holly have a soft bluish to grey fluorescence. Purpleheart emits a dim coppery glow. Badi exhibits a mellow pumpkin orange. In addition to normal sapwood and heartwood fluorescence, certain anatomical features such as resin canals, oil cells, vessel contents, bark, fungal stains and pigment streaks show selective fluorescence. In aspen, for example, a brilliant yellow fluorescence usually occurs at the margins of areas stained by fungi.

Fluorescence is of obvious value for identification purposes, but it also suggests interesting applications for the woodworker, expecially in carving or marquetry. Inspiring sculpture and religious statuary can have moving effects when viewed in darkness or subdued light with hidden ultraviolet lamps. With the increased use of black light for entertainment areas, such as game rooms and cocktail lounges, fluorescent figures, decorative carvings and items such as lightswitch covers are quite popular. Fluorescence can add extra excitement to already popular wooden jewelry and personal accessories. An African mask or Polynesian tiki carved in a fluorescent species makes an unusual pendant or pin.

Fluorescent woods can be used in combination by laminating or inlaying. Menacing fluorescing teeth can be set in the mouth of a carved dragon. Spooky yellow eyes that "light up" can be inlaid into a carved owl. Laminated woods can be carved or turned into unusual lamp bases—especially for black lights. And don't throw away carving chips or planer shavings, as children delight in gluing these to cardboard to create fluorescing designs or pictures.

Wood fluorescence is subject to surface chemical degradation, apparently associated with the familiar darkening or aging effect. Fluorescent wood is most rapidly faded by exposure to daylight, especially direct sunlight. A carving will retain its brilliance for years if kept in a dark place. In normal indoor light, a year's exposure will fade a piece to about half its original brilliance. A light recarving or sanding of the surface to expose unaged wood will renew the original fluorescence. Most finishes reduce the fluorescent brilliance, but in the long run may maintain brilliance by minimizing aging. Clear paste wax seems to be the least dulling. □

Scientific Name	Common Name	Color of Fluorescence
Acacia greggii	catclaw acacia	deep yellow
Annona glabra	pond-apple	dull yellow
Asimina triloba	pawpaw	faint yellow-green
Berberis thunbergi	Japanese barberry	bright yellow
Cercidium floridum	blue paloverde	yellow green
Cercis canadensis	eastern redbud	bright yellow
Cladrastis lutea	yellowwood	pale yellow-light blue
Cotinus obovatus	American smoketree	deep yellow
Gleditsia aquatica	waterlocust	pale yellow
Gleditsia triacanthos	honeylocust	bright yellow
Gymnocladus dioicus	Kentucky coffeetree	deep yellow, bright
Ilex verticillata	common winterberry	light blue
Magnolia virginiana	sweetbay	pale yellow
Mangifera indica	mango	pale orange
Piscidia piscipula	Florida fishpoison-tree	dull yellow
Rhus copallina	shining sumac	bright yellow
Rhus glabra	smooth sumac	bright yellow
Rhus typhina	staghorn sumac	bright to greenish yellow to pale blue
Robinia pseudoacacia	black locust	bright yellow
Robinia viscosa	clammy locust	bright yellow
Torreya taxifolia	Florida torreya	dull yellow
Yucca brevifolia	Joshua-tree	yellowish gray
Zanthoxylum clava-herculis	Hercules-club	sapwood pale yellow to light blue, heartwood bright orange

From *Fine Woodworking* magazine (May 1979) 16:81

Ash's distinctive bark, with its neat, contrasty striations, makes the tree easy to identify at any season of the year. Its compound leaves, composed of leaflets on a central stem, are among the first to fall in autumn. A distinguishing characteristic of black ash is the leaflets' close attachment to the stem.

Ash
Counterfeit oak or quality cabinetwood?

by Jon W. Arno

At a recent antiques show, I found a dozen or so turn-of-the-century commodes labeled "oak." The general public and a lot of antique dealers seem happy enough to identify every light-colored, open-grained wood as oak at a glance. The oak label serves as a convenience for pricing and dating such pieces, but it isn't always accurate. Two of the commodes at the show were of mixed wood construction (predominantly elm); the three nicest were unquestionably ash.

Most people may not have much reason to care. Ash and oak are both open-grained woods, with similarly attractive and somewhat racy figures. Furniture made from either wood has a look of solid quality. Yet I think ash outclasses oak in several important ways, at least from a cabinetmaker's viewpoint—the two woods have decidedly different characteristics. For starters, oak is a

member of the beech family, *Fagaceae,* which includes the oaks, the beeches and the chestnuts. Ash belongs to the olive family, *Oleaceae,* and is related to lilac and forsythia.

You don't have to be a botanist to quickly separate oak from ash. Oak has prominent rays that are easily visible on the flat-sawn surface, where they appear as bold lines called ray flecks. In some species of white oak, these flecks may be more than ¹⁄₁₆ in. wide and well over 1 in. long, while in the red oaks they are generally smaller and darker. In fact, the rays are such a dominant feature in white oak that it's often specially quartersawn to expose them as broad bands or ribbons. These are extremely hard and dense, and in stained wood you could call their appearance either fantastic or outrageous, depending on your taste. I person-

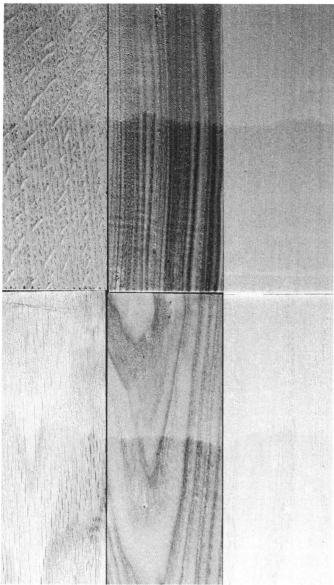

Oak and ash are easy to tell apart. Oak has prominent rays, most pronounced when it's cut radially (top left), but also visible as a needlelike pattern on the tangential surface (bottom left). Ash's rays are hardly visible, allowing both radially and tangentially cut lumber to be mixed in the same piece of furniture. Brown ash is in the center, white ash on the right. The lower half of all samples has been oiled.

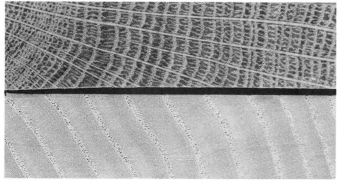

The rays, lines of cells extending from the pith to the bark, are much more prominent in oak (top) than they are in ash. Both woods are ring-porous: large cells produced in early spring are followed by more solid growth in summer.

ally don't like the effect, but if you do, score one point for oak, because no matter how you cut ash, it will not produce this pattern. Like all woods, ash has rays, but they are almost undetectable with the naked eye. As a cabinetmaker, I view this as one of ash's great virtues, because flatsawn and radially sawn boards can be used in the same piece with no surprises when the stain goes on.

Oak contains tannic acid. If you expose the wood to strong ammonia vapor, a chemical reaction will turn it dark brown. This staining process is known as fuming, and it won't work on ash. Personally, I use ammonia only on windows, but if fuming sounds like a good idea to you, score another point for oak.

Oak's acid content is a mixed blessing at best. A friend of mine once left a green piece of oak on his tablesaw overnight, and by morning it had permanently etched its shape as a black rust mark, which is still there after four years.

Ash's biggest advantage is that it is generally less dense than oak. If we cabinetmakers accept our two premier domestic hardwoods as having nearly ideal density—black cherry with a specific gravity of 0.47 (green to oven-dry) and black walnut at 0.51—we find that the various species of ash straddle this range, while the oaks are all somewhat denser. Ashes run from 0.45 to 0.55, oaks from 0.52 to 0.80. Ash is by no means a soft wood in comparison to pine, basswood, butternut, poplar or aspen, but it is relatively soft when you consider its ability to withstand pounding and stress. Ash yields an end product with great strength relative to both its weight and the amount of energy expended to shape or fashion it. And what could be nearer and dearer to a cabinetmaker's heart?

Because of these advantages, ash was one of several favored woods in Grand Rapids factories during the so-called "Golden Oak" era. Oak got all the publicity, but ash often was the dominant species in those utilitarian and now quaintly obsolete mixed-wood pieces: the dry sinks, commodes, cupboards and wardrobes that were cranked out by the thousands in the late 19th century for America's growing middle class. I'm grateful that nobody thought to call the stuff "Golden Ash"—the lack of publicity helps keep ash at a reasonable price.

While keeping a low profile in cabinetry, ash has established a worldwide reputation as the wood for baseball bats and as one of nature's most perfect materials for tool handles. For these purposes, second-growth trees with straight, evenly spaced grain are selected and specially graded. The white-ash sample shown on this page was cut from a friend's woodlot and wouldn't make a bad bat. Such ash has great strength-to-weight ratio and rigidity. Also, once the surface is smoothed, ash polishes well. Whether this is achieved by constant contact with human hands, as in the case of a tool handle, or by the deliberate effort of a woodworker, the end result is a definite plus.

Within each annual ring, ash has a honeycomb of porous earlywood followed by a layer of dense latewood, making it a sort of natural laminate. The American Indians discovered that they could separate the layers by soaking the quartered log and pounding it vigorously. As the earlywood broke down, thin strips of strong, highly flexible latewood peeled off, which the Indians used for basket splints and ribs in their canoes.

There are over a dozen species of ash native to North America, but only a few of them reach timber size. Those that do all produce ring-porous woods. There are, however, some subtle differences that relate not only to the species of ash, but also to the environment in which the tree grew. Generally speaking, the

From *Fine Woodworking* magazine (March 1985) 51:49-51

strong, straight-grained wood resulting from second-growth timber, which is so desirable for tool handles and sports equipment, is not the best for cabinetmaking. First-growth ash, or ash that has grown slowly for whatever reason, produces the nicest furniture lumber. For one thing, the ratio of heartwood to sapwood is greater in slow-growing trees. For another, these trees produce relatively more earlywood than latewood each season, which means that their wood is lighter in weight, more porous, and far more interesting in figure.

In the lumber trade, most of the wood marketed as "white ash" comes from two species: white ash (*Fraxinus americana*) and green ash (*F. pennsylvanica*), both of which are plentiful throughout the eastern United States. Although on the average white ash might be a little denser and tougher than green ash, variations in growing conditions make the two overlap considerably. Another species, blue ash (*F. quadrangulata*), is of little consequence in the lumber trade because of its limited and sporadic range (around the Ohio and Mississippi River basins). It produces a wood that is almost identical to green ash, and it too is marketed as white ash. Blue ash gets its name from a blue dye extracted from the bark, which was once used for dyeing cloth.

The so-called "white" ashes make nice cabinetwoods once the project is complete, but three other species of ash are noticeably softer and easier to work: black ash (*F. nigra*), pumpkin ash (*F. profunda*) and Oregon ash (*F. latifolia*). To my way of thinking, black ash is the connoisseur's choice. Native to the Great Lakes states, New England and Canada, its environment is a harsh one, which forces slow growth that results in a lighter, less dense wood with exceptionally pretty flatsawn figure. The heartwood is a beautiful soft brown in color (in some parts of its range, black ash is referred to as "brown ash" by lumber dealers) and produces a natural "fruitwood" tone with nothing more than a coat of clear varnish. Because of its narrow annual rings, black ash was the preferred species for basketweaving, and like all the ashes, its stratified nature makes it one of the better woods for steambending.

Pumpkin ash, a similar species, is found in the South. It's less dense than the white ash species and extremely variable as a result of environmental conditions. Pumpkin ash growing in swampy areas will produce a buttress-like base that yields light, soft wood, tending to brittleness. On the West Coast, Oregon ash produces a reasonably good cabinetwood. Its specific gravity of 0.50 makes it somewhat softer than any of the white ashes.

Price and availability of the ashes depend a little on how creative you are. Like the old saying "Water, water everywhere, nor any drop to drink," ash is abundant, but my favorite grades for furniture usually end up as shipping crates and pallets, not in retail lumberyards.

Until recently, local lumberyards didn't have much reason to stock ash. Customers always seemed to be asking for maple, cherry, walnut and oak—and if not these, then some exotic timber. Today, at least in my area of Wisconsin, times are changing. Without much trouble, I can get select, kiln-dried ash at between $1.40 and $2.00 a board foot (all 1985 prices). Unfortunately the mills aren't always careful to identify the species, so lumberyards don't always know what they have. Most of the time it's white ash, and of such high quality that it lacks character.

To find my favorite, black ash, I look around at the beginning of the distribution chain, either buying direct from a mill or going to a pallet manufacturer. The last time I did this, about a year

Turn-of-the-century pieces from the 'Golden Oak' era—like the author's commode above—often are not oak at all, but ash.

ago, I got lucky. The pallet manufacturer said: "Yeah, I got some ash, but it's just that soft brown stuff from up near Rhinelander; you can have it for forty-five cents a board foot...." "Well, maybe I can make it work," I muttered. I took all he had, about 200 bd. ft., stickered and air-dried it for a few months (with its low stump moisture content, ash dries well and easily), then had it planed for 10¢ a foot. Sure enough, it's a cabinetmaker's dream: beautiful, slow-grown northern black ash, at 55¢ a board foot. How sweet it is!

To conclude from all of this that ash is somehow an undiscovered, world-class cabinetwood to be ranked with walnut, cherry, rosewood and teak would be driving a point beyond its credible limits. Ash is nice in comparison to many woods, but it also has its faults. After praising ash for its laminate qualities, I should point out that the flip side of this feature is that the wood splits easily, as anyone who has spent much time chopping firewood knows (and appreciates). Ash is also very splintery, and unless your hands are calloused from constant shopwork, you may pick up some slivers when cutting and coarse-sanding it. Once shaped, however, it smooths out nicely. Given its extremely open grain, ash must be filled before you can finish it to the kind of glass-smooth surface required for some surfaces, such as tabletops. And, finally, ash does not weather well when exposed to moist, outdoor conditions. Powderpost beetles and other wood-eating bugs absolutely love the stuff. If resistance to the elements is important to your project, score one last point for oak, white oak in particular. It weathers well. Especially in antiques shops. □

Jon Arno is an amateur woodworker in Brookfield, Wis. He has also written on elm (pp. 66-67) and the pines (pp. 70-72).

Two Neglected Woods

Elm: modern power tools make it workable

by Jon W. Arno

From the founding of the first colonies, American cabinetmakers have been both blessed and spoiled by a choice of native woods unequaled anywhere else in the world. Virgin stands of both deciduous and coniferous trees stretched over a third of the continent. The variety and abundance have, to this day, retarded our thorough utilization of what we have. A perfect example is the elm tree *(Ulmus americana)*.

Elm is one of our most attractive hardwoods. It has always been plentiful, yet over the past three centuries, elm has been used only sparingly. Now, because of the Dutch elm disease, we are stacking it up and burning it by the hundreds of thousands of board feet annually. In some states it is the law that an infected tree be so destroyed. Yet the disease, a fungus carried by a bark beetle, could as well be controlled by slabbing the bark off and burning only that. The rest of the log could be used; kiln-drying would eliminate any unlikely contamination that had penetrated to the heartwood. Were we in the midst of a walnut blight, every board foot would be carefully gathered and used, but because elm has had no place in our past, its place in our future is in jeopardy.

Early on, elm must have had its opportunity, as did virtually every species an ax could fell. Our forefathers certainly came to know as much about elm as they did about other woods. They were quick to discover that cedar split well for siding and shingles, that our oaks equaled the oaks of Europe as dense, strong, durable woods. They were likely amazed by the properties of our hickory and ash, for nowhere else in the world are there better natural materials for tool handles. For beauty and workability, the broad array of hardwoods, nut trees and fruit trees must have excited them. Imagine cutting into American walnut, chestnut and cherry for the first time. They experi-

American elm
(Ulmus americana)

mented, often using several species in one piece of furniture; in doing so, they usually had a purpose in mind based on an understanding of the characteristics of each wood.

What was it, then, that caused the old master cabinetmakers to shun the use of elm? According to the U.S. Department of Agriculture's *Dry Kiln Operator's Manual*, elm would seem to have everything going for it. With an average oven-dry specific gravity of 0.46 it is a moderately dense wood compared to western white pine (0.36), but it is comfortably less dense than other prized cabinet hardwoods such as walnut (0.51) and white oak (0.60). Dried to 6% moisture content, elm's radial shrinkage of 3.4% and tangential shrinkage of 7.6% would indicate a high, but not inordinate susceptibility to warpage and checking. Sugar maple, by comparison, has 3.9% radial and 7.6% tangential shrinkage, while shellbark hickory comes in at 6.1% and 10.1%, respectively. Even the USDA's

Wood Handbook, which statistically compares woods in virtually every conceivable way, ranks elm well within the extremes in terms of working characteristics. It is listed as superior for boring, steam-bending, gluing and resistance to nail-splitting. Its weakest properties are its planing and shaping characteristics. Yet even here it outperforms aspen, cottonwood and sycamore, all of them widely used in cabinetry as secondary woods.

I recently bought a hundred board feet of elm, and after building several clock cases, a dry-sink top and several knickknacks I feel it deserves more respect than it has traditionally received. Elm is strikingly figured; light latewood pores in continuous wavy bands yield a wild, zigzag pattern on the tangential surface, an identifying characteristic of elm. It does not have the pronounced rays and sharp contrast between earlywood and latewood that make the oaks unpredictable to stain and often flashy in appearance. Yet it is far from bland.

Drawings: Christopher Clapp

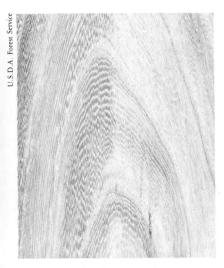

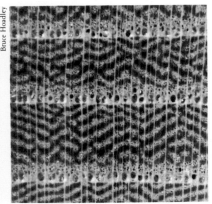

U.S.D.A. Forest Service

Bruce Hoadley

In elm, small and numerous latewood pores characteristically appear as wavy bands in end grain (above, 10× magnification) and create zigzag pattern on flatsawn board (top).

It is less porous than other ring-porous woods (ash, hickory, chestnut and the oaks) and seldom requires a filler. Stability is not its long suit, but my work has not warped severely once elm is structurally incorporated into the piece, and I am pleased with its sanding and finishing properties. Among the many domestic hardwoods I have used I would rank elm third, in terms of the end results achieved, behind only walnut and cherry.

However, I have also discovered what may well be the reason elm never made it with the old masters: Attempting to work it with the edged hand tools of the time—chisels and planes—borders on the impossible. Elm grain is interwoven, causing edge tools like a hand plane to either "dig" or "skip," often doing both in the same path. Elm will saw, rasp, sand and drill well, but jointing, channeling and shaping require high-speed power tools.

Also, because of its interwoven grain, elm is virtually impossible to

split or shatter. It will pit-check if dried improperly and it will fray under extreme stress, but it maintains its structural integrity under punishment few other woods can survive. Because of this it has been begrudgingly used where this feature is vital, in the ribs of wooden warships, for instance, and in the seats of rocking chairs. Elm was used sometimes because of its superior steam-bending properties and on occasion, especially in mixed wood pieces, simply because the board was handy and the project would be painted. However, it was seldom the primary material for major pieces or quality cabinetry, and it was never referred to as a selling point. Items made of elm were, and often still are, charitably referred to only as "hardwood."

Even after the advent of power machinery overcame the difficulties of tooling elm, tradition seems to have barred its elevation to the status of a popular cabinet wood. For a short time around the turn of the 20th century it came into more common use with furniture factories in the Midwest. However, here again it was often used in cheap, mixed-wood pieces along with oak, ash and hackberry, which it closely resembles, to satisfy the utilitarian needs of a low-income, rural market. Few who bought these articles knew or cared what they were made of, and elm's brief heyday, if you could call it that, was quickly ended by the golden oak era.

Now that its very existence is threatened by the Dutch elm disease, it is a shame that more cabinetmakers have not discovered elm. In the decades to come it is likely that the few examples of custom-made solid elm furniture will become as precious as chestnut pieces are today. When elm goes, its demise may very likely be complete. Its day of recognition must be now.

Unfortunately, elm is not always easy to find. Not all suppliers carry it. Elm is plentiful and cheap, at least here in the Midwest; however, lack of demand seems to be limiting distribution. When you find it, Select grades run around $1 a board foot (1980 prices). By way of comparison, red oak is running $2 or more, and Select walnut, when you can find it, is over $3. Even No. 2 ponderosa pine is more than $.50 a foot, and there is nothing cheaper.

In a supply/demand economy prices for these "familiar" woods can only go

up unless we tailor our demand to what is plentiful rather than using what is "traditional" or currently popular. If we demand elm, perhaps trees that must be cut anyway will go to the mill instead of to the fire pit. Any increase in the demand for this wood will actually help retard the blight by providing incentive to harvest infected trees. It was economically worked by the crude power tools of the late 1800s, and certainly it is workable today. If your confidence and skills have progressed to where you can work with oak or maple, you can surely handle elm. You may want to avoid it on pieces requiring hand carving or in items where the wood's stability is especially critical, but where a beautiful figure is desired, keep elm in mind. □

Chestnut: salvaging a blighted giant

by Victor O. DeMasi

Once the most important timber east of the Mississippi, chestnut is now seldom recognized in the forest, and its lumber is rarely seen at the local yard. Chestnut wood is still around, fairly common, in fact, but it's a treasure revealed only to the careful observer.

I live surrounded by chestnut. I salvage timbers from destruction sites and old farm buildings, saving them from ignominious ruin. I take great pride in giving this wood new life, and I save a buck while I'm at it. A New York supplier recently (1980) quoted a price of $7.50 a board foot for wormy chestnut, and clear grades were unavailable.

The chestnuts are members of the beech family. There are more than ten species worldwide, including the chinkapins, Chinese and Spanish chestnuts. All the chestnuts have sweet-tasting nuts but only the American chestnut (*Castanea dentata*), reaching a height of 120 ft. and a diameter of 7 ft. (17 ft. is the record), has ever been valued for its lumber.

Years ago the American chestnut was a highly valued tree. Besides supplying a valuable nut crop, tannin derived from its bark supported the animal-hide processing industry. As a shade tree, only elm was planted more widely. As lumber, it was not the best for any one thing but versatile enough to be used for everything. Chestnut's rot resistance rivals the heartwood of white oak, and abundant shingles, doorsteps and sills testify to its durability. Easy to work, it found wide service in barns, carriage houses and out-buildings. Chestnut also takes a fine finish, and was popular in the cabinet shop and for items as diverse as barrels and caskets. This tree's fast growth ensured a steady supply of posts and rails as America fenced herself in in the 1880s. When blight-infected trees flooded the market in the 1930s, telephone poles and highway guard rails helped absorb the glut. Boxes, crates, veneer core and railroad ties were also made from chestnut.

Chestnut was available. Usually growing in mixed hardwood forests, it composed from 15% to 50% of the standing timber. Pure stands also occurred. Chestnut trees can put on an inch in diameter in a year during their youth. One 70-year-old specimen was 5 ft. in diameter. With little effort, a farmer could get posts at 15 years, beams at 25, lumber at 50 and feed his hogs on the nut crop every fall in between.

In 1904, trees infected with a fungus, brought into this country on chestnut trees from the Orient, were noticed at the Bronx Zoo in New York City. The chestnut blight, as the fungus came to be known, attacked the bark of the tree, girdling the trunk with cankers. These cankers interrupted the vital flow of water from the roots and killed the tree. The wind-borne blight advanced 25 miles per year. It was first seen in central Connecticut in 1910, and uninfected trees were hard to find by 1915. In Pennsylvania, state foresters cleared large areas of forest, hoping to halt the epidemic's advance. But pockets of infection broke out far in advance of the blight's front and spread, eventually decimating the chestnut throughout its entire natural range. By 1940, loggers were sharpening their saws to drop the last big sticks in the South.

In the wake of the blight was economic disaster. Nuts disappeared as an important source of food for man and animal alike. Dead chestnut hulks inundated the sawmills, depressing lumber prices. In Appalachia, the tanning industry collapsed, adding more hardship to that already impoverished area. Upland soils eroded at an alarming rate with the sudden disappearance of such

a dominant forest member. In place of chestnut, less desirable trees grew. Land that gave timber now gives cordwood.

Chestnut persists today, but only as a shrub. It sprouts from the stumps of the former giants and grows several inches in diameter before the blight grabs it again. How long this cycle will last is anybody's guess, but these remaining small trees offer hope. Dr. Richard Jaynes, of the Connecticut Agricultural Experiment Station in New Haven, is working on a disease to infect the disease. In Europe and a few isolated areas in the U.S., chestnut trees with resistance to the blight have been found. In these trees, a virus infects the fungus. Dr. Jaynes is looking for a method to spread this virus to American chestnut sprouts. Success would be an economic miracle for our eastern timberlands.

Locating and using chestnut

Chestnut wood is often confused with oak, ash, elm and hickory, all ring-porous woods, but there are ways to distinguish it. I don't stress color because it is unreliable. Fresh cut, the wood is blond, but with aging mellows to a wide variety of reddish browns. The surest way to identify it is by looking at the end grain. The pores that form the earlywood rings, best seen with a hand lens, are oval in chestnut and frequently occluded with tyloses—shiny, bubble-like structures. The transition from these rings to the denser latewood rings is more gradual than in other ring-porous woods. An obvious difference between chestnut and oaks is that the oaks have prominent rays, which on the end grain appear as light lines radiating from the center of the tree and on the face grain (tangential view) appear as dark flecks. Rays are less prominent in elm, hickory and ash, but they are visible; they are not visible in chestnut. Chestnut is the lightest and softest of the ring-porous woods (with a specific gravity of 0.43). Lastly, chestnut because of its high tannin content will stain black in contact with iron salts. Boiling shavings in a ferric chloride solution will not distinguish it from oaks, which are also high in tannin, but elm and ash, low in tannin, will discolor only slightly.

Knowing where chestnut was commonly used is valuable when looking for wood to recycle. I pay close attention to sills, joists and other pieces close to ground level where rot resistance is a

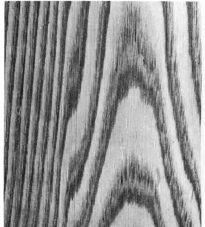

Usable pieces of plainsawn chestnut may be salvaged from framing members of turn-of-the-century buildings.

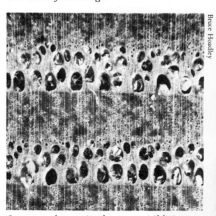

Bruce Hoadley

Large, oval pores in chestnut, visible in 10× cross-sectional view, are often occluded with tyloses. Earlywood/latewood transition is gradual. Rays are fine, barely discernible.

must. Fencing also merits close scrutiny. Buildings from early in this century are my favorite haunts. Two structures on my property are dated 1914, just when blighted trees were abundant. Not surprisingly, they are framed completely in chestnut. In general, white oak is the only other ring-porous wood commonly found as a framing member. In furniture, where finishes obscure the wood, identification can be tricky. Chestnut never hides beneath painted millwork and was usually considered too soft for flooring, although I do know of a few examples.

Heavy boots, gloves, a crowbar and a sharp knife are all the would-be chestnut hunter needs to bring along. Time-encrusted roughsawn lumber doesn't display its grain. If the wood cuts like pine to reveal an open grain, I give it a second look. Where an old house or barn is being torn down, the wood is often free for the asking.

When I've amassed a pile of wood, I

American chestnut
(Castanea dentata)

chestnut—whence the name wormy chestnut. The holes, if not too plentiful, are attractive. These holes are the excavations of the chestnut pole borer, which attacks moist heartwood in standing dead chestnut and oak. The cavities are packed with the borers' excrement, which looks like fine sawdust. It can be packed so tight as to obscure the hole. I use the air pump at a service station to clean the wood. Goggles and a mask must be worn because the dust is extremely irritating. Cleaning the holes with small pins is time-consuming and not very satisfactory.

No two pieces of chestnut are the same. In my haunts I occasionally come across pieces stained black on the outside. Always found in close contact with the soil (iron salts react with the tannin in the wood), these uglies conceal a real treasure. Inside, the wood is mellowed to a soft brown with creamy white streaks running with the grain. It's incomparably beautiful.

When dressing this rough stock, I rip off about ⅛ in. The stain on this surface has the best effect. If I saw too far into the board, I usually get regular-colored chestnut, and if too shallow, black wood. Cutting shallow is preferable though, because the surface can be planed to change the intensity of the stain. In constructing with this wood you must bear in mind that there is only one beautiful face; the other is either black or typical chestnut, and the edge shows the transition.

Salvaging from older structures is not the only way to obtain chestnut. One woodturner I know gets wood from old chestnut hulks he finds on the ground in remote forests. He goes as far as Ohio and South Carolina for logs passed over during the post-blight salvage. Often these choice pieces are inaccessible, perched on a steep hill miles from the nearest road. It is remarkable that after 30 or 40 years some hulks remain unrotted. Sometimes the center of the tree rots out, leaving a hard, useless shell. Crotch areas often remain solid, though, and are usually symmetrical with beautiful figure. Turning must proceed cautiously, as the wood splits easily if the tool catches. □

Jon Arno lives in Brookfield, Wis.; Victor DeMasi lives in Redding, Conn. Both are amateur woodworkers. De-Masi's article was prepared with the help of research by Roanna Metowski.

sort the pieces according to destination—the saw or the woodstove. I inspect the good pieces for rot and nails and crosscut these out with a bowsaw. Before pulling out individual nails, I mark the area around each with a red crayon in case the nail breaks off. Black spots should be crayoned too. These are iron stains from nails, pieces of which might still lie buried in the wood.

It helps to have a definite project in mind before you start ripping. You can then saw for the right sizes. I work backward, however, and must always see the wood before I can decide on a project for it. Plainsawn chestnut, which has wavy face grain, is more attractive, I think, than quartersawn stock. Most chestnut was plainsawn to begin with, so I cut parallel to existing edges and usually obtain attractive figures. I use a circular saw with a guide, or a bench saw for wider boards. Cheap blades are best; if I hit a big nail, I change the blade. After a few too many

damaged blades I got better at avoiding those nails. When all my stock is ripped I again crosscut to eliminate the few remaining nails that I missed. I don't send any wood that has nails into a planer. When the wood is surfaced and jointed, it is tightly stacked and weighted down to minimize warping.

Working with chestnut is a real pleasure. It rips cleanly with a sharp blade, but on older pieces the end grain always tears during crosscutting. The wood almost leaps together when it is glued. It sands easily, but grits below 100 should be avoided because they scratch the wood and make even more sanding necessary. The finest sanding stages can be frustrating, as a slightly raised grain persists. The problem can be solved by wetting the surface with paint thinner. Tung oil is a suitable finish for chestnut, and brings out the beautiful color on older, salvaged wood.

Small wormholes are common in

The Great American Pines
Forty species yield three distinct families of cabinet woods

by Jon W. Arno

The newspaper ad might read: "Common pine shelving boards, only 59¢ a board foot!" So the weekend woodworker, on his precious hobby budget, hustles off to load up. With just 100 bd. ft. of that affordable pine, he might reproduce that beautiful 17th-century New England china cupboard he's admired in the local museum.

Yet when the reproduction is finally done, something just isn't quite right. The joinery is accurate, the antique finish genuine, the hardware hand-forged. Nevertheless, there is something unmistakably 20th-century about the piece.

Our craftsman resigns himself to the apparent fact that it simply takes a couple of centuries for pine to develop its mellow, pumpkin-orange patina. The truth is, this particular pine lumber is never going to mellow, not in a thousand years. Why? Because pine isn't just pine. That bargain wood was a western yellow pine, probably *Pinus ponderosa,* while the Colonial original was almost certainly made of a decidedly different species: *Pinus strobus,* or eastern white pine. Both woods have a distinctly individual character. To a reproduction cabinetmaker, their lumber is not interchangeable.

The genus *Pinus* of the botanical family *Pinaceae* contains more than ninety species worldwide, several of which are among the most important in the timber and paper industries. The range of the pines is restricted to the Northern Hemisphere, except for one species that strays below the equator in Indonesia. As with fine hardwoods, North America is especially blessed with pines. Half of our 40 native pine species are important timber producers, and some have become major reforestation species, growing now where no true pine had grown before.

In Colonial days, the East Coast pines fit nicely into three basic groups. In the North were a "soft" (white pine), a "hard" (pitch pine), and an "intermediate" (red pine) which was very like Scotch pine, the wood that European cabinetmakers call "deal." In the South, the many kinds of pines were all very hard. In comparison with soft white pine, whose uniform texture works easily, some of the southern yellow pines have earlywood as soft as basswood, while the latewood within the same annual ring is as hard as rosewood. The southern yellow pines are therefore difficult to work, and have a showier grain pattern than the softer pines, especially when stained.

Throughout the Colonies, the hard pines provided building timbers, tough construction lumber and wear-proof floors. For furniture, the northern cabinetmakers favored the bland, easier-working white pine, but the southern cabinetmakers utilized the harder wood of the local trees. For this reason, museum curators today routinely find drawer runners and sides of southern Colonial furniture to be in good condition still, while in northern furniture the same parts have mostly worn out.

As local lumber stands were exhausted, loggers moved west and discovered other species of pine: two soft pines (western white pine and sugar pine), and a number of western yellow pines, the most important of which are much softer and more workable than the southern yellows. At the very least, today's cabinetmaker ought learn how to distinguish between the white pines as a group, the southern yellow pines, and the western yellow pines. Amateur lumberjacks might note that with one or two minor exceptions, the soft pines have needles growing in bunches of five, while the harder pines have them in bunches of two or three. The chart on the facing page compares pines within each of the three groups and shows macrophotographs of typical species.

Keep in mind that pine furniture has always been decidedly local in character. The Europeans made Scotch pine tables, New Englanders made white pine chests, and southern farmers built yellow pine cupboards with flashy grain. In the television show *Bonanza,* Ben Cartwright's furniture would have been of pure ponderosa pine. Country-style pine furniture was originally made of whatever pine grew in the particular geographic area.

The white pines—If you like traditional American furniture and want your projects to be "authentic," your first choice will naturally be eastern white pine. This is the "pumpkin pine" of early New England, so called because of the rich, golden-orange patina it develops with age. It's also the tree that Paul Bunyan harvested as he made his way from pinery to pinery along our northern border. The lumberjacks called it cork pine because its extremely low density caused it to ride high in the river as the logs were floated to the sawmill. For the cabinetmaker, this low density means that the wood is soft, easily worked, and lightweight. Wood from the white pine group is, in general, less dense than that of the species in the other groups. It is also not as resinous and has less contrast between earlywood and latewood. Thus the white pines cut more predictably, and can be finished to a mellower, more uniform tone.

The woods of eastern white pine and western white pine are so similar that I doubt whether a Colonial cabinetmaker could have told one from the other. The sapwood of both trees is light cream, almost white, in color, with the heartwood ranging from yellow to light orange-tan. Idaho has been the primary producer of western white pine, and the term "Idaho white pine" or the initials "IWP" stamped on a board identify one of America's finest softwoods.

Unless historical authenticity is important, however, I'd most likely choose the third major member of the group, sugar pine, for the primary wood in a furniture project. It has outstanding working characteristics (though it mars quite easily) and great stability, and it is available in large, wide, blemish-free boards—volumetrically, sugar pine is the largest true pine in the world. The wood is extremely consistent in

From *Fine Woodworking* magazine (May 1984) 46:62-64

THE THREE GROUPS OF PINE LUMBER

Group A: White pines
Prime lumber from trees in this group is soft, light, easily worked, and commonly available in lumberyards. As shown in the 10X end-grain macrophotograph at right, *Pinus strobus* (eastern white pine), which is typical of trees in this group, has a gradual transition from earlywood to latewood within each growth ring, and an evenness of cell-wall thickness throughout, which means that earlywood and latewood have similar densities. These characteristics make for good woodworking and staining properties.

BOTANICAL NAME	COMMON NAME(S)	RANGE	PROPERTIES OF THE WOOD
P. strobus	Eastern white pine, northern white pine, cork pine, Weymouth pine.	Northeastern United States and eastern Canada, Appalachians south to Georgia.	Creamy white wood with yellow to orange-tan heartwood; traditional pine of Colonial New England. Average specific gravity 0.34.
P. monticola	Western white pine, Idaho white pine.	Western Montana, Idaho, into Washington and Oregon.	Virtually identical to eastern white pine. Specific gravity 0.35.
P. lambertiana	Sugar pine.	Oregon, northern and eastern California.	Creamy tan color, prominent "fleck" marks; available in large, clear stock; excellent carving wood. Specific gravity 0.34.

Severe growing conditions make the woods of the following western trees extremely variable: Limber pine, *P. flexilis;* whitebark pine, *P. albicaulis;* the pinyon pines (four or more species and hybrids); bristlecone pine, *P. aristata;* and foxtail pine, *P. balfouriana.*

Group B: Southern yellow pines
Woods in this group vary according to growing conditions, but latewood is predictably very hard and sometimes wide, while earlywood is soft, making for hard-to-work woods with racy grain patterns. Wood is resinous, dense, strong. Not generally a cabinet-quality wood, except for period furniture that demands it and for a long-lasting secondary wood. Makes good pressure-treated decking. The 10X macrophotograph of *P. echinata* (shortleaf pine), typical of the southern yellow pine group, shows wide, dense latewood, abrupt transition between earlywood and latewood within each growth ring, and extreme differences in wall thickness between earlywood and latewood.

P. palustris	Longleaf pine.	Southeastern and Gulf coastal plain.	Hard; yellow to orange-brown color; very resinous. Specific gravity 0.54.
P. echinata	Shortleaf pine.	From Texas to Georgia, and from Kentucky to northern Florida.	Similar to longleaf; slightly less dense. Specific gravity 0.47.
P. taeda	Loblolly pine.	Similar to shortleaf, except more southerly.	Same as shortleaf. Specific gravity 0.47.
P. elliottii	Slash pine.	Florida, southern Georgia and Gulf coastal plain.	Much like longleaf pine; one of the denser southern yellow pines. Specific gravity 0.54.

Minor species include Virginia pine, or Jersey pine, *P. virginiana,* specific gravity 0.45; pond pine, *P. serotina,* specific gravity 0.51; pitch pine, *P. rigida,* specific gravity 0.47; spruce pine (cedar pine, poor pine), *P. glabra,* specific gravity 0.41; sand pine, *P. clausa,* specific gravity 0.46; and Table Mountain pine, *P. pungens,* specific gravity 0.46, not abundant.

Group C: Western yellow pines
Woods in this group are slightly denser and more yellow than the white pines, but are lighter, less resinous and more workable than the southern yellow pines. *P. ponderosa,* shown at 10X in the macrophotograph at right, is typical of the pines in this group. Transition from earlywood to latewood is abrupt, yet latewood is not as wide or hard as in the southern yellow pines. Wood works well, holds crisp edges. Stain accentuates grain pattern. Dimpled grain common. Commonly seen in lumberyards as moldings and trim. The minor species listed are of little importance as timber producers due to their limited range and/or poor quality.

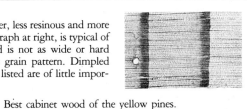

P. ponderosa	Ponderosa pine.	Inter Rocky Mountain region from Mexico to Canada, northern California and Oregon.	Best cabinet wood of the yellow pines. Specific gravity 0.38.
P. jeffreyi	Jeffrey pine.	Northern and eastern California, southeastern Oregon.	Virtually the same as ponderosa and marketed with it as "ponderosa" pine.
P. contorta	Lodgepole pine.	Northern Rockies, eastern California, Pacific Northwest.	Usually knottier than ponderosa or Jeffrey. Specific gravity 0.38.

Among the minor species are Torrey pine, *P. torreyana;* Monterey pine, *P. radiata;* Digger pine, *P. sabiniana;* and knobcone pine, *P. attenuata.* These may be available locally to western woodworkers. Some may be cut and shipped with the major species, especially in the lower grades and/or as dimension lumber.

The following species are not western trees, but are included in this group because of their wood's working characteristics:

P. banksiana	Jack pine.	Eastern Canada, northern Great Lakes states, New York and New England.	Wood most resembles lodgepole pine; knotty; light in color; wide sapwood; coarse-grained, may have dimpled grain. Specific gravity 0.40.
P. resinosa	Red pine, Norway pine.	Northeastern and Great Lakes states, eastern Canada.	Midway between the southern and western yellow pines in density; creamy white to yellow sapwood, orange to brown heartwood; less grainy and resinous than southern pines, but not as soft and workable as western yellow pines. Specific gravity 0.41.

Photos: John Limbach, Ripon Microslides

texture and a creamy light tan or beige in color, with a distinctive pattern in the grain caused by its characteristic resin canals. While all pines have numerous, fairly large resin canals (when compared to larch, spruce and Douglas fir), no other pine displays them so plentifully and prominently. This gives sugar pine the most distinctive—some think it beautiful—appearance of the white pines.

Several other western species—including limber pine, bristlecone pine and the pinyon pines—are listed in the chart as part of the white pine group, but their gnarly, short growth habit limits their value as lumber.

Southern yellow pines—These trees are hard, strong, dense and resinous, and a major source of paper pulp, plywood and construction timber. On the basis of commercial value and volume, the southern yellows are our most important pines, but very little lumber from this group finds a place in my shop. The trees produce a large band of latewood during the growing season, and they exhibit an abrupt transition between earlywood and latewood, with enormous contrast in density between the two zones. The knots are virtually impervious to stain. I don't like southern yellow pine, and much prefer to work with wood from either of the other two groups, yet I understand how southern yellow could be close to a period cabinetmaker's heart.

In reproducing a period piece in southern yellow pine, you would be better off trusting your eyes than relying on the differences listed in the chart. Woods from this group may be quite variable, but this seems less a matter of species than of growing conditions. Trees seeded on abandoned plantation lands grow faster than those that struggle up in mature forests. Producing broader annual rings and wider sapwood, the wood of these fast-growing trees may be considerably less dense than that of the typical southern yellow pine.

Western yellow pines—Most of the western yellow pines are less dense and resinous than the southern yellow pines. For a cabinetmaker, western yellows are a fine secondary wood, and some have novel grain patterns that can be attractive as a primary wood as well.

Ponderosa pine is one of the largest and most plentiful of the pines, which explains its ready availability and moderate price in lumberyards throughout the country. Unfortunately, it is not a rapid grower in the somewhat arid habitats of its range, and the day may come when this close-grained wood is no longer plentiful enough to hold its place as America's general-purpose, low-cost timber.

Ponderosa is only about 10% denser than the white pines, and therefore only a little harder, yet it is still undeniably a yellow pine in most ways. Just take the description of the southern pines and tone it down to the point where the wood's personality becomes amenable. The annual rings, for instance, are distinct and sometimes very showy, but there is less contrast in hardness between earlywood and latewood. Ponderosa has very narrow latewood, and the old-growth timber, with its narrow growth rings, can look surprisingly even-grained. The wood is superb for millwork: it machines beautifully and holds crisp edges.

Lodgepole pine is similar to ponderosa in color and density, but usually has smaller knots and many more of them. This species yields far less lumber per log than ponderosa. Growing in dense stands, the trees look like telephone poles with crowns of short needles, two to the bunch.

The ponderosa and lodgepole pines often exhibit a dimpled grain pattern. If you split a piece of the wood with an ax, small bumps on one side will be matched by dimples on the other. This abnormality, almost "normal" in these two pines, is caused by resin blisters in the inner bark which distort the cambium layer. The pattern is sometimes visible on the surface of plainsawn boards, and when the surface is tight enough to finish smoothly, it can resemble bird's-eye maple.

Northern yellow pines—Woodworkers may want to distinguish the northern yellow pines, species with which the first New England Colonists were familiar. Although two of these trees have working characteristics that assign them to groups we've already considered, the third, red pine, has qualities that help put all three groups in perspective.

Pitch pine is used primarily for pulp and only occasionally for lumber, although it was an important Colonial species before the stands were razed. Its wood resembles that of the southern yellow pines in color, resin content and hardness, and the lumber trade treats it as a "minor species" of the southern yellow pines. With a specific gravity of 0.47, it is by far the densest of the pines native to the northeastern United States.

Jack pine is a Canadian spillover invading the northern Great Lakes states and parts of New York and New England. It is a small tree which quickly seeds on burned-over land but is eventually displaced by more dominant species. Its wood—weak with wide sapwood, light in color, excessively knotty and somewhat coarse in texture—is something like inferior lodgepole pine, but jack pine seldom grows as straight. Like lodgepole, it sometimes has dimpled grain. In Canada, where their ranges overlap, these two trees will produce natural hybrids.

Red pine, the dominant yellow pine of the northeast, is a massive and beautiful tree. Legend has it that its other common name, Norway pine, stems from Norway, Maine, and has nothing to do with Scandinavia. In any event, it is definitely a native Northern American species. The wood of red pine falls somewhere between the western and southern yellow pines in most characteristics. It is slightly heavier than ponderosa, but substantially lighter than the southern yellow pines. The contrast between earlywood and latewood is more pronounced than in the western yellow pines, but substantially more gradual than in its southern cousins. Like the western yellow pines, its sapwood is light enough in color to resemble the white pines; its heartwood, however, is often a bright orange-brown. If carefully selected, the dark orange heartwood of red pine can be substituted for deal (Scotch pine) in the reproduction of European furniture designs.

Arbitrarily, I've assigned red pine to the western yellow pines in the chart, where it shows up as one of the worst cabinet woods. If I'd put it in with the southern yellow pines, however, it would be a star. So understand what your project requires and pick the group before you try to pick a species. And keep in mind that any wood comes in several grades—no woodworker should buy materials blindly. Yet getting to know the pines is an adventure no woodworker, and certainly no American woodworker, should miss. □

Jon Arno is an amateur woodworker in Brookfield, Wis. See also his articles on other woods: "Ash" (pp. 63-65) and "Elm: modern power tools make it workable" (pp. 66-67).

Packing Out Perfume

by Wayne J. Jacintho

My friend Mike and I were hunting pheasants on our home island of Kauai. We had just climbed out of a deep gorge to hunt a flat I hadn't been on for ten years, before I'd gotten interested in woodworking, trees and wood. We started our sweep, but before I'd gone ten yards I froze, all thoughts of pheasants forgotten. Unmistakably, in a small grove of trees about a hundred yards away stood a sandalwood tree!

Mike couldn't believe his eyes. "There's no *iliahi* around here," he insisted. "Everybody knows it's extinct."

The sandalwood trade of the 1800s is a shameful part of Hawaiian history. Island chiefs ordered the commoners to leave their fields and labor in the forests, sawing and hauling sandalwood for export. Pits the size of the holds of various ships were dug, then packed to capacity with the precious wood. Seeing none of the profits and suffering famine as a result of neglecting their farms, the laborers began to rip out every sandalwood sapling they saw. In a few short years the sandalwood forests were gone. Many people now believe *iliahi* to be extinct, but small trees, 3 in. to 6 in. in diameter, still grow in the high, dry plateau of Kokee. After a botanist friend pointed one out to me, I was able to identify the unique color and shape anywhere, even in the thickest tropical forest. But I had never seen, or heard of, any large trees with usable heartwood. At least not until now.

The tree was, in fact, three trees. From a short trunk three branches grew straight up. On one of them a banyan had started growing, and the branch had broken off under its weight. As we stared at the long-dead log, we realized our good luck. You can't cut a live tree on Forest Reserve land, but you sure can cut fallen timber.

Mike had never smelled sandalwood, so I grabbed a branch to break. It barely even moved. I put my gun on the side and gave it more grunt. It bent, but didn't break. I gave Mike the high sign and he put his charterfishing boat muscles to good use. The branch splintered, and we were enveloped in a cloud of the heavenly odor that had made this wood so valuable. Mike smiled and smiled, and I realized my mouth was stretched as wide as his.

Our problem was clear—the tree was nearly two miles from the nearest road. To get the lumber out, we would have to park the jeep, hike a quarter-mile almost straight down, cross a stream, climb straight back up, circle a domed hill, and then trek downhill for about a mile to the tree. We wanted to mill the log where it lay (I own a Granberg Alaskan mill with a Stihl 075 AVE powerhead), but the mill and its necessaries were too much for us to carry that far. We debated half-seriously about horses or mules and we even considered a helicopter, but blanched at the $400/hr. price.

But Mike and I think alike, and in a sandalwood-aroma

Author with sandalwood flitch.

high we mused, "We could cut the log into sections . . ." "Debi Wood just returned my pack-frame . . ." "And I've got mine and the one we found at the dump . . ." "We can carry your small Stihl easily . . ." "And your sister-in-law Jane and her boyfriend John are coming in from Colorado tomorrow. He's a mountain man . . ." "I doubt we'll ever see another sandalwood tree like that . . ." "It's settled then. *We'll carry it out on our backs!*"

Getting there was easy. John and Jane had come from cold Colorado to tropical Kauai, and their festive mood soon infected everybody. My wife Deborah loaded herself down with food and drink (lots of Gatorade), and Jane carried the gas-and-oil.

Under a glorious blue sky with white cotton clouds we laid out the cuts, fired up the saw, and soon were covered with the sweetest sawdust in the universe. It was the first time I'd ever seen anybody actually *trying* to get layered with itchy, scratchy sawdust.

Those few cuts seemed to take forever. But we finished and managed to lash the sections onto the packframes. Then it took two of us to lift each load high enough so the third guy could slip his arms into the packstraps. I ended up on my hands and knees while the others hoisted the pack onto my back. We were silent by that time, finally realizing the weight of our task. Mike looked at me mournfully for encouragement. I told him that the log on my back felt heavier than the 137½-lb. wild boar I had once helped pack out. Mike's face grew even longer.

We still talk about our adventure once in a while. We talk about that first, long, uphill, windless mile in the open afternoon sun, about the packs breaking and the loads coming undone. We talk about the downhill zigzags that turned our legs to hot jelly and about that last brutal straight-up hill, when we took each pack in relays, one-two-three up to the top, on hands and knees where the gravel was loose. We talk about unloading onto the truck and the long haul back down to the river for the next load. We can still see Jane carrying a branch almost as long as she is tall, so she could take a bit of heartwood home to Colorado. And we can practically taste again the much-anticipated iced beer that awaited us in the truck. When we finally milled those three sections, they scented the neighborhood for blocks around.

We swear we'll never have this adventure again, and then smile at each other in silent accord, thinking: "I wonder when those *other* two branches are going to fall down!" □

Wayne J. Jacintho of Kauai, Hawaii, builds cabinets and furniture at the Kauai Cabinet Works, in Kilauea.

Black Walnut Woes

A tree-grower learns from the roots up

by John R. Harwood

Like most woodworkers, I admit an emotional attachment to trees. When I decided to plant black walnut trees in an abandoned field on our property in Upstate New York, I understood that their lumber wasn't likely to ever find its way onto my workbench. Yet I wished to replace some of the trees cut, often before their time, to meet the demand for lumber that I was helping to place upon the forests. I chose walnut for its uncommon beauty and outstanding workability, as well as for the scarcity of this valuable species in our area. Needless to say, I did not know what I was getting into. Stick a bunch of seedlings into the ground and sit back and watch them grow, right? Not quite! I found that if you sit back after planting hardwoods, you won't have much to watch grow except weeds.

I began in the winter of 1976 by placing an order with Van's Pines, in West Olive, Mich., for 100 black walnut

A woodworkers' rite of spring: the black walnut tree beginning to bloom.

bare-rooted seedlings, 3 ft. to 4 ft. tall. For the remainder of the winter I read anything I could find about tree-planting in general or walnuts in particular, and I also enrolled in courses in environmental science and forestry. Most of the literature I found was directed toward establishing conifer stands. The little bit of available material about walnut plantations presumed machinery far superior to my lawn tractor, and manpower greater than my two hands. I found that I would have to learn as I went along.

Spring came, and with it two parcels—a long, soft one containing the seedlings, and the other, which looked like a manual jack-hammer, my dibble bar. A dibble bar is a planting tool used for conifers, but ignorance, if not bliss, is at least a postponement of unhappiness. I decided to plant that day since the weather was gray and drizzly—the seedlings would not dry out as they were being handled and the trees would not need immediate watering. I sloshed my way up to the "plantation" site, with visions of walnut trees dancing in my head.

Ceremoniously, I extracted the first seedling for planting, only to find that its taproot was a good 4 in. longer than the spade on the dibble bar. The ground was so saturated, however, that I was able to force the bar far enough down to place the root without breaking it. Fortunately, the average root on the remaining seedlings was only slightly longer than the spade. As I untangled the bundle, the quantity of seedlings seemed to grow, as did the effort required to plant each of them. I began to wonder why I had ordered so many. The final count was 112 walnut seedlings standing proud, albeit in crooked rows, at a spacing of 8 ft. by 8 ft., or two big steps and one little one—a rather small plantation of less than 6,000 sq. ft., barely an eighth of an acre. Though my goal was 10 acres of walnuts, I proudly gazed upon my modest accomplishment, then headed home for a hot bath and some muscle liniment.

Two weeks later the still-dormant walnuts could barely be seen through the lush growth of spring grasses. By midsummer the seedlings showed signs of transplant shock, insect damage, and stress from competition. I mounted furious warfare against the weeds. Somewhere between blisters and backaches, I decided that a gasoline-powered weed whacker was just what I needed, only to learn that this monster does a fine job of gashing the tender bark off of seedlings when its operator grows weary. The insects had already eaten most of the sickly leaves, so pesticides seemed of no use at this point.

I could see that my simplistic approach to planting hardwoods was futile, so I began to plan the next spring's endeavor with a little more forethought. I continued my part-time

Drawings: Christopher Clapp

studies. I met with the regional state forester. Meanwhile, to my amazement, most of my bedraggled walnuts set healthy winter buds, and were obviously interested in surviving. I ordered another 200 seedlings.

As spring drew near, I finalized my plans. I would again plant in wet weather, and this time I would discourage the weeds by scarifying the soil around each hole with a shovel. I would drop a timed-release fertilizer tablet into each hole, and I was prepared to apply insecticide at the first sign of damage. I theorized that the dibble-bar method might cause trapped air around the bottom of long taproots, so I had ordered smaller planting stock. I had also ordered 50 black alders to intermix as trainers: alders grow faster than walnuts, encouraging the slower-growing trees to head straight up for light and not branch out too much. When the alders began to suppress the more valuable walnuts, I would thin them out for firewood. I was becoming a more sophisticated tree-planter.

As I trudged through my plantation that spring, I discovered that deer and rabbits love healthy walnut buds—only two trees, fortuitously planted within a blackberry bramble, had escaped the forage. Discouraged, I nevertheless resolved to stick to my plans, and I set to work. After several hours of back-breaking scarifying, though, I gladly dropped that idea. It was all for the best: by midsummer no difference could be detected between the seedlings whose sod I had scarified and those I had not. By then the alders had all perished, presumably due to root damage. Their roots are really too crooked and multi-branched for dibble-bar planting.

Things looked pretty bad at that point, but I was due for a little beginner's luck. While contemplating the relative costs and benefits of fencing the whole plantation versus constantly spraying various animal repellents, I decided to salvage some old 4-ft. welded-wire fencing. I had only enough to make six 3-ft. dia. cages, but at least I would be able to protect the

In a nutshell

by Charles Leik

My father has spent his life farming within sight of where he was born in central Michigan 78 years ago. Over the years he has planted acres of corn, wheat and beans, but nothing has given him as much pleasure as growing trees. His stands have included tens of thousands of pine planted in the poorer soil and more severe winter climate a short distance to the north, yet his greatest satisfaction comes from the one hundred black walnut trees surrounding the farmstead in Portland. As a youngster, I learned real patience picking out nut meats over the kitchen table on wintry Sunday afternoons—but the black walnut was a delicacy well worth the effort. Now, with Dad's careful attention, each year these trees progress a bit more toward the quality veneer logs that my children will harvest toward the middle of the next century.

Black walnut (_Juglans nigra_) develops best on deep, moderately well-drained, nearly neutral soils that are generally moist and fertile. It is native to the area from the East Coast to the Missouri Valley and from the Southern Appalachians to the Canadian border. Dad's walnut plantings are on the northern fringe of their natural habitat, and growth is considerably slower than, say, in the Shenandoah Valley of Virginia. Slower growth isn't all bad, though, as the most desirable veneer patterns result from the smaller annual rings of trees from north of the Ohio Valley. It isn't unknown for unscrupulous sellers to truck southern logs to northern locations and represent them as locally grown.

Dad dates his interest in growing walnuts from the Depression era, when he shucked walnuts from trees growing wild in fencerows and sold the nuts for a dollar a bushel in Detroit. He planted his first trees from nuts in 1929. These trees are now 50 ft. tall and 19 in. in diameter at breast height (DBH). In late autumn of 1968, Dad made preparations for his largest planting. After shucking the nuts, he placed them in a leaf-lined pit, where they would be kept moist but would not freeze. He planted these nuts the following spring. In some cases germination was delayed quite a while, as seedlings continued to appear for several springs. Before long, the stand was so thick that many trees had to be transplanted. After 15 growing seasons, these trees average 32 ft. in height and over 8 in. DBH.

A danger of planting nuts instead of seedlings is that squirrels and chipmunks may mistake them for a winter food cache. Some foresters recommend burying the nuts in a perforated tin can, which deters animals while allowing the nuts to germinate. Tin cans (don't use aluminum cans) soon rust away, posing no problem for a growing seedling.

Dad's goal is to produce 16-ft. logs, so he approaches training and pruning with considerable thought. He trims the branches as high as possible without shocking the tree by taking off too many in a season. Trees planted in open country will usually fork, and then Dad has to decide which branch should be lopped off and which can be trained as a new leader. He studies the alternatives like a gem cutter, solicits opinions from visitors, and by fall has generally made his decisions for pruning.

After a new leader has been established, or when a tree leans away from the prevailing westerlies, a guy rope is necessary to encourage straightness. At first Dad installed a taut rope between the limb and a stake, but in high winds either the tree or the rope was liable to snap. Now he runs the ground end of the rope through a pulley-type device and attaches a weight to the end. This allows the tree to flex in a wind, yet continuously tugs the tree or branch in the desired direction.

If a tree does break off, or has undesirable characteristics, Dad cuts it off at ground level. A 4-ft. to 5-ft. leader usually comes back the first year. Without such drastic cutting, the stub would just send out bushy branches, which would make the tree useless for lumber.

Now that the 1969 planting is well along, Dad has started a new enterprise. My brother and I bought a small farm several years ago that has eight acres of small hardwoods, many of them walnuts. Dad is trimming these trees and eliminating less valuable species that compete for sunlight and moisture. This approach to walnut-growing gives him a 10- to 20-year head start by utilizing already thriving trees.

Walnut-growing is not a short-term proposition, but Dad gets satisfaction from the thought that his efforts will allow those not yet born the opportunity to make fine furniture from this premium lumber. □

Charles Leik is a banker and woodworker who lives in Great Falls, Va.

best-looking survivors from the first year's planting. I secured each cage with two 5-ft. long stakes woven through the fencing. Then in July I discovered that several seedlings I had written off had resprouted from the root, and were growing at a rate far greater than those with original stems. I thought I was finally on to something.

I was not positive the cages would provide total protection. They were also expensive, averaging $6 per cage (1984) plus the stakes and time required. And I had to consider the risk of rot in stems resprouting so near the ground, especially with dense grass maintaining a moist environment. The books emphasized the grave importance of avoiding all injuries to the bark, since a walnut tree with heart rot is of no value. I would just have to wait and see. Perhaps it was cabin fever that drove me to complete madness—that winter I ordered 400 new seedlings.

As to why my lunacy doubled every year I cannot say; perhaps I hoped to overwhelm the odds. I decided to drop the dibble-bar method. Though no walnut mortality could be attributed to its use, no tree had gotten off to a good start being forced into such a small hole. I rented a hand-operated, gas-driven post-hole digger and purchased several cubic yards of weed-free topsoil.

Planting day arrived and the weather was beautiful, 70°F with bright sun and a steady breeze. Perfect for the friend I had persuaded to help me, but bad for the seedlings. The weatherman had promised rain, so I had made no provision

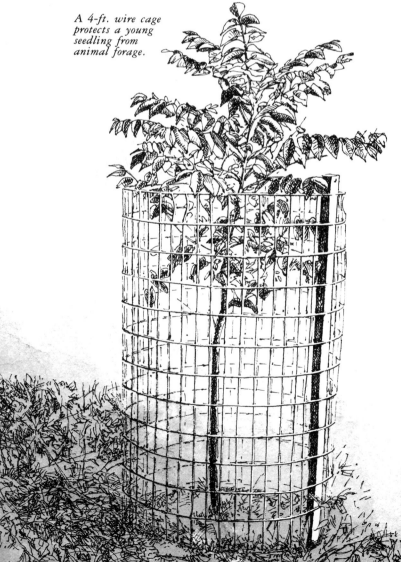

A 4-ft. wire cage protects a young seedling from animal forage.

for carrying enough water up to the field to give the seedlings a good soaking. The post-hole digger, which I was to operate, was like a lawn mower connected to a 6-in. auger drill by a flexible shaft—a real torture machine. My companion was to fill each hole with a tree and soil brought up in a small cart, towed by the lawn tractor, from where the truck had dumped it. Somehow, we managed to plant all 400 seedlings. The rain clouds I had been watching as the sun set dropped a foot of snow that night, and the temperature dropped 50°F. Nature's watering remained frozen above the ground long enough to either kill or hopelessly weaken most of the trees within a week.

• • •

Each of the past four springs, I have ritually planted about 100 trees, though I've concentrated on species with a greater chance of success, such as spruce and larch, plus small numbers of birch and oak. Because it takes so long for a particular acre to grow quality cabinet lumber, I've made an experimental planting of 30 Japanese larches, as a cash crop, intermixed with 10 black cherries.

I have by no means forsaken the walnuts, or hardwood reforestation in general, and have continued to care for the trees that have survived. The only trees that have had a predictable chance have been those placed in cages, so I dutifully purchase several rolls of fencing each year and delegate its use as best as possible. I have managed to cage, and in some cases cut back and resprout, more than 50 of the trees in the walnut plantation. Two years ago I begrudgingly applied simizene, a pre-emergence herbicide, around some. With one application, second- and third-year seedlings grew above their cages that year, and out of the reach of the insects in the surrounding high grass the following. All of the first six trees caged were treated, and they are now true saplings, beyond the possibility of deer and rabbit browse, so I've moved their cages on to other needy recipients. The trees without cages resemble gnarled bushes.

This year I have the inclination to plant walnuts again—no, not 800, but maybe 25. Last spring I sprouted nuts collected from local trees, and knowing that the parents had good growth habits and were well adapted to our climate gives me confidence. But I will not be tempted to plant more than I can care for. With a garden tiller on the tractor, I'll be able to loosen the soil and subdue competition without much effort. I'll consider one application of herbicide next spring, if called for based on the competition present late this summer. If planted and cared for properly, walnuts can grow 3 ft. or more a year, allowing the cages to be reused after three or four years. Once the trees are out of the cages, I have only to worry about insect infestation and disease, winter die-back, and storm damage. I have learned a lot, and I have gained a great sense of satisfaction from helping the trees grow. □

John Harwood, a designer and woodworker, operates Grassy Lane Studios in Cazenovia, N.Y. For more on how to grow black walnut trees, read Nut Tree Culture in North America *edited by Richard A. Jaynes (Northern Nut Growers Association, Broken Arrow Rd., Hamden, Conn. 06518),* Black Walnut for Profit *by Bruce Thompson (Graphic Publishing Co., Inc., Lake Mills, Iowa 50450), and* Black Walnut as a Crop *(publication #S/N 001-001-00403-1, available from the U.S. Government Printing Office, Washington, D.C. 20402).*

Stalking Mesquite
Sleek sculpture from scrawny trees

by Stanley T. Horn

Rock collecting may seem distant from woodworking, but there are times when the two interests are complementary and produce unexpectedly pleasing results. After many years of field trips for gems and minerals, I am well aware of the eccentricities of collectors. Even so, I was amazed to watch otherwise normal rockhounds working hard to gather gnarled, weathered branches of scrawny desert trees they called ironwood or mesquite. Some were so happy that they nearly neglected the usual target material of the area, agate and jasper. The wood certainly did not look like potential lumber or anything useful, even firewood. The scene was near Blythe, Calif., in the Wiley Well area. Trees either don't exist or are scarce in the deserts of southern California, Nevada and Arizona, but here there were many, following dry washes and underground water courses. They seemed to be about equally divided between mesquite and smoke trees. Both run about 12 ft. to 15 ft. tall, with mesquite a dusty grey-green color from small leaves. Branches are twisted, with no main trunk after the first few feet from the ground.

The best I could get when I cautiously inquired as to why the excitement over the mesquite was that it was "real purty." I dismissed further interest and turned to more serious and sane activities. Too bad. Months later I began to notice at various shows small Navajo sculptures of birds and animals carved from a dark, chocolate-brown wood, sculptures that took advantage of the wood's wild and twisted shape. It was the same mesquite I had snubbed, and it was a lot more than "real purty." Its subtle colors sing out with grain patterns to wood lovers, and I had been in that fraternity long before discovering the parallel joys of lapidary art.

Mesquite is not usually available from exotic wood dealers, so one must gather it oneself. It is widely distributed in the Colorado River basin, Arizona, New Mexico and Texas. Therefore, some months later I returned to Indian Pass, east of El Centro, Calif., and north of Yuma, Ariz. Rocks and minerals were still the primary objective, but this time mesquite had equal time. One looks for branches long dead on living trees, or unattached branches or roots—scarce because previous collectors have picked up all the easy pieces. There are two reasons for gathering dead wood only: It's already cured, and live trees are protected in some areas, such as Wiley Well, and a citation and fine could be expensive.

The best saw for cutting the mesquite is one designed for cutting firewood, with widely spaced teeth and plenty of set, but in dire emergency an ordinary saw may do the job, with time and patience. An ax is useless—mesquite's alternate name of ironwood is well earned. Even with the right saw, be prepared for a lot of work. My usual performance is about a half-hour for a 6-in. limb—three minutes of sawing and three

Stanley Horn, a retired aeronautical engineer, pursues woodworking, lapidary and silver work, and no work at all.

'The Spirit soars, and returns to the source,' Horn's Moebius-strip sculpture, carved from mesquite. Base is dumortierite, a desert stone.

Photos: Stanley T. Horn

Gathering wood the hard way: When cut, this mesquite branch weighed 60 lb. It is shown second from right in photo inset.

From *Fine Woodworking* magazine (March 1979) 15:44-45

minutes of puffing recovery, in cycles. Even winter days on the desert can be warm, and at other times, forget it.

Because the wood may have been drying for 50 years or more, the usual problems of curing self-collected wood do not exist. Mesquite can be used as soon as you want. I tried some small natural shapes and trays to get the feel of it (and the deep tannin stains on my hands), and found that ordinary woodworking methods apply almost to the end. Traditionalists may cringe, but at this point metalworking files are the most practical tools, because the wood responds much the same as medium brass. It even takes on a polished appearance with fine-cut files, but successive grades of abrasive paper, ending with wet-or-dry #600 used dry, provide the ultimate base for final polishing. Plain carnauba wax, lightly applied and vigorously rubbed with an old wool sock, gives a beautiful deepening of tone and a fine lustre. Your own pet schedule of finishing would probably work equally well, but I've never wished to go beyond this, in view of the results.

The photo at left shows one of my efforts that had a most satisfying end. The basic idea is an adaptation of the old Moebius strip, dearly loved by topology and math buffs. The natural branch had just the right amount of undulation, and luckily there were no voids or inclusions at the wrong places. As most art texts insist, the material itself will pull the craftsman inevitably toward a fine result. It seemed to here. The human element is there to respond of course, but it is the man/material combination that is required. Synergy is becoming a cliche, but is the only word to describe what happens in the process of developing a piece such as this. Part of the pleasure at the last stages of refinement is the tactile thrill of smoothly flowing surfaces and clean sharp edges that please the eye at the same time. The exact shape is not definable before starting, nor is a theme necessarily in mind. The finished piece may suggest a name or title, as mine did.

This mesquite harvest is the result of several field trips.

What, then, could be more fitting than a base of dumortierite, from the same earth that nurtured the branch? This stone varies from an almost black-purple through blue as bright as lapis lazuli and on into a granite-like grey. So as not to distract from the sculpture, the brightest blue was passed over in favor of a subdued shade, with veining suggestive of the distant galaxies of the Milky Way. A less-than-intense polish was given the stone, again to avoid overpowering the main item of interest. The combination of weathered branch arising from the Great Void, developing into the smooth Spirit shape and returning to the origin, seems a natural flow.

If you can acquire a piece of mesquite, try it for an interesting experience. It is a challenge any woodworker can enjoy. □

EDITOR'S NOTE: One source of mesquite is Dubose Architectural Floors, 916 Jackson St., San Antonio, Tex. 78212.

Drying Wood

The fundamental considerations

by R. Bruce Hoadley

It is ironic that our environment has us surrounded by trees—yet wood seems so inaccessible and expensive for the woodworker. Actually, abundant tree material is available to those who seek it out from such sources as storm damage cleanup, construction site clearance, firewood cuttings and even direct purchase from local loggers. With chain saws, wedges, band saws and a measure of ingenuity, chunks and flitches for carving or even lumber can be worked out. Also, it is usually possible to buy green lumber, either hardwood or softwood, at an attractive price from small local sawmills.

But what to do next? Many an eager woodworker has produced a supply of wood to the green board stage, but has been unable to dry it to usable moisture levels without serious "degrade" or even total loss. Certainly, the most consistent and efficient procedure would be to have the material kiln dried. Unfortunately, however, kilns may simply not be available. The cost of custom drying may be prohibitive, or the quantity of material too meager to justify kiln operation. But by understanding some of the basic principles of drying requirements and techniques, the woodworker can dry small quantities of wood quite successfully.

The so-called "seasoning" of wood is basically a water-removal process. Wood in the living tree has its cell walls water saturated and fully swollen with "bound" water and has additional "free" water in the cell cavities. The target in drying is to get the wood moisture content down to the equilibrium level of dryness consistent with the atmosphere in which the finished product will be used (see the article "Water and Wood," pp. 6-10). In the Northeast, for example, a moisture content of about seven percent is appropriate for interior cabinetwork and furniture; in the more humid Southern states, it would be higher; in the arid Southwest, lower. Since removal of bound water is accompanied by shrinkage of the wood, the object is to have the wood do its shrinking *before*, rather than *after*, the woodworking.

Wood dries first at the outside surface, creating a moisture imbalance. This moisture gradient of wetter interior and drier surface zone is necessary to cause moisture in the interior to migrate to the surface for eventual evaporation. On the other hand, if a piece of wood is dried too quickly, causing a "steep" moisture gradient (i.e., extreme range between interior and surface moisture content), excessive surface shrinkage will precede internal shrinkage; the resulting stress may cause surface checking or internal defects (collapse or

R. Bruce Hoadley, who teaches wood science at the University of Massachusetts in Amherst, is a carver who is never without a pile or two of drying wood.

Small quantity of lumber piled for indoor drying is shown at left. Double wedges are tapped in tighter to maintain restraint as lumber shrinks. Above, an assortment of log sections and blocks for carving is arranged for indoor drying.

later honeycomb). Gradual drying with a moderate moisture gradient allows moisture from the interior to migrate outward, replacing moisture as it evaporates from the surface, thus maintaining gradual and more uniform shrinkage. Shrinkage in wood per se is a natural and normal part of drying which should be expected and accommodated; *uneven* shrinkage due to uncontrolled drying, however, is the culprit which we must deal with. On the other hand, drying cannot be too slow or unnecessarily delayed, lest fungi causing decay, stain, or mold have a chance to develop. In other words, the key to drying is manipulating conditions of humidity, temperature and air circulation to attain a compromise drying rate fast enough to prevent fungal development, but slow enough to prevent severe uneven shrinkage.

The practice of drying includes (1) proper cutting and preparation of the pieces, (2) appropriate stacking and location to allow regulated drying (and in lumber, restraint of warp), and (3) systematic monitoring of the drying progress. Let's review the application of these basic concepts to typical situations of drying small quantities of wood. We will consider the drying of short log segments or short thick stock, commonly used for wood carvings or stout turnings, as well as regular lumber or boards. We will also assume that fairly small quantities such as several log chunks or up to a few hundred board feet are involved—as occurs when one suddenly falls heir to a storm-damaged tree or purchases enough lumber for a single piece of furniture.

First let's look at proper preparation of the material. Selection of pieces should favor those with normal structure and straight grain. If possible, avoid pieces with large obvious defects. Lumber from trees with special grain will invariably twist upon drying. Irregularities such as crotch grain or burls are esthetically interesting but chancy to dry, since their cell structure usually has unpredictable shrinkage. Knots are troublesome if they are large enough to involve grain distortion. Logs with sweep or from leaning trees having an eccentric cross-sectional shape probably contain reaction wood and will almost surely develop warp and stress due to abnormal shrinkage.

Whether preparing lumber or carving blocks, remember that normal shrinkage is about double tangentially as radially. My initial rule in splitting carving chunks from logs is to avoid pieces containing the pith. A half log or less which does not contain the pith can dry with a normal distortion of its cross-sectional shape (like slightly closing an oriental fan).

Another advantage of not boxing in the pith is being able to see if any overgrown knots are present which may not have been apparent from the bark side. Every knot-causing branch

developed from the pith, so it is important to examine pieces from the pith side to discover hidden branch stubs, especially if they have decay. Additionally, the pith area is often abnormal juvenile wood that might best be eliminated.

In sawing lumber, cup will be minimized by favoring quartersawed boards, which have no tendency to cup, or flatsawed boards taken furthest from the pith. Boards sawed through the center of the log, containing the pith or passing very close to it, will usually cup severely (or split open if restrained) along the center and might as well be ripped into two narrower boards before drying.

End drying is about 12 times as fast as drying through side-grain surfaces. Consequently, the regions near the ends of pieces drop below the fiber saturation point first. As the ends begin to shrink while the rest of the piece is still fully swollen, end checking usually results. In boards that are relatively long compared to their thickness, most moisture will leave slowly via the side surfaces; the influence of the end-checking problem is confined to a zone near each end of the board (about 6 inches from the ends of 1-in. boards). With relatively thick material, e.g., an 8 x 8-in. chunk 20 in. long, the end checking under uncontrolled drying can extend inward so far from each end that it riddles the entire piece.

To prevent the rapid end drying which will ruin carving chunks and the ends of lumber, the end-grain surface should be coated. Any relatively impervious material (such as paraffin, aluminum paint or urethane varnish) in ample thickness will do nicely. End coating can be applied to relatively wet surfaces by giving a primer coat of latex material first. It is important to end coat as soon as possible after sawing, before even the tiniest checks can begin to develop. Once a check develops, the cell structure failure will always be there even if it later appears to have closed. Also, when normal drying stress develops, a small check can provide the stress concentration point for further failures which otherwise might not have even begun in check-free wood. The purpose

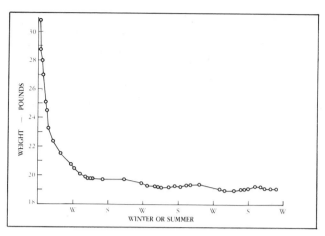

Periodic weights of drying wood plotted on a graph show equilibrium moisture content has been reached.

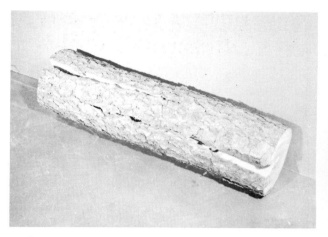

As shown in this cherry log, the greater tangential than radial shrinkage is relieved by radial cracking.

of end coating is to force all moisture loss to take place from lateral surfaces.

In some species, radial drying may be significantly faster than tangential drying. Therefore, if the bark on larger carving blocks is tight (as with winter-cut wood), it may best be left on to slow the radial drying. If the bark has been removed from a heavy slab, it should be watched carefully during the early drying stages for signs of surface checking. Another reason for prompt end coating is to prevent ever present airborne fungal spores from inoculating the surface. If the bark is loose, it should be removed; otherwise the layer of separation will become a fungal culture chamber with undesirable results.

Don't forget to mark a number and date on each piece. It is amazing how easily your memory can fail once you have several batches of wood in process.

Next, consideration must be given to the correct piling and location of the material so proper drying will result. Piling must ensure maximum air circulation around virtually every surface of the material. Some means of elevating the bottom of the stacks should be provided and some sort of sticker strips are usually recommended to separate adjacent pieces. With irregular carving blocks, merely piling them loosely may suffice, as long as flat surfaces do not lie against one another. No attempt should be made to restrain distortion of large chunks. With lumber, however, carefully designed systematic piling is best.

The usual piling method is to arrange boards in regular layers or courses separated by narrow strips or stickers. This permits the free movement of air around the lumber, uniformity of exposure of the surfaces, and restraint to minimize warp. The stickers should be dry and free of fungi and at least as long as the intended width of the pile. In planning the pile, stickers should be placed at the very ends of each course and at least every 18 inches along the length of the boards, since loose ends hanging out of the pile lack restraint and dry too rapidly (resulting in excessive warp). It is best to have lumber uniform in length, but if random lengths are unavoidable, they should be arranged in a pile as long as the longest boards; within each course, stagger the position of alternate boards so their alternate ends are lined up with the end of the pile. This "boxed pile" system prevents excessive drying of overhanging ends. To prevent excessive drying degrade to the top and bottom courses or layers, extra outer

courses of low-grade lumber or even plywood might be added to the pile. Stickers should be lined up in straight vertical rows. To ensure uniform restraint in a course, lumber and stickers should be as uniform in thickness as possible.

In large piles, the majority of the boards are restrained by the weight of others above. In small piles, extra weight (old lumber, bricks, cinder blocks, etc.) should be placed atop the pile. An alternate method of applying restraint is to assemble rectangular frames to surround the pile. The pile can be wedged against the frames and the wedges tapped further in to maintain restraint as the pile shrinks. Obviously the weighting or wedging should not be so extreme as to prevent shrinkage of the boards across their width.

In a commercial dry kiln, the operator can manipulate air circulation, temperature and humidity to dry the lumber gradually. He begins with a moderately low temperature and high relative humidity until the lumber (based on monitored samples) drops to a certain moisture content, say, near the fiber saturation point. He then establishes a slightly higher temperature and drier condition which he holds until the next lower prescribed moisture content is reached. Then he again establishes another warmer, drier level and so on until the lumber is dried. The so-called "kiln schedule" is a sequence of successively drier conditions which are regulated according to the moisture content of the lumber.

In home drying of wood, we must therefore try to choose locations or regulate conditions to allow only moderate drying at first, followed by more drastic conditions once the lumber has reached a lower moisture level. One logical starting place is out-of-doors. Except for especially arid regions, the relative humidity is usually moderately high. For example, in the New England area the humidity averages around 75 to 80 percent, which would give an equilibrium moisture content of 12 to 14 percent. Piles of blocks or stacks of lumber should be kept well up off the ground to avoid dampness, and should be protected from direct rainfall and sun rays as well. Any unheated building which has good ventilation, such as a shed lacking doors and windows, is ideal. Most garages serve well and even unheated basements are suitable if plenty of air space around the pile is provided. In air drying out-of-doors, some rather obvious seasonal variations will be encountered. In many Eastern areas, slightly lower humidity and more prevalent winds favor drying in spring months. In winter, if temperatures drop to near or below freezing, drying may be

End grain surface of a basswood half log which was not end coated in time shows a large number of end checks.

Cross-cutting has revealed that the surface checks have penetrated deep into this white oak board.

brought to a standstill. You must therefore interpret conditions for each particular area. If wood is intended for finished items that will be used indoors, outdoor air drying will not attain a low enough equilibrium moisture content. The material must be moved indoors to a heated location before it is worked.

Surface checking should be closely watched. Minor shallow surface checking that will later dress out can be ignored. However, deeper checks should be considered unacceptable. The worst type are those which open up but later reclose. Often they go unnoticed during subsequent machining operations only to reveal themselves when staining and finishing of a completed piece is attempted. If any serious end checks develop, don't pretend they don't exist, or will ever get better or go away. For example, if a large carving block develops a serious check, this indicates fairly intensive stress; it is probably best to split the piece in half along the check, thus helping to relieve the stresses, and be satisfied with smaller pieces.

If wood must be located indoors from the very start, drying may be too rapid. Any signs of surface checks in the material suggest that some retardation may be necessary. This can be accomplished by covering the entire pile with a polyethylene film. Moisture from the lumber will soon elevate the humidity and retard the drying. However, this arrangement must be closely watched, since air circulation will likewise be stopped. Moisture condensation on the inside of the plastic covering or any mold on the wood surfaces may mean the pile has been turned into a fungi culture chamber and signals the need for speeding up the drying again. Common sense and intuition will suggest how often to check the wood and how to modify the storage location to speed up or slow down the drying. The seasonal humidity fluctuation commonly encountered in heated buildings must also be allowed for in determining the equilibrium moisture level.

Drying progress can be monitored by weight. Weights should be taken often enough to be able to plot a fairly coherent graphical record of weight against time. Weighing should be accurate to within one or two percent of the total weight of the piece. A large chunk in the 100-pound range can be weighed on a bathroom scale. Pieces in the 10 to 25-pound category can be weighed with a food or infant scale. Small stacks of boards can be monitored by simply weighing the entire pile if this is convenient. In larger piles, sample boards can be pulled and weighed periodically. Electrical moisture meters are perhaps the simplest means of keeping track of the drying progress in boards.

The last stage of drying should be done in an environment similar to the one in which the finished item will be used. The weight of the pieces will eventually level out and reach a near constant equilibrium with only faint gains and losses of weight in response to seasonal humidity fluctuations.

When material comes into equilibrium weight with the desired environment, it's ready. Don't pay attention to overly generalized rules like "one year of drying for every inch of thickness." Such rules have no way of accounting for the tremendous variation in species' characteristics or in atmospheric conditions. Basswood or pine decoy blanks four inches thick dry easily in less than a year, whereas a four-inch thick slab of rosewood may take much longer to dry without defects. In general, the lower density woods are easier to dry than higher density woods. Since the average cell wall thickness is less, moisture movement is greater and this results in faster drying. In addition, the weaker cell structure is better able to deform in response to drying stresses, rather than resisting and checking. After some experience is gained for a particular species and thickness dried in a certain location, a fairly reliable estimate can be made as to the necessary drying time. Here, the initial date you marked on the piece will serve you well.

Whether drying log sections or boards, remember that the drying must be somewhat regulated; usually at the beginning, indoor drying proceeds too quickly and needs slowing down.

In drying your own lumber or carving wood, one common problem is hesitation. You can't wait! If you do, fungi or checks will get ahead of you. Try to think out all the details *before* you get your wood supply; don't wait until you get it home to decide how you are going to end coat or where you are going to stack it.

But perhaps the greatest pitfall is greed. Most woodworkers never feel they have enough material put aside and tend to overstock if the opportunity presents itself. With green wood, this can be disastrous. Don't try to handle too much. Don't even start if you can't follow through. More material is ruined by neglect than by lack of know-how.

Finally, in drying wood, nobody has ever proved that it doesn't pay to cross your fingers. □

Air-Drying Lumber
Usable stock comes from a carefully stickered stack

by Paul Bertorelli

Air-drying your own lumber can be a cheap alternative to expensive and sometimes unavailable kiln-dried wood. If you live near a sawmill or have your own woodlot, green wood can be had for a fraction the cost of commercially dried stuff. But once you've got the wood, the real challenge is converting it into a material you can use in the shop. Conventional wisdom recommends air-drying green stock for one year per inch of thickness. That seems easy enough, but having seen more than a few piles of stained and checked boards, I suspected there was more to it. I visited Paul Fuge to find out.

Fuge, of Shelton, Conn., has made a business of buying sawmill-green lumber and air-drying it himself. After air-drying, he runs it through his small kiln before selling it. He got into drying his own for the same reason most of us do: he couldn't find decent wood at a price he could afford. Six years and several hundred thousand board feet later, he has learned that there's a bit more to lumber seasoning than neat piles.

Fuge dries thousands of board feet at once, but his techniques can be successfully applied in seasoning any amount of wood. Here's how he does it.

Sites and foundations—The worst checking, staining and warping is liable to happen very soon after the lumber is cut from the log. Therefore, Fuge picks drying sites before he buys lumber, allowing him to quickly stack, sticker and, if conditions warrant, cover his wood. He avoids swampy, damp, low-lying spots, and sites where high winds will dry the wood too quickly. Fuge's stacks are on south-facing slopes where nearby trees and shrubs moderate the winds. He places gravel or tarpaper under the stacks to control ground moisture.

Lumber piles should be oriented with the wood's final use in mind. Some checking is acceptable in siding and structural lumber, for instance, so such stacks can be placed to achieve a high drying rate. That means exposing their sides to the prevailing winds, on a site with plenty of sun. Furniture lumber, on the other hand, should dry more slowly, so pick a more sheltered area and aim the ends of the stack into the wind, so the stickers will prevent it from blowing through the pile.

Fuge builds sturdy foundations for his stacks, and he is careful to keep the boards in parallel planes as the stack is built. The foundation should be high enough to keep the bottom layer of wood 1 ft. off the ground. For a foundation 10 ft. long, Fuge places two rows of three concrete blocks on their sides, each on relatively level ground. The rows are 30 in. apart and the blocks in each row are 36 in. apart. Atop the blocks, Fuge sets a pair of 10-ft. 4x6 timbers called mudsills. He sights along both mudsills to make certain they lie in the same plane, and shims under each concrete block to ensure uniform support. Next, six 4x4 bolsters go across the mudsills on 24-in. centers. With all the bolsters in place, Fuge uses a long, straight board to check them for alignment, and shims any that are not in line. If everything is in the same plane but still isn't level, Fuge is pleased. A pitched stack will shed any water that finds its way inside.

Stacking and stickering—Fuge keeps a large supply of carefully dimensioned stickers on hand. "I like white oak but if I have sassafras or locust, I'll use them too because they're lighter," he says. A 4-ft. long sticker, 1-in. square in section, seems the ideal size. Smaller stickers slow air movement and larger ones waste lumber and add weight. Don't use stickers with sapwood because it harbors the fungi that cause blue or sticker stain, a major source of lumber degrade. Stickers with bark are also rejected, says Fuge, because they deform under the pile's weight. Stickers can be grooved or coved along their length to reduce contact and moisture build-up on the lumber that can also cause stains.

With a sticker on each bolster, Fuge begins his pile with a layer of low-grade lumber that will act as a shield against ground moisture. If he is mixing lumber of various thicknesses, the heavier stock goes in the lower third of the pile where slower drying rates make it less likely to check. Fuge takes great pains to align each sticker vertically with the one below it, and to keep all the stickers over the bolsters' 24-in. centers. If the stickers creep out of line, the boards won't be supported evenly and those at the bottom will kink.

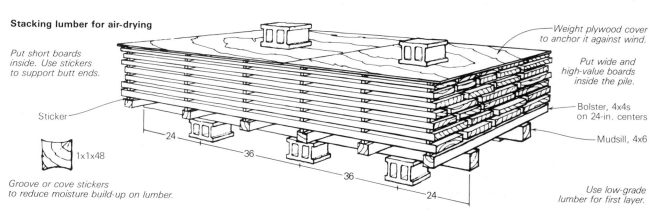

Stacking lumber for air-drying

Put short boards inside. Use stickers to support butt ends.

Sticker

1x1x48

Groove or cove stickers to reduce moisture build-up on lumber.

Weight plywood cover to anchor it against wind.

Put wide and high-value boards inside the pile.

Bolster, 4x4s on 24-in. centers

Mudsill, 4x6

Use low-grade lumber for first layer.

24   36   36   24

Drawing: Claudia Westerbeke Chapman

As he stacks, Fuge also sorts boards by length and width. The longer stock goes to the outside of the pile, the shorter stock to the inside. High quality and extra-wide boards also go on the inside where slower drying makes degrade less likely. Extra stickers can be placed at odd locations inside the pile where the butt ends of short pieces meet between the fixed 24-in. centers. Bowed boards should be stacked with the bows facing each other, allowing the weight of the pile to straighten them. Cupped boards are stacked with cups down, permitting water that seeps into the stack to drain.

As the pile rises, Fuge sometimes finds that the sawmill has given him lumber tapered or wedge-shaped in thickness. To keep everything in the right plane, he keeps some odd-sized stickers around so he can shim out the variations. If the stack is building neatly, Fuge isn't afraid to make it plenty high—those in his yard go 10 ft. and better. "I figure if I'm going to go to the trouble to build a good foundation, there's no point in starting another pile unless I have to," he says. Mixing species is okay too, but you must remember that different woods have different drying rates. If the stack will be taken down all at once, it should be air-dried long enough to suit the slowest-drying wood.

When the stack is complete, Fuge tops it out with a layer of low-grade lumber followed by a roof of sawmill slabwood, plywood or other materials, canted to shed water, and anchored against the wind. Fuge advises against using plastic for roofs because it slows ventilation in the top layer and quickly decomposes and starts falling apart in sunlight. "Besides," he adds, "it looks like hell."

Moisture control and maintenance—With the lumber stacked and roofed, Fuge turns his attention to controlling the drying rates and minimizing degrade. If he has built his pile during the peak drying months—April to October in the Northeast—he coats the butt ends of wide and heavy boards with glue or latex paint. This slows end-grain moisture loss and thereby reduces checking. "But if you don't coat them in the first two or three days, forget it, because the damage will be done already," Fuge warns. If a stack goes up in late fall or winter, little need be done until warmer weather approaches. And when spring does arrive, Fuge is ready. He shields his lumber against severe drying rates of hot, dry days by covering the pile with burlap or old blankets. The fabric is porous enough to slow (but not stop) moisture loss from the wood. As the weather moderates, Fuge uncovers the piles. If a stack end faces into the sun, it should be shielded with fabric or plywood throughout the drying cycle.

Fuge likes to leave 4/4 and 5/4 stock air-drying for a full season, that is, April to October. So a stack that goes up in the middle of the summer isn't considered dry until the middle of the following summer. Stock 6/4 and thicker may need two but certainly no more than three full drying seasons.

"After it's been out that long, it isn't going to get any drier and you might as well move it inside," Fuge says. He monitors moisture content with an electric moisture meter but an ordinary household oven and an accurate scale or balance will work just as well. Find moisture content by cutting a 1-in. cube about 2 ft. in from the end of a sample board. Weigh the cube and cook it in the oven at 212° to 221° until it no longer loses weight. Calculate moisture content by subtracting the oven-dry weight from the sample's wet weight. Then divide that figure by the oven-dry weight and multiply by

Paul Fuge makes sturdy foundations for his lumber stacks. He checks alignment of bolsters with a long, straight board fresh from the sawmill. To build a foundation with lighter stock, shore up with more concrete blocks or make a smaller pile.

100. If he is in a hurry, Fuge checks the stack's moisture content every two weeks. When it reaches the 18% to 22% range, it's ready for the kiln even if it hasn't been out for a full season. The one year per inch guide is hardly written in stone. Vagaries in climate and species moisture content and drying characteristics make monitoring the lumber a must.

If you don't have a kiln, bring your air-dried lumber indoors to dry for final use. Fuge recommends stacking and stickering it in a heated, dry room for an entire winter. A small fan to circulate air through the stack will speed things along and by spring the lumber should be ready. "If you're willing to live with your wood in the house and treat it like you treat yourself, there's no reason you can't dry it entirely without a kiln," Fuge says. If domestic considerations make indoor drying impossible, Fuge suggests a dry garage, attic or shed. Any space in fact, will work except the basement—even the driest of basements is probably too moist for further wood seasoning. Once wood is dried down to about 12% it will pick up moisture in a damp basement.

With air and inside drying complete, stack your lumber tightly without stickers in a dry place. Further air movement through the pile will only restore part of the moisture you've worked so hard to remove. ☐

Paul Bertorelli is editor of Fine Woodworking. *For more on drying lumber, see these articles:* "Water and Wood," *pp. 6-10;* "A Barn for Air-Drying Lumber," *pp. 84-85;* "Alternative Wood-Drying Technologies," *pp. 86-89;* "Measuring Moisture," *pp. 90-91;* "A Dehumidifier Kiln," *pp. 92-94;* "Dry Kiln," *pp. 95-99;* "Shop-Built Moisture Meter," *pp. 100-102;* and "Solar Kiln," *p. 103.*

A Barn for Air-Drying Lumber
Pennsylvania Dutch tobacco sheds inspire design

by Sam Talarico

About ten years ago I came across a huge red oak burl left to rot by lumbermen who had no use for this natural rarity. It led to more than a career in woodworking. I now pursue burls, rootwood and highly figured flitches. I have gathered thousands of board feet, involving many hours of searching, felling, hauling and sawing. I came to be known as a source of hard-to-find, special pieces. I stacked these treasures carefully with stickers, waxed the ends and protected them from the weather with roofing tin. This worked until winter winds wreaked havoc. Too many times I found myself gathering the scattered tin to re-cover the stacks. Piling cement blocks on top caused another problem. Every time someone came for wood, I would have to uncover and unstack many piles to find just the piece or pieces to satisfy him. All of my lumber is bookmatched, so it took extra care to go through a stack. Numbering the pieces with marking crayon

as they came off the sawmill helped. But I needed a shelter for air-drying that would provide easy access to the piles I was constantly shuffling through. It had to be spacious, sturdy and as maintenance-free as possible. I wanted an attractive building with a character to suit its purpose, one that would harmonize with the existing buildings on the property. And it had to be economical and easy to build.

Ideas for this barn came not from books or studies of convection and ventilation, but from everyday farmers, mostly of the Mennonite and Amish sects, whose livelihood depends on getting a good price for their money crop, tobacco. Their tobacco sheds, sound and handsome structures found throughout Pennsylvania and New England, are designed to generate and regulate air flow to eliminate fungus and mold, plagues also to the woodman trying to season green lumber. The pitch of the roof, for instance, not only beautifies the barn and

The drying barn under construction, top left. The floor will be poured concrete, leaving a 6-in. gap below the siding for air to flow in. Open-ended gables will vent air out. At left, the completed barn. Four sets of doors give easy access to lumber racks in the front and flitch piles throughout the lower level. Under front gable, above, stairs, deck and double doors provide access to upper level. Hoist beam extends halfway into length of building and is braced by 4x4s running obliquely into door framing. Swallow hole in gable serves no purpose, except 'for nice,' as the Mennonites put it.

Photos: Jim Penta; Illustration: Christopher Clapp

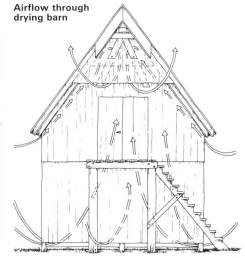

Gaps in flooring of upper level ensure airflow to dry burls and rootwood stored here.

allows headroom upstairs; it also moves air better than a lower roof would. The corrugated aluminum (traditionally tin) conducts the sun's heat, causing the air inside to rise. Fresh air is drawn in through a gap around the bottom of the barn and through spaces under the eaves. Openings under the gable ends serve as exhaust vents, and a 3x5 window in the top of the rear wall provides light upstairs. In a tobacco barn, long narrow doors, rather like louvers all around the building, can be opened and, in conjunction with the open-ended gables, provide maximum draft to inhibit mold and rot. For seasoning lumber, I didn't feel I needed as much draft. The eight wide doors on the side of the barn are mainly for access to the stacks, though in hot, humid weather, I open one or two sets for added ventilation. They also provide adequate light without windows on the lower level; direct sunlight bleaches some woods and its heat can cause surface checks and warp. A stairway on the front of the barn (easier to build than one inside, and it saved storage space), two doors and a hoist beam under the gable provide access to the second floor. The barn is 20 ft. by 40 ft., with the stairs added on to that; it is 23 ft. to the ridge.

I am experienced in the old methods of mortise-and-tenon contruction, held together with oak or locust pins, but these methods are too costly and time-consuming for today's economy. I compromised and used treated-pine pole construction with green oak framing, spiked and lag-bolted together. The lag bolts were old black steel, four 5-gal. buckets of them in various sizes I found for $5 a bucket. Beware of the new zinc-coated ones. I've had many bad experiences with their heads twisting off when you start to bear down on them. It's well worth hunting for the old black lag bolts.

The fifteen main posts, 10 ft. apart, and the two extra posts to frame the stairs and deck are 15-ft. 6x6s resting on concrete footers surfaced exactly the same depth using a transit. Before uprighting them, the posts are notched with saw and slick (a 3-in. to 4-in. wide paring chisel with a long offset handle) to receive the 2x12 rafter plate at the top and the 2x12 joist plate for the second floor 1 ft. below that. When the 4-in. thick concrete floor was poured, I still had almost 10 ft. of clearance below the second floor. The lower level has no sill, joists or wooden floor.

With the upper floor-joist plates bolted to the posts, braces are nailed flush with the outside of the posts to serve as nailers

for the pine siding. At the top of the center posts a 6x8 girder runs the length of the barn. Two-by-eight joists cross the girder from plate to plate, and 1x8 green oak flooring gets nailed on to make the second floor. The gaps that shrinkage produces in this flooring provide good air flow from the lower level of the building through to the top.

The roof is composed of 23 2x6 trusses, laid out on a 15/12 pitch. They're put up on 24-in. centers with poplar lath and 1x6 pine diagonal wind bracing let into the rafters for support. The 6x6 hoist I added serves as part of the ridge pole. It extends 19 ft. into the building, braced into each truss and supported where it overhangs at the front by two 4x4s run diagonally back into 4x4 framing for the upper door. The aluminum roof is nailed on, and then the siding. Rather than paint this, I've chosen to let it weather. I've removed pine siding from barns well over 100 years old, and the boards were sound enough to be used in other constructions.

After the siding is on, hanging the doors is easy. Basically, you frame each 10-ft. opening between the posts with 2x10s notched horizontally into the posts and braced with two diagonals. Cover these with siding, fasten your hinges, cut right down the middle and open the doors. It's best to set your circular saw at an angle inward so the doors can open and close without binding.

For lumber racks I framed out a 10-ft. by 10-ft. area in each front end of the barn to be used for easy access to dimensional lumber and smaller flitches. I lapped horizontal 2x6s into 4x4 uprights and into the 6x6 posts. I stack my large flitches on the floor throughout the rest of the barn on 4x4 blocks. All my shortest pieces, burls and rootwood I store upstairs. To add some extra storage I hung racks from the floor joists and posts in the back center. I've used all the space available and managed to keep things well enough in order to be able to quickly to pull a particular flitch upon request.

I'm very happy with this barn; it's served me well, drying large and highly figured pieces with little degrade. It took me and my Mennonite neighbors just seven days to build, except for the concrete and lumber racks, which I did later. It cost me a little under $4,000 when we built it three years ago, and has required no maintenance to speak of since. ☐

Sam Talarico makes furniture from his prize flitches in Mohnton, Pa.

Alternative Wood-Drying Technologies
Solar energy and dehumidification

Two-thirds of the energy used to manufacture lumber goes into drying it. Burning mill residue supplies only part of the energy used by conventional kilns; most of it is fossil fuel and electrical energy. In the United States, we use more than 10^{13} BTUs of fuel each year to dry lumber. Energy-efficient solar and dehumidifier kilns are important alternatives both to industry and to the individual woodworker.

Drying green wood involves removing both free water and some bound water. Free water is water in the cell cavities, and it evaporates relatively quickly and easily. But at the fiber saturation point (30% for most species) bound water must be extracted from within the cell walls, and shrinkage begins. If a board is dried too quickly, the moisture gradient between the surface and the core becomes too steep. Excessive surface shrinkage precedes internal shrinkage, causing stresses that can result in surface checks, casehardening or internal collapse (honeycomb). Proper drying requires careful pacing and close control of both temperature and humidity throughout the process. (For more on water and wood, drying lumber, and kiln operation, see other articles in this section, as well as "Water and Wood," pp. 6-10.)

Solar drying—Solar kilns are basically greenhouses that trap the sun's energy and circulate the heated air through stickered stacks of lumber. Most solar kilns consist of a rigid framework with one slanted side facing south for maximum solar exposure. Within the kiln, or mounted on the slanted side, are collectors—either metal plates or some other material painted flat black—to absorb energy. These collectors contact a transfer fluid, usually air. Water-transfer systems have higher heat capacities, but require expensive pipe-embedded plates and more demanding maintenance. Because of the relatively low temperatures required, because it is air that must ultimately be heated to effect the drying, and because of their simplicity and low cost, it is generally agreed that air-transfer systems are more appropriate for solar kilns.

The collectors must be covered with some transparent or translucent material that will allow solar energy to pass through to the collectors while inhibiting the escape of heat. The material should resist deterioration from ultraviolet light, weathering and heat. Glass is an obvious choice—low-iron, tempered glass is best, but more expensive than plain window glass. Glass requires substantial framing and expensive replacement when broken. A number of lighter, less expensive and, in some cases, more transparent materials have been developed specifically for solar-energy applications. They include Teflon and Tedlar solar films (Dupont, Wilmington, Del. 19898), a fiberglass material called Sun-Lite

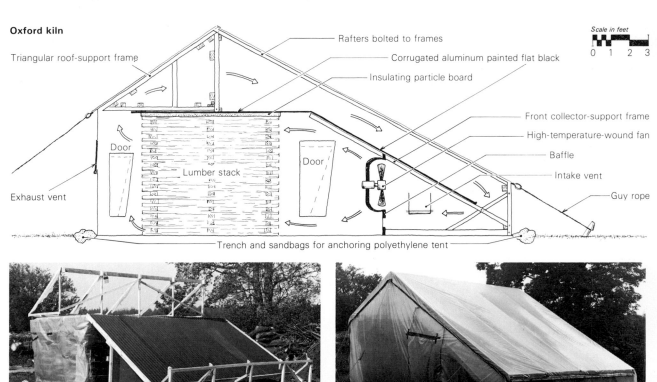

Oxford kiln

Triangular roof-support frame

Rafters bolted to frames

Corrugated aluminum painted flat black

Insulating particle board

Door

Door

Lumber stack

Exhaust vent

Front collector-support frame

High-temperature-wound fan

Baffle

Intake vent

Guy rope

Scale in feet
0   1   2   3

Trench and sandbags for anchoring polyethylene tent

The Oxford kiln with rafters and polyethylene tent yet to be mounted, left, and in operation, right, is light enough to be carried by two or three people from one stack to another. It was designed for use in energy-poor countries.

Illustrations: Christopher Clapp

(Kalwall Corp., Box 237, Manchester, N.H. 03105) and ultraviolet-resistant polyethylene and polyester (S.U.N., Box 306, Bascom, Ohio 44809). The polyethylene commonly available from building-supply houses deteriorates in ultraviolet light and cannot be expected to last more than a year.

The other important components of most solar kilns are a fan and vents. Temperature within the kiln can rise above 150°F, so fans with plastic components that may melt should be avoided. Proper air circulation ensures that the lumber will dry evenly and at the safest rate. A timer is generally used to turn the fans on during the day and off at night. It is important that the relative humidity within the kiln be allowed to rise at night, to slow down evaporation from the wood surface. As moisture from the core continues to migrate to the shell, stress is relieved and the moisture gradient is kept moderate. The most critical time is the first week; the kiln should be monitored daily (preferably in the afternoon when the kiln is hottest), lest too rapid drying cause checks. Vents are kept closed at first or opened only a little, to keep moisture exhaust to a minimum and the humidity high. Moisture content should be checked regularly with a commercial moisture meter or by weighing a sample board.

Paul J. Bois describes a small, permanent solar kiln ("Solar Kiln," p. 103). A cheaper, simpler, easier-to-construct kiln was designed by R. A. Plumtree at Oxford University, England. It is portable enough for two or three people to move it from one stack of lumber to another. The design has been particularly effective in developing countries, where drying timber instead of exporting it unprocessed generates badly needed employment and revenue. It consists of two wooden frames, some sheets of corrugated aluminum painted matte black, a couple of fans and a roll of polyethylene that gets draped over the framework.

One of the frames is a triangular truss that sits atop the pile of stickered lumber, the pile having first been covered with an insulating layer of particle board, then with half the sheets of corrugated aluminum. The other frame forms a slanted surface on which the remainder of the aluminum sheets lie. This frame is positioned on the side of the lumber pile where it will receive the most solar exposure. It includes a plywood baffle that houses the fans. The polyethylene tent is draped over the frame and made taut with guy ropes from the top periphery and sand bags around the bottom.

Doors cut into the polyethylene—one between the stack and the baffle, another at the rear of the stack—give access to the lumber for moisture-content readings. The fans draw fresh air through two vents cut on either side of the kiln in

EDITOR'S NOTE: This article was prepared, with help from Roger Schroeder, from material published by the Forest Products Laboratory, Box 5130, Madison, Wis. 53705; the Forest Products Research Society, 2801 Marshall Court, Madison, Wis. 53705; and the Department of Energy, Washington, D.C. 20545. Contact these agencies for more information on wood drying and solar energy. Other publications serving as resources in solar technology include *Harvest the Sun* by Nick Nicholson (Ayer's Cliff Center for Solar Research, Box 344, Ayer's Cliff, Quebec, Canada J0B 1C0; 210 pp., $9.95), *The Solar Age Resource Book*, edited by Martin McPhillips (Everest House, 1133 6th Ave., New York, N.Y. 10036; 242 pp., $9.95), *Solar Age* magazine (Box 4934, Manchester, N.H. 03108; $20 for 12 issues), and *The People's Solar Handbook* (Solar Usage Now, Box 306, Bascom, Ohio 44809; 350 pp., $5.00). Solar kilns and dehumidification systems are undergoing continuing development. All prices and information in this article are current as of publication in 1980. —*R.M.*

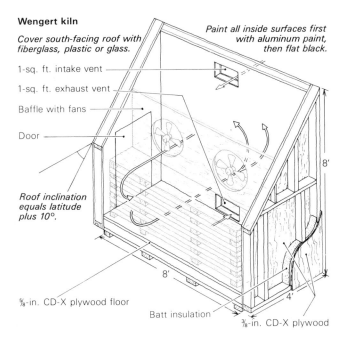

Wengert kiln

Cover south-facing roof with fiberglass, plastic or glass.

Paint all inside surfaces first with aluminum paint, then flat black.

1-sq. ft. intake vent

1-sq. ft. exhaust vent

Baffle with fans

Door

Roof inclination equals latitude plus 10°.

⅜-in. CD-X plywood floor

Batt insulation

⅜-in. CD-X plywood

8'

8'

4'

front of the baffle, and moist air escapes through a vent cut midway on the back side of the kiln. Velcro, a self-sticking material that can be bought in fabric stores, seals the doors and vents.

According to A. Frederick Prins, professor of forest science at Oxford, a kiln that can successfully dry 3,500 bd. ft. of 3-in. oak over the course of an English summer was built for around $1,600 in materials. Prins says the Oxford kiln can be scaled down, at a considerable reduction in cost, using only one fan, less polyethylene and fewer collectors.

Another solar kiln, developed and tested by Dr. Gene Wengert at Virginia Polytechnic Institute in Blacksburg, functions without metal collectors, an expensive component of most kilns. The plan calls for 2x4 stud walls covered inside and out with ⅜-in. exterior-grade (CD-X) plywood insulated with batt between the layers. The south-facing roof is covered with two layers of fiberglass, plastic or glass. Wengert suggests the angle of the roof be 10° steeper than the latitude of the kiln's location, which is between 30° and 50° in the continental U.S. Making it equal to the latitude gives best average exposure, but making it steeper improves winter performance, and summer performance is best moderated anyway. Multispeed, high-temperature-wound fans, mounted in a baffle that sits on a plywood covering atop the lumber stack, can be controlled with timers or thermostats. Instead of metal collectors, Wengert paints the baffle, plywood stack-cover and inside walls first with aluminum paint, then with flat black. The aluminum paint acts as a vapor barrier against the plywood, and the flat black absorbs enough heat to raise the temperature within the kiln, without a charge of lumber, up to 100°F above the outside temperature. A vent at the top of the north wall allows fresh air in and a vent at the bottom exhausts moist air, but the flow of new air is kept to around 5%. As with most kilns, humidity is kept high in the initial days of drying by keeping the vents closed. Doors in the east and west walls provide convenient access to the stack for moisture readings.

Wengert says a kiln of this design, with a capacity of 1,000 bd. ft., can be built for as little as $500. Size is flexible, but there must be at least 1 ft. between the walls and the stack to allow air to circulate, and the proportion of roof area to capacity must remain at about 1 sq. ft. to 10 bd. ft. As with all solar kilns, performance depends on the time of year and the weather conditions, but in good drying weather Wengert has taken green oak down to 6% moisture content in 30 days.

Both the Wengert and the Oxford kilns are open-flow systems that cycle air into and out of the drying chamber. As much as 25% of the heat generated in a solar kiln can be lost in venting. A couple of kilns have been designed as closed systems, employing condensation rather than venting to eliminate moisture. Condensation naturally occurs in solar kilns as a result of daily temperature fluctuations. It reduces degrade by relieving the stresses that build up in lumber as it dries.

Timothy Lumley and Elvin Choong at Louisiana State University have designed and tested a closed-flow solar kiln that incorporates a modification of the traditional flatplate collector, as used in the Oxford kiln. Their collector resembles a large box cut diagonally through two opposite corners, providing four surfaces instead of one for absorption. The diagonal surface is glazed, and vents located in the bottom of the box allow heated air to pass into the drying chamber. The design more than doubles the absorption area of a flatplate collector with the same amount of glazing.

A further advantage of the box-type collector is that because each of its four surfaces is oriented differently, it will pick up solar radiation from different angles during different seasons or times of the day, and energy reflected off any one surface, instead of passing uselessly out through the glass, may be absorbed by another surface. The kiln tested in Louisiana has two box-type collectors, one above the stack and the other in front of it, and has a capacity of 25,000 bd. ft. It was constructed for half the cost of a similarly sized conventional kiln and successfully dried lumber in only twice the conventional-kiln time, and at a fraction of the operating costs. Lumley and Choong believe their design may be commercially competitive with conventional kilns, but that the greatest potential for solar kilns is to replace air-drying before finally kilning down to 6% moisture content. Performance is too dependent on solar conditions to match the control possible in conventional kilns.

Dehumidification—Both conventional and solar kilns dry wood by increasing the temperature of the drying air, which decreases its relative humidity, making it possible for it to take on more moisture as it is circulated through the lumber. The same principle can be inverted: The temperature of the drying air *after* it has circulated through the stack can be *decreased* until it reaches its dew point, when the water vapor evaporated from the wood condenses. Dehumidification is a closed-flow system that employs a heat pump to effect condensation and the drying process. A heat pump transfers thermal energy by compressing a volatile fluid in one section of its circuit (the condenser), then piping it to another section where it is allowed to evaporate. The evaporator section takes on heat from the atmosphere; the condenser gives heat off. In a wood-dehumidification system, both the lumber stack and heat pump are in an insulated chamber. Fans draw air through the stack and past the evaporator section of the heat pump. Here moisture that the air has absorbed from the wood condenses on the cooling coils and is drained away. Now cool and drier, the air passes through the condenser section, where it is reheated with the energy that was extracted from it in the evaporator section. The air is blown back through the stack warm and dry.

The dehumidifier requires only half the energy of a conventional kiln and reaches an operating temperature of around 120°F; each pound of water condensed produces 1,000 BTUs of energy. Still, this is a relatively low-temperature process and as such produces lumber with little degrade. The system is simpler to operate and maintain than a conventional steam kiln and can require less initial investment. Canadian-based Merkara, Inc. (7290 Torbram Rd., Mississauga, Ont.) distributes a dehumidification system called Westair that can dry 5,000 bd. ft. of green oak to 6% moisture content in 30 days. At $15,000 the system is about half the price of a comparable conventional kiln. Other manufacturers include Irvington-Moore (Box 40666, Jacksonville, Fla.) and Ebac Ltd. (Greenfield Industrial Estate, Bishop Auckland, Co. Durham, England). The latter sells a dehumidifier with a 1,000-bd.-ft. capacity for $800, excluding the drying chamber. Unfortunately this product is not yet distributed in the U.S.

But the fact that dehumidification uses half as much

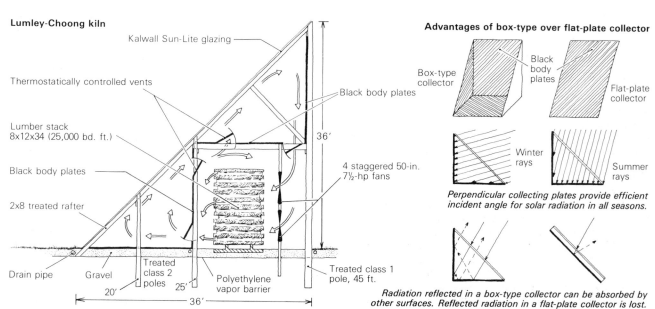

Lumley-Choong kiln

Kalwall Sun-Lite glazing

Thermostatically controlled vents

Lumber stack 8x12x34 (25,000 bd. ft.)

Black body plates

2x8 treated rafter

Drain pipe   Gravel

Treated class 2 poles

Polyethylene vapor barrier

Black body plates

36'

4 staggered 50-in. 7½-hp fans

Treated class 1 pole, 45 ft.

20'   25'

36'

Advantages of box-type over flat-plate collector

Box-type collector

Black body plates

Flat-plate collector

Winter rays   Summer rays

Perpendicular collecting plates provide efficient incident angle for solar radiation in all seasons.

Radiation reflected in a box-type collector can be absorbed by other surfaces. Reflected radiation in a flat-plate collector is lost.

Typical dehumidification system

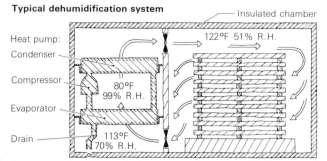

As moist air from the stacks is cooled in the evaporator section of the heat pump, water vapor condenses out and is drained away. The cool, dry air (the relative humidity is high only because it is cool) passes through the condenser section where it is heated with the energy absorbed from it in the evaporator section. This lowers the relative humidity, and it is blown back through the stack warm and dry.

energy as conventional kiln-drying must be weighed against the fact that it is electrical energy, which can be three to four times as expensive as fossil fuels. Also, for a heat-pump compressor to begin operating, the ambient temperature must be at least 70°F, necessitating pre-heating outdoor facilities. Most systems must incorporate an electrical coil preheater.

Ultimately, comparing dehumidification with conventional kiln-drying comes to a question of cost effectiveness, and the energy costs at particular installations vary. Where electricity is cheap and for medium-sized lumber-drying businesses (1,000 to 1,000,000 bd. ft./year), dehumidification is worth considering. But on the properties of individual craftsmen and enterprising woodworkers faced with the rising cost of conventionally dried lumber, greenhouse-like structures will be the more common sight.　□

Q & A

Fit between frame and panel—*I made a sugar pine cabinet with raised-panel doors, my first attempt at making this type of door. I didn't want a gap to show between the panel and the frame, so I made the panels fit tightly in their grooves. Is there a potential problem that the stiles will crack if the panel expands? Is it really that important to allow for expansion?*
　　　　　　　　　　　　　—George Fitzgerald, Detroit, Mich.
SIMON WATTS REPLIES: If you made your frame and panel as in the drawing, the stiles won't crack. Fortunately, wood is relatively compressible, and the fibers will just crush slightly as the panel swells.

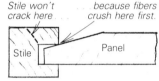

Stile won't crack here / because fibers crush here first. / Stile / Panel

You need make no allowance for expansion along the length of the grain because wood moves scarcely at all in that direction. But across the grain is another story, and you ignore it at your peril. For each foot of panel width in a red oak panel, you should allow about ⅜ in. for expansion (³⁄₁₆ in. on each side); for a mahogany panel, only about ¼ in. White oak moves even more than red oak, but sugar pine is almost as stable as mahogany.

I usually pin my panels to the rails at the center, top and bottom, so that any movement has to take place equally on both sides of the centerline. This also stops the panel from sliding around in the wintertime.

Casehardened boards—*When I resawed some 1-in. kiln-dried oak, the resulting ¼-in.-thick boards warped badly as I was sawing. The 1-in. boards weren't warped, but sometimes the resawing would even cause the stock I was cutting from to warp. I tried resawing some 1-in. air-dried ash and the ¼-in. boards came out straight, but after a couple of days they too were warped. What am I doing wrong?*　　　　*—Michael L. Buza, Alpena, Mich.*
GENE WENGERT REPLIES: Your kiln-dried oak has residual drying stresses, a condition known as "casehardening." Casehardening is often to blame whenever lumber warps or crooks immediately while machining, and can occur whenever lumber is dried in a kin or dehumidifier. To eliminate the stresses that cause casehardening, kiln operators usually subject lumber to a high-temperature (180°F), high-humidity (80% relative humidity) treatment, called conditioning, for 12 hours at the end of the drying cycle. Casehardening isn't often seen in

air-dried or solar-dried wood because there are usually some high-humidity days during the drying cycle.

Your air-dried ash (which, in Michigan, probably had a moisture content over 15%—too high for interior use) warped a few days after resawing because the inside of the board probably had a higher moisture content than the outside. So your resawn boards had one moisture content on one face and another moisture content on the other. When the wetter face dried out, the shrinkage caused the boards to cup. To prevent this delayed warp, dry the 1-in. ash to the moisture content that it will have in use, and store it at this same relative humidity. Remember that dried lumber will regain moisture when the humidity increases.

Ridges at countertop seams—*Last month I made a kitchen countertop using 2¼-in. tongue-and-groove red oak flooring. It was purchased from a mill specializing in hardwood flooring, then further dried in a school workshop. An ample quantity of non-waterproof white glue was spread on a panel of ¾-in. fir ply and the pieces of oak assembled on it. The pieces were pulled together by clamping across the counter temporarily, but no glue was applied between the pieces. At the same time, by using 2x4s on edge over and under, the oak was clamped to the ¾-in. ply. Several days later, after vigorous planing, scraping and sanding (during which time no ridges were evident), I applied successive coats of Watco Exterior Danish Oil (still no ridges). After another two-day wait, the first of four coats of #91 clear satin Flecto Varathane was applied.*

The counter is earning its keep now, but there are slight ridges at most of the seams. I don't think they're oak or glue, so that seems to leave finish.
　　　　　　　　　　　　　—Gary Buchfink, Talkwa, B.C.
R. BRUCE HOADLEY REPLIES: From the information given, I would guess that the oak strips were fairly dry when installed. During sanding, sealing and finishing, the strips may have dried a little more, increasing the opening at the joint slightly. This joint would have become filled with a combination of finishing material and sanding debris. The finish may have set hard but not absolutely rigid, and as later increase in moisture content caused the strips to swell (red oak is a fairly unstable and responsive wood), the cracks would close up and force the finishing material upward along the joint. I believe that this physical squeeze-out of material is responsible for the ridge. A light sanding with fine abrasive paper should remove it.

Measuring Moisture

Portable meters prevent guesswork and grief

by R. Bruce Hoadley

Problems that result from using wood at the wrong moisture content continue to be among the most common frustrations and failures plaguing the woodworker. Many of the symptoms are all too familiar—warp or dimensional change in parts, opened glue joints, raised grain, end checks, finish imperfections—all because the moisture content of the stock was inappropriate.

Perhaps the excuses are also quite familiar. The job just had to get started and there simply was no time to allow the material to come to equilibrium in the shop. Or, the boards were bought from a dealer's bin; the oven-drying of samples just wasn't possible. Such woes can be avoided by using modern moisture meters, which give immediate and highly accurate readings. These magical little meters use the electrical properties of wood, and their development has followed the usual trend in electronics toward portable and miniature units with simplified operation. A wide range of models is now available to suit virtually every situation, from the hobbyist's use to production operations, in the shop or in the field.

For typical woodworking applications two principal types of meters are available. One is based on the direct-current electrical resistance of the wood and involves driving small, pin-type electrodes into the wood surface; the other uses the dielectric properties of the wood and requires only surface contact of the meter with the board.

The resistance meter takes advantage of the fact that moisture is an excellent conductor of electricity but dry wood is an effective electrical insulator. The meter itself is simply a specialized ohmmeter which measures electrical resistance. The piece of wood is arranged as an element in an electrical circuit by driving the two pin electrodes into it. The current (usually supplied by a battery) flows from one electrode through the wood to the other, then back through the ohmmeter. Actually, by simply driving pairs of nails into a piece of wood for electrodes and taking resistance measurements with a standard ohmmeter, readings could be obtained that would indicate relative moisture content. Perhaps some useful values could be obtained this way, but resistance varies nonuniformly with moisture content and a mass of data would have to be accumulated to make a useful and versatile meter. Commercially manufactured meters have the meter scale printed directly in percent moisture content instead of ohms of resistance. Because electricity follows the path of least resistance, the wettest layer of wood penetrated by the electrodes will be measured. For boards that dry normally, a drying gradient usually develops from the wetter core to the drier surface with an average moisture content about 1/5 or 1/4 the board thickness from the surface. Thus for 1-in. lumber, the pins should penetrate only 1/4 in. to measure average moisture content. In the smallest models, the electrodes are a pair of pins extending from one end of the unit, which can be pushed into the wood by hand. More commonly the electrode pins are mounted in a separate handle, attached by plug-in cord to the meter box. Electrodes of various lengths, up to 2 in. or more, are available for measuring thick material so the same meter can be used for thin veneer and heavy planks. Electrodes should be inserted so current flow is parallel to the grain. Electrical resistance is greater across the grain than parallel to it, although the difference is minor at lower moisture-content levels.

Meters using the dielectric properties of wood have a surface electrode array which generates a radio-frequency field that extends for a prescribed distance when placed against the wood. Some meters measure the power-loss effect which varies according to moisture content, whereas others respond to changes in electrical capacitance. Different models have electrodes designed for field penetration to various depths. Field penetration to about half the stock thickness is usual. Where moisture content is uneven, a more or less average reading will be given.

Green wood may have an extremely high moisture content, but woodworkers are most concerned with moisture measurement of seasoned stock. Depending on geographic location, air-dried wood will reach moisture equilibrium levels in the 12% to 15% range. For interior products, stock must usually be kiln-dried or conditioned to the 6% to 8% range. Fortunately, the electrical properties of wood are most consistent at moisture levels below fiber saturation (25% to 30%), the range of most interest to woodworkers. Dielectric meters can indicate moisture contents down to zero. The electrical resistance of wood becomes extreme at low moisture contents, limiting the lower end of the range of resistance meters to about 5% or 6%. More elaborate meters sometimes have scales extending to 60% or 80% moisture content; however, electrical properties are less consistent above fiber saturation so readings in this range must be considered approximate.

Moisture meters usually give scale readings of percent moisture content that are correct for certain typical species at room temperature. Instruction manuals give correction factors for other species and different temperatures. Since density has little effect on electrical resistance, the species corrections are usually less than two percentage points for resistance meters; correction factors may be greater with power-loss meters. Resistance readings must also be corrected about one percentage point for every 20° F departure from the calibration standard. With dielectric meters the correction is more complicated,

From *Fine Woodworking* magazine (Fall 1977) 8:78-79

but is well explained in the instruction manuals. For anyone using meters under regular conditions—with one or a few common species and always at room temperature—correction factors either are not applicable or become routine.

The values obtained with a resistance meter can be expected to agree within one-half a percentage point with those obtained by oven-testing for samples in the 6% to 12% range; within one point in the 12% to 20% moisture-content range, and within two percentage points in the range from 20% to fiber saturation.

It is important to appreciate that a meter in good condition will faithfully and accurately measure the electrical properties of the wood being sampled. The operator must understand the vagaries of wood moisture and interpret accordingly. For example, a new owner of a meter might discover a variation of two or three percentage points up and down a given board. The common reaction is, "the meter is only accurate to within three percent" or, "it gives variable readings." But in fact the meter is properly measuring moisture variations that exist in the board. Thus one must measure average or typical areas of boards to avoid the ends or cross-grain around knots, which dry most rapidly.

Each type of meter has its strengths and weaknesses. Resistance meters have the disadvantage of leaving small pinholes wherever the electrodes were inserted, which might be unacceptable in exposed furniture parts, gunstocks and the like. On the other hand, a given meter can be used with a variety of electrodes in a wide range of situations. Resistance meters with a 6% to 30% range are available down to pocket size, with both built-in short pin electrodes and separate cord-attached electrodes, for about $150. Radio-frequency power-loss meters in compact hand-held models, with electrodes for one-inch field penetration and scaled from 0 to 25% moisture content, cost about $400 (all 1977 prices). Their big advantage is the ability to take readings without marring surfaces, thus allowing measurements of completed items, even after the finish is applied. These meters are quick to use, but are less versatile because a given electrode style works only for a particular area and depth of field.

The actual dollar value of moisture measurement is very difficult to assess. It should be given serious thought, however, as it is most commonly underestimated. Many woodworkers buy machinery costing hundreds of dollars to attain close dimensional tolerances that are later lost when parts shrink or swell because there was no way of measuring moisture. What is the real cost of a solid cherry dining table that is ruined because of the errant moisture content of just one edge-glued board in its top?

Nobody would buy meat without knowing the grade, or a used car without the mileage, and nobody should buy lumber without knowing its dryness. Yet some lumber dealers sell millions of board feet a year and don't own a moisture meter. A relatively tiny investment would allow them to provide this valuable service to their customers. □

[Author's note: For more about moisture meters, see *Electric Moisture Meters for Wood* by William L. James (U. S. Forest Products Lab. Gen. Tech. Rpt. FPL-6, 1975), available from the Superintendent of Documents, U. S. Govt. Printing Office, Washington, D. C. Portable moisture meters are made by Delmhorst Instrument Co., 607 Cedar St., Boonton, N. J. 07005; Moisture Register Co., 1510 W. Chestnut St., Alhambra, Calif. 91802; Electrodyne Inc., 2126 Adams St., Milwaukie, Ore. 97222; and Valley Products and Design, Box 396, Milford, Pa. 18337.]

Electrode array of dielectric meter, left, generates radio-frequency field when pressed against face of board, right. Strip arrays for edge measurement are also available.

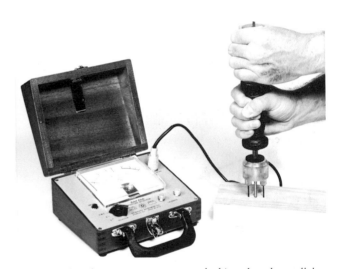

Pin electrodes of resistance meter are pushed into board, parallel to grain. Center pin gauges penetration.

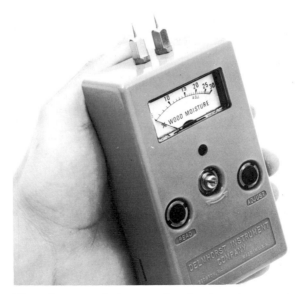

Electrodes are attached to case of pocket-size resistance meter.

A Dehumidifier Kiln
Home-dried lumber with no frills

by Donald Klimesh

For the past few years, I've been drying my own lumber in a kiln that I designed and built around a 22-pint/day Montgomery Ward dehumidifier. It will dry 300 bd. ft. of lumber in 8-ft. lengths, at a cost of about $.10/bd. ft. for electricity. The dehumidifier cost about $170 when I bought it, and the other materials totaled another $75.

The skeleton of my kiln is a wood frame of 1x6s covered with 4-mil clear plastic sheet, overlapped at the seams, and attached to the frame with wood strips and staples. I covered the plastic with 3½-in. fiberglass insulation. Don't fasten the insulation to the lid, because the insulation's removability is part of the kiln's temperature control. The dehumidifier sits inside, with its drain hose passing through a hole in the plastic and emptying into a catch pan outside the kiln. The water that collects here must be weighed daily to monitor the operation of the kiln. There is also a small electric fan inside, which runs continuously to circulate the air. I used a fan from an old appliance, but a small household fan would work fine.

The lumber to be dried is loaded on 4x4 supports, which for 1-in. lumber should be spaced no more than 2 ft. apart. To prevent the end grain from drying faster than the side grain—the main cause of checking—I liberally coat the ends of the boards with oil-based enamel paint. I use ¾-in. stickers to separate the layers of boards and to allow air to circulate. Space the stickers about 18 in. to 20 in. apart, and keep them one above another to minimize kinking.

It's easy to dry wood, but it's relatively difficult to end up with useful lumber. The first time I used my kiln, I ran the dehumidifier full-tilt. The wood dried much too quickly. The boards bent badly when ripped, and many were filled with internal checks, a defect called honeycombing. I've since overcome these problems with controlled drying and conditioning.

Wood will gain or lose moisture depending on the relative humidity of the air that surrounds it. As long as the relative humidity remains the same, a piece of wood will eventually reach a point where it neither gains nor loses moisture. The moisture that remains in the wood when it has reached this balance with the air is called its equilibrium moisture content, or EMC (see pp. 6-10). I operate my kiln until the wood reaches an MC (see p. 94) of about 7%.

To measure the relative humidity inside the kiln, I use a wet- and dry-bulb hygrometer (available from Edmund Scientific Co., 101 E. Gloucester Pike, Barrington, N.J. 08007). It consists of a standard thermometer mounted side by side on the same base with a wet-bulb thermometer which has a cloth wick fitted over the bulb. The other end of the wick dips into a small reservoir, which I fill with distilled water to prevent mineral buildup and to ensure accurate readings. The hygrometer hangs inside the kiln, and I cut a hole in the fiberglass so that I can read it through the plastic. I cover this window with a piece of insulation when I'm not reading the hygrometer, so that condensation won't fog up the plastic.

To determine the equilibrium moisture content, you need to know the relative humidity, but since the EMC is a more useful number to me than the RH, I've eliminated the need for calculations by making a chart that gives me the potential EMC of the wood directly from the wet- and dry-bulb readings. Just remember that the hygrometer actually measures the condition of the *air* inside the kiln, not of the lumber. It takes some time at any given relative humidity for the wood to reach the EMC shown on the chart—how long depends on the species and thickness of the wood. To lessen drying time and minimize degrade, you should air-dry dead-green lumber to below its fiber saturation point (25% to 30%

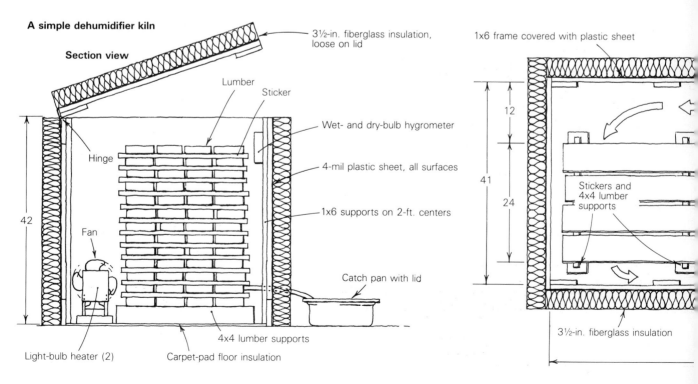

A simple dehumidifier kiln

Section view

3½-in. fiberglass insulation, loose on lid

1x6 frame covered with plastic sheet

Lumber

Sticker

Wet- and dry-bulb hygrometer

Hinge

4-mil plastic sheet, all surfaces

1x6 supports on 2-ft. centers

12

41

24

Stickers and 4x4 lumber supports

42

Fan

Catch pan with lid

3½-in. fiberglass insulation

Light-bulb heater (2)

4x4 lumber supports

Carpet-pad floor insulation

Photo: Jack Glaser; drawing: Ken Daniel

moisture content) before kilning it. (The article on pages 82-83 explains how.)

To keep track of the drying process, I use a data sheet with the following headings: date, time, wet-bulb temperature, dry-bulb temperature, EMC, total weight of water collected, and rate of drying as measured by pounds of water per day. I start a fresh load with the humidistat control on the dehumidifier set about one-quarter of the maximum dry setting. Then I monitor the drying rate by daily weighing the water that collects in the catch pan, and I compare this to the maximum allowable weight of water listed in my drying schedule. If the daily catch of water exceeds the maximum recommended in the drying schedule, the wood is drying too fast, and I turn the humidistat down. If the catch is less than half the amount listed in the drying schedule, I turn the control up to speed the drying rate. Keep the catch pan covered, or else water will evaporate and weights will be inaccurate.

I maintain the kiln temperature at 105°F to 115°F throughout the drying cycle. Higher temperatures would speed drying, but might also harm the dehumidifier. In commercial kilns, dry-bulb temperatures go as high as 180°F, but these kilns must dry wood quickly to make a profit. I don't have to rush.

I can control the temperature in three ways: by changing the humidistat setting, by removing the insulation cover on the lid, or by adding auxiliary heat. Although the main function of the humidistat is to control the relative humidity inside the kiln, the dehumidifier motor also produces heat. If the temperature exceeds 115°F, I remove insulation from the lid to cool it down. If the temperature is below 105°F and the lid is totally covered, I add heat by turning on one or both of the two shielded light-bulb heaters (detail A, below).

The lumber is dry enough for me when, with hygrometer readings of 7% EMC, the daily catch of water amounts to 0.2 lb./100 sq. ft. (not bd. ft.) of lumber, which indicates a moisture content of approximately 7%. You can measure the moisture content of the wood itself to be sure, but if you

Controlling the kiln

Regulate drying by monitoring EMC, which is indicated by the point at which the diagonal lines in the EMC chart intersect the wet- and dry-bulb temperatures. Find this EMC in the left-hand column of the drying schedule. The right-hand column shows the maximum weight of water you can remove (per 100 sq. ft. of lumber) without degrade.* Turn down the humidistat if you get more; turn it up if you get less than half.

* These figures derive from experimentation, and your results may differ.

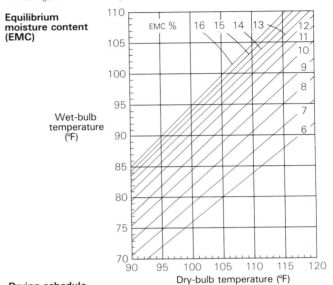

Equilibrium moisture content (EMC)

Wet-bulb temperature (°F)

Dry-bulb temperature (°F)

Drying schedule

Equilibrium moisture content (EMC) from chart above	Maximum water collected per day per 100 sq. ft. of lumber	
16% and above	11.0 lb./day	
15	8.0 lb./day	
14	7.0 lb./day	Note:
13	6.0 lb./day	100 bd. ft. of
12	5.0 lb./day	1-in. lumber = 100 sq. ft.
11	4.5 lb./day	
10	4.0 lb./day	100 bd. ft. of
9	3.0 lb./day	2-in. lumber = 50 sq. ft.
8	2.0 lb./day	
7†	2.0 lb./day	

† When water yield is less than 0.2 lb./100 sq. ft., lumber has reached approximately 7% moisture content.

Top view

Light-bulb heaters *(see detail A)*

Continuously running fan

Airflow

Dehumidifier

Hygrometer

Hygrometer viewing port

Catch pan

Drain hose

— 120 —

Detail A: Auxiliary light-bulb heater

Tin-can shield
(top and bottom removed)

Light bulb
(60- to 100-watt)

Porcelain
lamp socket

1-in. air gap

Sheet-metal
support (3)

4-in. electrical
ceiling box

2x8 base

don't have a moisture meter, you'll have to sacrifice part of a board. Here's how: Crosscut a strip 1 in. wide about 1 ft. in from the end of a board. Weigh this section on any sensitive scale—a gram scale, beam balance, food-portion scale or postage scale—anything that will give you an accurate reading in small increments. Write down the weight. Now bake the piece of wood in a 225°F oven for several hours to drive off all moisture. Weigh this dried piece and subtract its weight from the wet weight, to find out how much water it contained. Now divide the weight of the water by the oven-dry weight of the wood, multiply by 100 (move the decimal two places to the right), put a percent sign (%) after this figure, and you have the moisture content. But even if you've reached 7% MC, your wood isn't ready to use yet.

As lumber dries, it develops residual compression stresses in the outer fibers. This condition is called casehardening, a misnomer since the "case" is not really harder than the inside. It is most noticeable when you're resawing or ripping boards. Even if the board being cut is dry and straight, a casehardened board will bend when it is cut, sometimes severely. Commercial kilns solve the casehardening problem by adding a step called conditioning. Steam is introduced into the kiln to add moisture, which swells the outer fibers and causes them to yield, so they will be under less stress when they are redried. I also condition my dried lumber, but my process is less sophisticated. After the boards are dry, I remove them from the kiln and spray both sides of each board with warm water from a garden hose. Then I immediately restack the lumber in the kiln and redry, following the drying schedule.

The final drying step is called equalizing. When the lumber has dried again after conditioning (less than 0.2 lb. of water per day per 100 sq. ft. with hygrometer readings of 7% EMC, which is approximately 7% MC), I continue to operate the kiln for one week for each inch of lumber thickness, with the auxiliary heater lamps turned off. By this time I'm usually tired of the daily chore of weighing the water, so I just let the dehumidifier run with the humidistat set to give approximately 7% EMC, as measured by the hygrometer.

How long does it take? A batch of 320 bd. ft. of green, 1-in. red oak took me 60 days—46 days to dry and another 14 days for conditioning and equalizing. A total of 563 lb. of water was removed during the drying process. Drying time varies for different species, and thicker lumber takes longer.

So far, I've used the kiln and my drying schedule to dry oak, white pine, maple and cherry. While it may seem that the process is time-consuming, it takes only a few minutes each day to weigh the water, read the thermometers and occasionally adjust the humidistat. □

Donald Klimesh, of Birmingham, Mich., is an amateur woodworker and an engineer with Ford Motor Co. For more information on drying, read Dry Kiln Handbook *by J.L. Bachrich, published by H.A. Simons (International) Ltd., 425 Carrall St., Vancouver, B.C. V6B 2J6.*

Don't let that dry look fool you

Wood is only as dry as the air that surrounds it, and once dried it doesn't necessarily stay that way. Instead, wood always seeks a moisture equilibrium with its environment.

No matter how long wood has been seasoned, whether or not it has been kiln-dried, lumber still contains some water. This is called its moisture content (MC), and is usually expressed as a percent. The moisture content changes as the relative humidity (RH) of the air around the wood changes.

An example: Two identical boards of, say, white oak are kiln-dried to a moisture content of 7%. One is shipped to the Northeast, where the relative humidity outdoors averages 75% year round. The other goes to the Southwest, where the relative humidity averages 38%.

In the 75% RH of the Northeast, the board picks up moisture from the air and eventually reaches a moisture content of 14%, where it stops absorbing moisture and stabilizes. The board has now reached the equilibrium moisture content (EMC) for that relative humidity, and will hold at 14% as long as the relative humidity stays at 75%.

In the Southwest, at 38% RH, the board loses moisture to the air until its moisture content stabilizes at about 6%. This board also has reached the EMC for that relative humidity.

When the relative humidity of the air changes, the moisture content of the wood changes, until it reaches a new equilibrium moisture content.

Wood should be dried to a moisture content close to the EMC it will reach in the environment in which it will be used. In the Northeastern winter, in a heated, non-humidified room, the relative humidity might average 25% or less. Wood exposed to this low RH would reach equilibrium around 5% moisture content. In summer, when windows are open, inside humidity levels are close to those outside.

Why is all this important? Because wood expands across the grain when the moisture content increases, and shrinks across the grain when the moisture content decreases. Furniture must be designed to allow for this movement.

Here are some terms woodworkers should know:

Moisture content (MC): The ratio (expressed as a percentage) of the weight of water in a piece of wood to the weight of the wood when it has been completely dried in an oven. To calculate, subtract the dry weight from the wet weight, and divide the result by the dry weight, as in the equation:

Klimesh loads his kiln with green, 2-in. pine boards.

$$MC = \frac{W_{wet} - W_{oven\text{-}dry}}{W_{oven\text{-}dry}} \times 100$$

Relative humidity (RH): The ratio (expressed as a percentage) of the amount of water vapor in the air to the maximum amount the air could hold at a given temperature. Saturated air is said to be at 100% RH.

Fiber saturation point (FSP): The moisture content (which varies with the species) where all water has evaporated from the cell cavities, but the cell walls are still saturated. Wood shrinkage occurs only when the cell walls begin to dry.   —D.K.

Dry Kiln

A design to season 500 board feet

by William W. Rice

A number of years ago in a small New England town I met a man drying oak flooring. He cut the oak into 1 x 3-1/2-in. random-length strips while it was green. These were carefully stacked in his garage on sticks until the garage was full, except for a 3-foot space to the wall on one side and about 4 or 5 feet on the other. The lumber reached from the back wall to the doors. A thin partition extending down from the ceiling to the top of the load contained three 18-in. window fans spaced along the length of the lumber pile. On the wall hung two thermometers, one with a piece of wicking surrounding the bulb and dangling into a pan of water.

This man had a dry kiln. When he fired up his wood stove, he could heat the garage to about 100 degrees. The fans circulated the hot air through the lumber pile; when the humidity got too low he misted the pile with the garden hose. After a month, his flooring was flat, check-free and at a low moisture content.

The operation succeeded because the man knew what he was doing as he manipulated the heat and humidity to produce flooring that would machine, finish and perform well in service. For those of us who need small quantities of dry wood, a homemade kiln may be the answer.

Wood is a cellular material (see the articles on pp. 2-5 and pp. 6-10) that in the tree, log or freshly sawn board contains two forms of water. Free water is located in the cell cavities in a liquid state and can move by capillary action from cell to cell. Bound water is held in the cell walls by molecular attraction and moves by diffusion. During drying, the loss of free water does not change the dimensions of the cells and the effect can be likened to emptying a coffee cup. However, as bound water is released from the cell walls, the cellulosic strands move closer together and the wood shrinks. In very small pieces of wood, the free water leaves the wood first, followed by the bound water. But larger pieces dry from the surface towards the center and bound water evaporates at the surface while free water is still traveling from the interior. This creates moisture gradients in the wood, which cause drying stresses, and the result is checks, splits and warp.

The three factors to be controlled in drying wood are temperature, humidity and air movement through the pile. In that New England garage, the wood stove undoubtedly produced erratic temperatures. Control of humidity was probably minimal—the moisture evaporating from the wood maintained the necessary relative humidity, occasionally supplemented by the garden hose. Only the air circulation was con-

stant throughout the kiln run. How fast the load dried depended on the way the man handled these factors, plus the characteristics of the species.

In general the higher the temperature, the faster the drying. Heating the wood also heats the water and water vapor it contains and reduces the molecular forces bonding the water to the wood. Thus water moves more easily through the wood to the surface where it can evaporate. Temperatures below 70° F do not promote drying; temperatures above 212° F are likely to cause structural damage, especially in hardwoods. High temperatures over periods longer than three days can reduce the strength of wood and make it brittle.

Most kilns operate between 100° and 180° F. The normal sequence is to maintain low to moderate temperatures (100° to 140° F) until the free water has been removed and then to raise the temperature to accelerate the process. As the wood becomes drier, it takes more energy to break the bound water loose from the cell walls.

In large commercial kilns the usual heat source is steam generated in a boiler and distributed by finned pipe similar to home baseboard convectors. While steam has proven to be the most economical, hot water, electricity, radio frequency and solar energy will also work. A steam system has the added advantage of easily furnishing vapor for humidification. An electric heating system is usually lower in initial cost and easy to control, but expensive to operate.

Relative humidity is the amount of moisture air contains, expressed as a percentage of the maximum amount it could contain at that temperature. Air at low relative humidity can absorb large amounts of water vapor before becoming saturated. Air at high humidity has little capacity for additional moisture. Heating air without admitting additional moisture reduces its relative humidity; cooling the air will reverse the process and increase the relative humidity. By manipulating the relative humidity of the air, we can control the drying of wood.

The hygroscopic property of wood allows us to predict how it will react to various combinations of temperature and relative humidity. A piece of wood will release or absorb moisture until its moisture content is in balance with that of the surrounding air. This is called equilibrium moisture content (EMC) and it is expressed as a percentage.

Thin pieces of wood arrive at equilibrium with the atmosphere in minutes and react quickly to fluctuations in relative humidity. The surfaces of thicker pieces of wood also arrive at equilibrium quickly. However it takes a long time, even years, for lumber to reach equilibrium throughout its mass. This "reaction time" results in moisture gradients during

---

William Rice, a former kiln operator, teaches wood science and technology at the University of Massachusetts.

drying. Wet wood subjected to a low relative humidity (and therefore a low EMC) will dry quickly because the moisture gradient is steep. The differential between internal moisture content and surface moisture content causes water vapor to flow to the drier zone. The larger the differential, the faster the rate. The kiln operator adjusts the temperature and relative humidity to control the drying rate without excessive stress formation and consequent degrade.

Humidity is easily increased in the kiln by spraying steam into the chamber through a perforated pipe. Small kilns can be humidified by steam released from open, shallow water tanks equipped with immersion heaters. A third, and very economical, way of controlling humidity is to use the moisture evaporated from the wood by not venting it from the building. This sometimes retards drying since the exact humidity called for in the schedule may not be achieved, but it saves fuel because less outside air must be warmed and humidified. A skillful kiln operator can do an excellent job of drying and never use the steam spray until the end of the run, when it is needed for stress relief.

Air circulation is necessary to carry the evaporated moisture away from the lumber surface and to heat the lumber to accelerate evaporation. The air circulation system also vents wet air from the kiln and brings in fresh, dry air to aid in humidity control. The air is moved by fans. In modern kilns, velocities of 500 feet per minute through the load are desirable, although speeds as low as 200 fpm can be effective. Whatever the air speed, it is essential that the air move uniformly through the stack so that the lumber dries evenly. Thus baffles are used.

With regard to species characteristics, low-density woods give up moisture faster and with less stress development than do the high-density species. Part of the difference is due to

the thickness of the cell walls and the resulting volume of free water. Structural characteristics that affect the permeability of wood, such as the formation of tyloses or other deposits within the cell, slow down the drying rate and increase the risk of degrade. This is why white oak takes longer to dry than red.

How a kiln operates

Briefly, a lumber dry kiln is operated as follows: The boards are carefully stacked in the kiln chamber with uniformly thick stickers between the layers. Stickers should be spaced on 16-in. or 24-in. centers along the pile and vertically aligned in successive courses of lumber. The ends of the boards should be supported because even a 10 or 12-inch overhang will droop during drying. Good stacking is critical to obtaining flat, dry lumber.

As the lumber is stacked, the operator selects and sets aside several boards that represent the wettest and the driest material in the load. He may be guided by a moisture meter, by weight (heavy generally means wet), or by other knowledge about the initial wetness of the load. A commercial kiln operator takes four to eight samples in 20,000 to 50,000 board-foot loads. Even with loads as small as 500 BF, two or more samples should be taken to ensure control.

The operator cuts sections about 30 inches long from the centers of the sample boards, to avoid being misled by previ-

Final desired average moisture content	Moisture content to which driest sample should be dried	Equilibrium moisture content at which charge should be equalized	Desired moisture content of wettest sample at end of equalizing	Equilibrium moisture content values for conditioning treatment	
				Softwoods	Hardwoods
5 %	3 %	3 %	5 %	7- 8%	8- 9%
6	4	4	6	8- 9	9-10
7	5	5	7	9-10	10-11
8	6	6	8	10-11	11-12
9	7	7	9	11-12	12-13
10	8	8	10	12-13	13-14
11	9	9	11	13-14	14-15

From wet-bulb and dry-bulb readings, operator uses large chart to find relative humidity (above diagonal line) and equilibrium moisture content. Chart below left gives typical kiln schedules; chart at right determines EMC values for stress relief at end of kiln run.

CHERRY 4/4, 5/4 and 6/4

Moisture Content	DB	Dep.	WB	RH	EMC
Initial to 35%	130°	7°	123°	81%	14.0%
35 to 30	130	10	120	73	12.1
30 to 25	140	15	125	64	9.6
25 to 20	150	25	125	48	6.9
20 to 15	160	40	120	31	4.3
15 to Final	180	50	130	26	3.3

CHERRY 8/4

Moisture Content	DB	Dep.	WB	RH	EMC
Initial to 35%	120°	5°	115°	85%	16.2%
35 to 30	120	7	113	80	14.1
30 to 25	130	11	119	71	11.5
25 to 20	140	19	121	56	8.4
20 to 15	150	35	115	35	5.0
15 to Final	160	50	110	21	3.2

WALNUT (Black) 4/4, 5/4 and 6/4

Moisture Content	DB	Dep.	WB	RH	EMC
Initial to 50%	120°	7°	113°	80%	14.1%
50 to 40	120	10	110	72	12.1
40 to 35	120	15	105	60	9.7
35 to 30	120	25	95	40	6.6
30 to 25	130	40	90	21	3.8
25 to 20	140	50	90	14	2.6
20 to 15	150	50	100	18	2.9
15 to Final	180	50	130	26	3.3

WALNUT (Black) 8/4

Moisture Content	DB	Dep.	WB	RH	EMC
Initial to 50%	110°	5°	105°	84%	16.2%
50 to 40	110	7	103	78	14.1
40 to 35	110	11	99	67	11.4
35 to 30	110	19	91	48	8.1
30 to 25	120	35	85	23	4.4
25 to 20	130	50	80	10	2.0
20 to 15	140	50	90	14	2.6
15 to Final	160	50	110	21	3.2

Psychrometric chart — **WET-BULB DEPRESSION (°F)**. Left and right edges: **TEMPERATURE DRY BULB (°F)**. Columns of wet-bulb depression: 2, 4, 6, 8, 10, 12, 14, 16, 18, 20, 22, 24, 26, 28, 30, 32, 34, 36, 38, 40, 45, 50. Each cell shows relative humidity (upper value) over equilibrium moisture content (lower value).

Dry Bulb °F	2	4	6	8	10	12	14	16	18	20	22	24	26	28	30	32	34	36	38	40	45	50	Dry Bulb °F
30	78/15.9	57/10.8	36/7.4	17/3.9																			30
40	83/17.6	68/12.9	52/9.9	37/7.4	22/5.0	8/1.9																	40
50	86/19.0	74/14.4	62/11.5	50/9.4	38/7.6	27/5.7	16/3.9	5/1.5															50
60	89/19.9	78/15.6	68/12.7	58/10.7	48/9.1	39/7.6	30/6.2	21/4.9	13/3.2	5/1.3													60
70	90/20.6	80/16.5	71/13.7	62/11.6	54/10.1	46/8.8	38/7.4	31/6.6	23/5.5	16/4.3	12/2.9	6/1.5											70
80	91/21.0	82/16.9	75/14.3	67/12.3	60/10.9	52/9.7	45/8.7	41/7.7	35/6.8	29/5.8	23/5.0	18/4.0	12/3.0	7/1.8	3/0.5								80
90	92/21.3	84/17.3	77/14.7	70/12.9	63/11.4	57/10.2	52/9.4	47/8.6	41/7.6	36/6.8	31/5.8	26/5.1	22/3.9	17/3.8	12/2.8	8/2.1	5/1.3	1/0.4					90
100	93/21.5	85/17.9	80/15.1	73/13.1	67/11.8	60/10.6	55/9.6	50/8.9	45/8.1	41/7.4	37/6.5	32/5.7	28/5.1	24/4.5	19/3.7	15/2.8	13/2.4	9/1.7	6/1.1	4/0.7			100
110	93/21.4	87/18.2	81/15.5	75/13.7	70/12.3	65/11.1	60/10.0	55/9.2	51/8.5	45/7.6	42/7.0	38/6.2	34/5.6	30/5.0	26/4.4	22/3.8	19/3.3	15/2.7	11/2.0	8/1.5	4/0.7		110
120	94/21.6	88/18.4	82/15.7	77/14.1	71/12.7	67/11.7	61/10.6	57/9.8	53/8.9	49/8.2	43/7.3	41/6.6	38/6.1	33/5.5	30/5.0	26/4.5	23/3.9	20/3.5	17/3.1	13/2.5	10/1.9	5/1.1	120
130	94/21.8	89/18.5	83/15.9	79/14.4	73/12.9	69/11.9	64/11.0	60/10.2	56/9.4	52/8.7	48/8.0	45/7.5	41/6.8	38/6.2	35/5.7	32/5.3	29/4.9	26/4.4	23/4.0	20/3.5	12/2.7	10/2.0	130
140	95/21.9	90/18.7	84/16.1	80/14.7	75/13.3	70/12.2	68/11.4	62/10.6	58/9.8	54/9.2	51/8.5	47/7.9	44/7.4	41/6.9	38/6.3	35/5.8	32/5.4	29/5.0	26/4.6	24/4.1	18/3.3	13/2.6	140
150	95/22.0	90/18.9	85/16.4	80/15.0	76/13.6	72/12.6	68/11.7	65/11.0	62/10.3	58/9.6	54/9.0	50/8.5	47/8.0	45/7.4	41/6.9	38/6.5	35/6.0	33/5.5	29/5.1	28/4.7	23/3.9	18/3.1	150
160	95/22.2	91/19.0	86/16.6	82/15.2	77/13.9	73/12.9	69/12.1	66/11.4	62/10.7	59/10.1	55/9.4	52/9.0	49/8.4	46/8.0	43/7.5	40/7.0	37/6.6	35/6.2	32/5.7	30/5.3	25/4.4	21/3.7	160
170	96/22.3	91/19.1	87/16.8	83/15.5	78/14.2	74/13.2	71/12.5	67/11.8	64/11.1	61/10.6	58/10.0	55/9.4	51/8.9	48/8.4	46/8.0	42/7.5	40/7.1	37/6.6	35/6.3	32/5.8	28/5.1	24/4.2	170
180	96/22.5	92/19.3	87/17.0	83/15.7	79/14.4	76/13.5	72/12.8	69/12.1	66/11.5	63/10.9	60/10.3	57/9.8	54/9.3	52/8.9	48/8.4	46/8.1	43/7.6	41/7.2	38/6.8	36/6.4	31/5.6	27/4.8	180
190	96/22.6	92/19.5	88/17.2	84/15.9	80/14.7	77/13.9	73/13.1	70/12.4	67/11.8	64/11.3	62/10.7	59/10.2	56/9.7	53/9.3	51/8.9	48/8.5	45/8.0	43/7.7	41/7.3	38/6.9	33/6.0	29/5.3	190
200	96/22.8	92/19.7	88/17.4	85/16.2	81/15.0	77/14.2	74/13.5	71/12.8	68/12.2	65/11.6	62/11.1	59/10.6	58/10.1	55/9.7	52/9.3	50/8.9	47/8.5	45/8.1	43/7.7	39/7.3	34/6.5	30/5.7	200
210	95/22.9	92/19.7	88/17.6	85/16.3	81/15.1	78/14.4	75/13.7	72/13.0	69/12.5	66/11.9	63/11.4	60/10.9	58/10.4	55/10.0	53/9.6	51/9.3	48/8.8	46/8.4	44/8.0	41/7.6	36/6.7	32/5.9	210

ous end drying. Then he cuts 1-in. wafers from the ends of each sample, immediately weighs them, and dries them in an oven at 220° F until they stop losing weight. He calculates the moisture content of the wafers from the formula:

$$\text{moisture content (MC)} = \frac{\text{original wt.} - \text{oven-dry wt.}}{\text{oven-dry weight}} \times 100$$

While the wafers are drying he weighs each sample board to .01 lb. and seals the ends with paint or glue. The sample boards are assumed to contain the same percentage of moisture as did the oven-dried wafers. The boards go back into the kiln and stay there, to be retrieved periodically and weighed to gauge the progress of the drying. Based on these control samples, the operator manipulates temperature and humidity to dry the lumber as rapidly as possible with a minimum of degrade.

By calculation, the oven-dry weight of the sample board can be found. This value is used to determine current moisture content of the sample as the load dries. The formulas:

$$\text{calculated oven-dry wt.} = \frac{\text{original sample wt.}}{100 + \text{MC}} \times 100$$

$$\begin{array}{l}\text{current MC} \\ \text{of sample}\end{array} = \frac{\text{current wt.} - \text{calc. oven-dry wt.}}{\text{calculated oven-dry weight}} \times 100$$

Research and experience in the drying of various woods have resulted in kiln drying schedules which guide the operator in applying the right combinations of temperature and humidity. But only with a great deal of experience can a kiln be run on a rigid schedule. More information about kiln operation can be found in the *Dry Kiln Operator's Manual.* This manual also presents a wealth of information about wood-moisture relationships, degrade and storage.

The kiln load is started at the temperature and humidity corresponding to the moisture content as determined by sampling. It is held there, and the sample checked daily, until the moisture content has dropped to the next line on the schedule, when the kiln is adjusted accordingly.

All kiln schedules start with low temperature and moderate to high relative humidity, and become hotter and drier as the wood moisture content drops. Generally, hardwoods for furniture and other interior uses are dried to 6% to 8% MC. Softwoods such as white pine should also be dried to this level for furniture, although often softwood millwork is only dried to 10% MC.

At the end of the drying period the wood will contain drying stress (often misnomered as casehardening). This stress is normal but it should be relieved before the wood is machined, by raising the humidity in the kiln until moisture enters the surface fibers, swelling them slightly and relaxing the stresses. This is called equalizing and conditioning.

Total drying time in the kiln varies with the initial moisture content, species, thickness, and final moisture content. Low-density species dry quickly. Thick, dense woods dry slowly. Examples of comparative drying times from green to 7% MC are:

4/4 white pine	8- 9 days
4/4 red oak	21-28 days
8/4 white pine	25-30 days
8/4 red oak	56-72 days

While kiln drying green lumber has the advantage of placing the drying process under control from start to finish, thereby reducing degrade, it does cost more in terms of capital investment and energy consumption. Commercial operators much prefer to kiln dry most species after they have been air dried as low as possible. This cuts the kiln residence time in half.

Properly air-dried stock (well stickered, good pile foundation, roofed) can be started in the kiln at its current moisture content, partway through the drying schedule. The higher temperatures and lower humidities safely accelerate drying since the danger of checking was passed during air drying. A combination of air and kiln drying is especially desirable when seasoning 8/4 and thicker lumber.

Dry kiln construction

Basically, a dry kiln is a well-insulated box equipped with devices to control the environment inside. Size depends on how much lumber is to be dried in one charge and may range from a unit about the size of a garden shed to one 50 feet square by 30 feet high or larger. Kilns are usually sized by their holding capacity of 4/4 lumber, expressed in board feet. A 20,000-BF kiln would be about 15 feet wide by 50 feet long.

Kiln length to width ratio is often determined by the length of the lumber or by combinations of lengths. In small kilns, the length of the unit must be carefully considered. A kiln designed to hold 12-foot boards cannot accommodate 16-foot boards. On the other hand, a compartment designed for 16-foot stock and then operated most of the time with shorter lengths will be inefficient and, because air cannot circulate evenly, drying quality may be poor. In a well-loaded and properly run kiln, the drying time will not vary significantly with the volume of lumber.

Craftsmen using less than 5,000 BF at a time find it prohibitively expensive or impossible to obtain space in commercial kilns. But a craftsman can build and operate his own small kiln. The plan offered here is for a kiln of 500-BF capacity, in 8 ft.-2 in. lengths. This kiln should be sheltered inside a barn, garage or shop; if it is to be used in a small area such as the basement of a house, it should be vented to the outside like a clothes dryer.

Kiln structure

It is important that the kiln be well insulated to minimize heat loss, with a good vapor barrier on the inside of the insulation. This is to prevent the high humidity generated in the kiln from penetrating the insulation and destroying its effectiveness. The roof is especially vulnerable to moisture penetration. Wherever wires or pipes pass through the kiln wall or roof, they should be in a conduit that can be sealed. In this design the conduits pass through framing members rather than stud spaces and insulation. Doors and vents should fit snugly with gaskets to prevent leaks.

If masonry construction is used, the interior walls should be sealed with an asphalt-base sealer. Two coats of aluminum paint are also advisable for both a moisture barrier and reflective insulation. Our plan calls for conventional frame construction with studs and joists 16 in. on center. It is assumed that the unit will be located on a level floor and that the bottom plate will be sealed to the floor with caulking. A few anchor bolts tying the plates to the floor will ensure that the kiln stays put, but they are not essential. If a floor is poured specifically for the kiln, an inch of Styrofoam insulation under the concrete will reduce heat losses. It is also useful to install a floor drain for those times when the kiln is extra wet.

Apply kraft-backed or foil-backed fiberglass insulation to the framing with the backing to the inside of the kiln. Then install a continuous film of 6-mil plastic to the inside framing, to line the walls and ceiling completely. Fold the plastic at the corners rather than cutting it. If it is cut, caulk the joint.

The inside wall covering is 15/32 Homasote board. It has good moisture resistance and insulating properties. It is available in large sheets which minimize the risk of leakage through internal joints. Since Homasote swells slightly with moisture gain, carefully follow the manufacturer's installation instructions. Two coats of aluminum paint will improve moisture resistance.

Almost any material is satisfactory for the exterior of the kiln, as long as it protects the insulation. We recommend 1/2-in. plywood for general rigidity. Door construction is the same as for the walls.

Air circulation

A single 1/2-horsepower motor drives the two fans that circulate the air. Flanged bearings (pillow blocks) can be bolted directly to the face of the kiln for the outside shaft bearing. Inside on the fan deck, the rigid-mount pillow blocks should be fastened to stands devised by the installer to align the fan

in the fan wall. These internal bearing mounts must be braced to the fan deck and ceiling so they remain fixed. Install the fans so they blow in the same direction; the fans needn't be reversible because the load is small.

Heating/humidifying

The builder can adapt the heat and humidity system to available materials. Our kiln should be capable of temperatures from 80° to about 180° F. The heating system should be able to develop 15,000 BTU per hour although it will take, on the average, about 8,500 BTU per hour. This is about the amount of heat obtained by burning a pound of dry wood; it is also the heat an average room requires. Heating systems with less capacity will not generate the higher temperatures and drying time will be extended. Drying quality should not be affected, so if time is not critical less heating capacity is not a drawback. On the other hand, a system with a high heat output will give greater flexibility and somewhat faster drying. Also, it may permit the installation of additional kilns.

The electric baseboard type of heater is quite straightforward and easily controlled. Each heating coil has its own manual switch so that the kiln can be operated on only that energy actually required to hold the desired temperature. This results

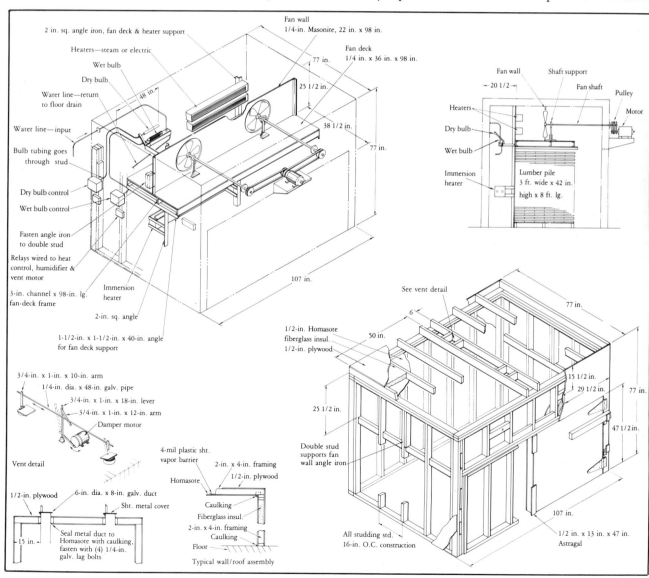

in more uniform drying as well as energy conservation.

One drawback of electric heating is the need for an additional energy source for humidification. Our kiln uses an open water tank containing a conventional water-tank heating element. The immersion heater creates steam which is circulated by fans. A float valve keeps the tank filled.

A kiln builder can tap the steam system used to heat his residence or install a separate system. Again, a heating capacity of 15,000 BTU per hour is desirable. In place of the electric heaters, install 36 linear feet of 1-in. finned pipe (or 100 square feet of equivalent heating surface). This amount of pipe surface is based on the assumption that the boiler will operate at between 2 and 5 pounds per square inch pressure. Higher pressures require less heating surface to generate the same BTU output. As with the electric heaters, individual steam-coil control by means of hand valves is desirable.

Humidification with a steam system is accomplished by connecting six linear feet of 1/2-in. black pipe perforated 6 in. on center with 1/8-in. diameter holes. When called for by the controller, the steam will spray from the holes and circulate. Be sure to aim the spray away from the lumber to avoid staining the load.

Automatic heater and spray control valves can be solenoid-operated so the same remote-bulb thermostats and relays shown in the plan can be used. Depending on the solenoids, relays may not be needed. To conserve steam even on a 2-psi system, it would be advisable to install steam traps in the heating coils.

The kiln could also be heated by hot water (electric or oil-fired) or solar energy. Likewise, a hot-air furnace ducted to the kiln can be satisfactory. We have not worked out the details for these alternate systems but offer them as suggestions to trigger the imagination of the reader.

Ventilation

An experienced operator can run his kiln with practically no use of the vents, except when drying white pine green from the saw. However, vents are a desirable feature. For most schedules the vents can be set partially open for the entire run. Experience with various species and moisture contents will give the operator a feel for manual vent control.

Controllers

In the old days, dry kiln operators had only hand-valve control and glass-stemmed thermometers, and of course one can still do this. But a more accurate and convenient control system includes remote sensing bulbs that activate solenoid valves. The type of thermostat required for our kiln is relatively inexpensive and accurate to within 5° F. With experience the operator can set them quite closely to the desired temperatures.

The units should have a temperature range of about 80° to 200° F. Bulb capillary length of 5 ft. is sufficient. These thermostats do not indicate temperature except at the setting device. If the operator wants to see the actual temperature, we

recommend he obtain some glass-stem thermometers with the scale etched in the glass. These are available at chemical supply houses for about $6 (1977).

The wet-bulb thermometer is controlled by having a second remote-bulb thermostat and on the bulb placing a wick which is constantly wet from a water reservoir. Do not use the humidification tank for a reservoir as this water is too hot and gives a false wet-bulb reading. Keep clean wicks on the bulb. Old undershirts or diapers make fine wicks.

The remote-bulb thermostats will trigger solenoid-operated heater and spray control valves in a steam system. In both electric and steam systems, the wet-bulb relay can energize a vent motor of the type normally used to open louvers for large exhaust fans. Enough differential should be set into the relay so that the spray and vents can never be open at the same time; trial and error will determine the differential setting.

Kiln modification

The capacity of the kiln can be increased to 1000 board feet simply by doubling its length and keeping its width and height the same. The heating units, humidification system and fans should also be doubled. The same temperature controllers will do, although they should be moved to the middle of the kiln length for accuracy.

Other modifications and improvements will occur to the operator as he builds and uses the kiln. In the meantime, we estimate that the 500-BF kiln will cost about $760 to build (1977). Perhaps it will help some woodworkers get around the problem of finding wood. Dry it yourself. □

[Author's note: The *Dry Kiln Operator's Manual* by E. F. Rasmussen (Ag. Hdbk. No. 188) is available from the Superintendent of Documents, U.S. Govt. Printing Office, Washington, D.C. 20402.]

Shop-Built Moisture Meter

Printed circuit guides you through electronic maze

by Rick Liftig

Even though I've occasionally had problems with wood warping and cracking or joints coming loose because of moisture-related wood movement, I never could justify spending $100 or so to buy a moisture meter to check my stock before I used it. I've always been interested in electronics, so I decided to build my own meter. My home-built version, shown in the photo on the facing page, cost $30. I've relied on fairly simple electronic procedures, so even if talk about soldering and circuits makes you uncomfortable, you should be able to build the meter.

The moisture content of wood can range from 0% for oven-dried samples to more than 100% for soaking-wet green wood, where the water in the wood weighs more than the wood tissue itself. Traditionally, technologists determined the moisture content by weighing a wood sample, oven-drying it until it was bone-dry, then weighing it again. The weight difference divided by the oven-dry weight, multiplied by 100, gives you the percentage of moisture content. This time-consuming method requires such an extremely accurate scale that it's impractical in most shops.

My meter, and many commercial models, bypasses drying and weighing by taking advantage of the fact that wet wood conducts electricity, while dry wood, a good insulator, resists the flow of electricity. By measuring this electrical resistance (expressed in units called ohms) and comparing your reading with standards developed by the U.S. Forest Products Laboratory and other agencies, you can determine wood's moisture content. The system works fine if the wood moisture content is in the 6% to 30% range, which is fairly common. Depending on the season and locale, most air-dried wood has 12% to 15% moisture content. Properly kiln-dried wood should be 6% to 10%. The electrical resistance in very wet or very dry samples is too erratic to give accurate readings.

Since we are measuring ohms, you might think that any off-the-shelf ohmmeter could measure resistance in wood. Wood is such a good insulator, however, that only a high-range ohmmeter capable of measuring in megohms (one million ohms) can be used. Early instruments used vacuum tubes and expensive high-voltage circuits, but my unit uses a modern, integrated circuit called an operational amplifier which can be wired to compare the wood resistance to known resistances in the meter circuit. The details aren't too important; what's important is that the meter is sensitive enough to measure the moisture in a wood sample. Once I worked the bugs out of the system, I modified my meter dial

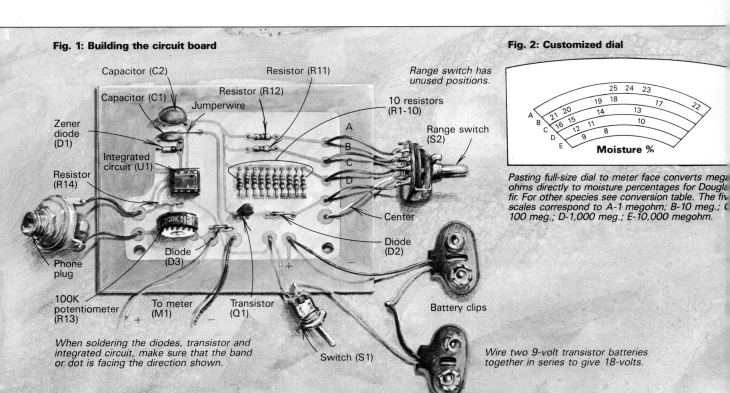

Fig. 1: Building the circuit board

Capacitor (C2)
Capacitor (C1)
Jumperwire
Resistor (R12)
Resistor (R11)
Resistor (R1-10) — 10 resistors
Range switch has unused positions.
Zener diode (D1)
Integrated circuit (U1)
Resistor (R14)
Range switch (S2)
A
B
C
D
Center
Diode (D2)
Phone plug
Diode (D3)
100K potentiometer (R13)
To meter (M1)
Transistor (Q1)
Switch (S1)
Battery clips

When soldering the diodes, transistor and integrated circuit, make sure that the band or dot is facing the direction shown.

Wire two 9-volt transistor batteries together in series to give 18-volts.

Fig. 2: Customized dial

A 21 20
B 16 15
C 12 11
D 9 8
E
25 24 23
19 18
14 13 10
17
22

Moisture %

Pasting full-size dial to meter face converts megohms directly to moisture percentages for Douglas fir. For other species see conversion table. The five scales correspond to A-1 megohm; B-10 meg.; C-100 meg.; D-1,000 meg.; E-10,000 megohm.

Drawing: Mark K

how percentage directly, as shown in figure 2 on the facing page, so I wouldn't have to keep checking resistance charts. Just glue figure 2 to your dial face with rubber cement and you're ready to go. I find my readings, based on Douglas fir standards, are accurate enough for most uses, but if you want more accurate readings that account for the physical differences of each species, use figure 5. If the species you are testing isn't listed, you can assume its readings would be much the same as one of the listed species from the same geographic area and with similar density and structure. The values are probably within 2% of each other. Even within one board, you may find that much of a variation because of wood structure, uneven drying and contamination.

Construction—The simplest way to build the meter is to make a printed-circuit board from the pattern shown, drill holes to accept components, then solder the components on. The completed board, along with its gauge and switches, can be housed in any type of box—I used a cherry case fitted with a ¼-in. walnut deck. The printed circuit is not as mysterious as it looks—it's just a way of replacing wiring with thin copper lines drawn and etched on a board. All you have to do is buy a printed circuit kit from Radio Shack, or some other supplier, and follow the instructions in the package to the letter.

The probe is a 1¼ in. dia. piece of Plexiglas rod drilled to accept the probe leads, which are soldered to the steel points (taken from a cheap drawing compass) epoxied into the rod. I spaced the electrodes about ¾ in. apart, but the spacing isn't critical. Make the probes long enough to penetrate one-fifth to one-quarter the thickness of the boards you want to test. If you don't want to bother with a probe, drive a pair of nails into the wood and connect them to the meter with alligator clips.

Calibration and use of the meter—The meter must be calibrated before use. Solder four 10-megohm resistors together in a four-unit "daisy chain" series. Touching the ends of the chain to the probe tips, adjust R13 (the 100-K potentiometer) to read 14% moisture content, with the meter set to scale C. Do not touch the

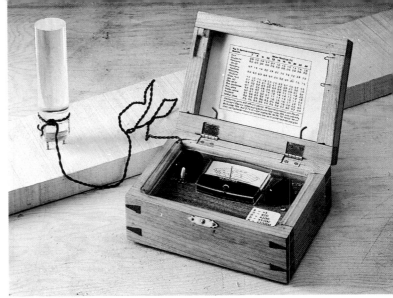

A few common electronic components, a plastic probe and species chart let you gauge moisture levels and anticipate wood movement for about $30. Jazz the unit up with a custom made box.

Fig. 5: Species corrections	Meter Readings (%)										
Species	7	8	9	10	12	14	16	18	20	22	24
Birch	0.9	1.0	0.8	0.7	0.7	1.0	1.0	1.3	1.4	1.6	1.6
Douglas Fir	0.0	0.0	0.0	0.0	0.0	0.0	0.0	0.0	0.0	0.0	0.0
Mahogany, African	0.7	1.4	1.6	2.0	2.8	3.2	3.6	3.8	3.8	3.8	3.8
Mahogany, Honduras	0.3	0.3	0.3	0.4	0.6	0.5	0.2	0.0	-0.5	-1.0	1.5
Mahogany, Philippine	-1.2	-1.2	-1.5	-1.9	-2.4	-2.8	-3.3	-3.7	-4.5	-5.2	-5.8
Maple, hard	0.7	0.7	0.4	0.1	-0.2	-0.1	-0.2	0.0	0.2	0.5	1.0
Oak, red	-0.4	0.0	0.0	0.0	0.0	0.0	0.0	0.0	0.0	-0.2	0.0
Oak, white	-0.1	-0.2	-0.4	-0.5	-0.5	-0.5	-0.8	-1.1	-1.5	-1.8	-2.0
Pine, ponderosa	0.4	0.6	0.7	1.0	1.4	1.6	1.6	1.4	1.2	1.2	1.6
Pine, white	0.0	0.1	0.2	0.3	0.7	1.1	1.3	1.3	1.2	1.1	0.4
Poplar, yellow	0.1	0.6	0.7	0.7	1.2	1.6	1.6	1.6	1.7	2.0	1.7
Redwood	0.0	0.0	0.0	0.0	-0.2	-0.5	-0.8	-1.0	-1.0	-0.2	0.0
Walnut, black	0.5	0.6	0.4	0.4	0.4	0.5	0.3	0.2	0.0	-0.2	-0.4

Conductivity varies with different species. All species compared with Douglas fir standard. Example: When testing birch and meter reads 10%, look opposite Birch under 10%. Add 0.7% to meter reading for 10.7%. For woods not on chart, use figures for species of similar hardness and grain configurations.

Adapted from *Furniture and Cabinet Making* by John L. Feirer ©1983, Bennett & McKnight, Peoria, Ill.

Fig. 3: Printed circuit

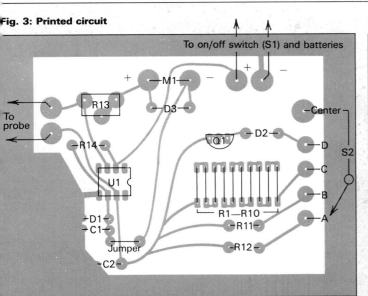

To on/off switch (S1) and batteries

+ M1 −

R13   D3

To probe

R14   Q1   D2

Center

D   S2

U1   C

B

D1   R1—R10

C1   R11   A

Jumper   R12

C2

Use diagram to lay out printed circuit and add components. Black lines are connections on the top of the board. Grey patterns are circuits printed on underside of board. Underside of board is shown here. The parts are coded and refer to the parts list at right.

Fig. 4: Parts list

Qty.	Radio Shack Part Number	Diagram Code	Description
1	270-1752	M1	0-1 milliamp DC meter
1	276-561	D1	6.2 volt, 1 watt zener diode
1	None	U1	LM308 N Op Amp
1	276-2009	Q1	MPS2222 Transistor
	276-1576		Printed circuit fabrication kit
	276-1577		Direct etching dry transfers
2	276-1620	D2 & D3	1N914 Silicon diode
1	271-220	R13	Printed circuit potentiometer 100K
15	271-1365	R1 - R11	10 Megohm resistors ¼ watt
1	271-1325	R14	2200 ohm resistor ¼ watt
1	271-1356	R12	1 Megohm resistor ¼ watt
1	275-625	S1	On-off switch (SPST)
1	275-1385	S2	One pole 12 position rotary switch
2	270-325		9-volt transistor-battery clips
1	274-252		Phone Plus
1	274-256		Phone jack
1	274-414		Knob for switch
2	272-134	C1 & C2	0.05 UF disk capacitors

Misc: 5 in. section of 1¼-in. diameter Plexiglas rod, 22-gauge wire, solder for electronics.

Parts available from Radio Shack; Jameco Electronics, 1355 Shoreway Road, Belmont, Calif. 94002; or Digi-Key Corp., P.O. Box 677, Thief River Falls, Minn. 56701. Unless you're very familiar with electronics, don't try to substitute electronic components.

Gauging wood movement

by Tom Lieb

Many people will tell you woodworking is a simple enough craft—the right tools (with plenty of horsepower), the right glue, no problems. Then, when your beautiful tabletop cracks even though you glued and screwed hefty cleats across its underside, you wonder if maybe there's more to it.

"That's wood movement for you," the pros say as they scan your cracked top, but what does that mean? With a careful reading of Hoadley's *Understanding Wood*, the fundamental characteristics of wood will become clear, but in the workshop we are more often interested in how much movement than why. Few of us can get too excited about searching out just the right book, wading through a bewildering mass of data aimed at scientists, not craftsmen, then tracking down a pocket calculator just to figure out how much slack to build into a set of drawerfronts.

You could wing it, but cutting it too close could bring a summertime house call and a tarnished reputation. Leaving a ¼-in. gap would be playing it safe, but doesn't do much for looks. To solve this dilemma, I developed this chart on the movement and tendency to cup of most commonly used wood species.

I use the wood movement chart most, and when I combine potential movement with the cupping tendency of flatsawn lumber, I get a good idea of a species' dimensional stability. If I had a choice between red or white oak for a tabletop, I'd lean toward the white.

To use my chart, you must know three factors: the width of the piece, its annual ring orientation and the moisture content (MC) range where you live. The table is based on 12-in. wide boards, a convenient size for measuring expansion and contraction. Ring orientation may be either tangential (flatsawn) or radial (quartersawn). When in doubt, assume tangential since they move more than quartersawn.

After wood has been kiln- or air-dried

Dimensional changes

Species	Movement of 12 in. wide board over 7% change in moisture content		T/R[1]
Hardwoods	Radial	Tangential	
Ash, white	.14 in.	.23 in.	1.6
Basswood	.19	.28	1.4
Beech	.16	.36	2.2
Birch, yellow	.22	.28	1.3
Butternut	.10	.19	1.9
Cherry	.11	.21	1.9
Elm, American	.12	.28	2.3
Hickory	.22	.35	1.4
Locust, black	.13	.21	1.6
Maple, sugar	.14	.30	2.1
Oak, red	.13	.31	2.1
Oak, white	.15	.31	1.8
Sassafras	.12	.18	1.6
Sycamore, American	.14	.25	1.7
Walnut, black	.16	.23	1.4
Willow, black	.09	.26	2.6
Yellow, poplar	.13	.24	1.8
Softwoods			
Baldcypress	.11	.18	1.6
Cedar, Alaska	.08	.17	2.1
Douglas-fir (coastal)	.14	.22	1.6
Pine, eastern white	.06	.18	2.9
Redwood (second growth)	.08	.17	2.2
Spruce, Sitka	.12	.22	1.7
Imported Woods			
Khaya	.12	.17	1.4
Lauan, Dark red	.11	.22	2.1
Mahogany	.14	.20	1.4
Teak	.08	.16	1.8

Decimal equivalents
.03 = 1/32-in. .125 = 1/8-in. .31 = 5/16-in. .44 = 7/16-in.
.06 = 1/16-in. .25 = 1/4-in. .38 = 3/8-in. .50 = 1/2-in.

[1] *Ratio of tangential to radial shrinkage (green to oven-dry) indicates tendency to cup in flatsawn lumber. Higher ratio means a greater chance of cupping.*

to equilibrium with its environment, it will continue to shrink and swell with any change in relative humidity. You can determine your annual moisture range by monitoring local conditions or by consulting a moisture-change map, like the one in Hoadley's book.

I feel that for my area (and much of the midwest and the northeast), a 7% change in MC (5% to 12%) is appropriate for

wood that has been treated with a moderately moisture resistant finish, like polymerized oil. Wood with a highly resistant finish (lacquer, shellac or varnish) might change as little as 3%. For many coastal areas, plus much of the south, a 3.5% range would work nicely.

Think of the measurements in the table as baselines, which you can adjust for changes in width, MC, or both by simple arithmetic. For example, take an 18-in. flatsawn red oak door panel. The table gives a movement of .31 in. over a 7% MC cycle for a 12 in. width. Since movement is directly proportional to width, the calculation is simple—18 is 1.5 times 12, so the movement for an 18-in. board is 1.5 times the movement of a 12-in. board or 1.5 × .31 = .46 in.

The MC range is figured in the same way. If you live in a 3.5% area (half of our 7% baseline), simply halve the result of your movement calculation.

For best results, you also must determine the current moisture content of the wood, usually with a meter like the one shown on page 101. If we want to install the 18-in. panel in a frame, our answer of .46 means that we must allow for at least a .23 in. movement in each side slot, but we must know the panel's current moisture content to decide whether to fit tight or loose.

Fitting tight in the summer and loose in the winter is a general rule. In any case, it's best to allow a little extra for movement, especially if you can't determine the current MC or face condition that could produce extreme variations— say, furniture built in the dry southwest being shipped to the Pacific northwest. Once you understand how moisture affects wood movement, almost any situation can be anticipated. □

Tom Liebl designs and builds furniture and boats in Madison, Wisc.

---

probe tips or resistors with your hands as this will change the reading. The meter is now calibrated for all ranges, and should remain accurate as long as the batteries are good.

To use the meter, jam the probe straight into a clear area of the board's face, so that an imaginary line between the points runs parallel to the grain. For the most accurate reading, measure the wood at room temperature. Also, don't insert the probe towards the end of a sample, which will probably be drier than the rest of the board. When measuring, switch the meter ranges from lowest to highest (i.e. A to E) and stop at the position that gives a mid-range reading, usually the most accurate and easiest to read. If you can't get a reading, the sample probably has a moisture content of

6% or less. Readings may vary from one part of the board to another due to improper drying, abnormalities in grain structure, dirt and other surface contamination. If you have any doubts about a reading, probe several other areas of the sample.

I've found that having such a useful and inexpensive instrument in the shop is a real plus. If you're contemplating working with wide panels it would be wise to determine the moisture content of the stock before you begin work. The time and trouble you'll save is well worth the effort. □

Rick Liftig lives in Meriden, Ct., where he dabbles in woodworking and electronics.

From *Fine Woodworking* magazine (July 1985) 53:48-50

Solar Kiln

Boards emerge bright, check-free

by Paul J. Bois

Solar panels on Johnson's kiln are tilted to catch early morning and late afternoon rays. Small door gives access to rear of solar collector, large door to stickered lumber.

Curtis L. Johnson, of Madison, Wis., has designed and built a sun-powered kiln for drying small quantities of furniture-grade lumber. His kiln is slower than a steam kiln (see pp. 95-99), but it is gentler. The boards emerge bright and clear, with virtually no checking.

The kiln is an insulated, stud-framed wooden box that measures 10 ft. wide and 12 ft. long at floor level. It holds 800 bd. ft. of lumber in two stickered piles. The south wall slopes 40° from the vertical and is enclosed by storm windows of single-strength glass facing solar collector panels. Each collector consists of a flat box whose front is sheet metal painted flat black and whose back is a sheet of hardboard. An air space of 1-1/2 in. separates the glass from the collectors. The bottom of each collector is vented and the top is open.

Johnson piles the lumber in equal stacks, well stickered,

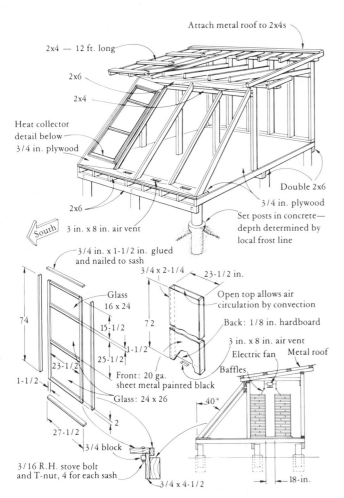

leaving a central plenum 18 in. wide. Two overhead fans, spaced evenly atop the 8-ft. load, each deliver 1,200 cubic feet of air per minute into the plenum. Hinged baffles hanging from the fans ensure that all the air is driven down between the two stacks and out between the stickered boards. A thermostat turns on the fans when the interior temperature reaches 80° F. Two floor vents, each 4 in. by 10 in., admit outside air to the central plenum. The vents are screened against rodents and can be gradually closed as drying progresses, to keep the relative humidity as low as possible.

The sun heats the kiln as high as 130° F in summer and 90° F in the Wisconsin winter. The temperature climbs as the moisture content of the lumber drops below 20%, because evaporation is slower and its cooling effect is less.

To monitor the drying, Johnson cuts a sample from a representative board, weighs it, dries it in an oven and reweighs it. This allows him to calculate the initial moisture content, and he repeats the process throughout the run. Drying time depends on species, initial moisture content, thickness, season and latitude. Madison's latitude is 43° north.

On July 15, 1975, Johnson loaded a green stack of 4/4 cherry at 60% MC and a stack of 4/4 white oak that had been air dried to 15% MC. Fifty-two days later, the cherry had dried to 6% MC and the oak to 7-1/2% MC. The following July 14, he loaded the kiln with 2x4 cottonwood studs at 130% MC and 4/4 black walnut at 85% MC. After 47 days of excellent drying weather, moisture contents had reached an average of 10% and 12%, respectively.

Johnson figures that about 80 summer days will dry most hardwood species from green to 8% MC or less. These figures assume 70 days of sunshine, or 400 hours of direct sunlight. Winter drying takes longer, from 150 to 200 days. A load of mixed green and air-dried stock will dry only at the rate of the green stock, but a full charge of lumber that has already been air dried to 15% MC will dry considerably faster. □

This article is taken from Forest Products Utilization Technical Report No. 7, by Paul J. Bois, a wood drying specialist with the U. S. Forest Products Laboratory in Madison, Wis. The report is available from FPL.

Index

FINE WOODWORKING
Editorial Staff, 1975-1986

Paul Bertorelli
Mary Blaylock
Dick Burrows
Jim Cummins
Katie de Koster
Ruth Dobsevage
Tage Frid
Roger Holmes
Cindy Howard
John Kelsey
Linda Kirk
Nancy-Lou Knapp
John Lively
Rick Mastelli
Nina Perry
Jim Richey
Paul Roman
David Sloan
Nancy Stabile
Laura Tringali
Linda D. Whipkey

FINE WOODWORKING
Art Staff, 1975-1986

Roger Barnes
Kathleen Creston
Deborah Fillion
Lee Hov
Betsy Levine
Lisa Long
E. Marino III
Karen Pease
Roland Wolf

FINE WOODWORKING
Production Staff, 1975-1986

Claudia Applegate
Barbara Bahr
Pat Byers
Mark Coleman
Deborah Cooper
Kathleen Davis
David DeFeo
Michelle Fryman
Mary Galpin
Dinah George
Barbara Hannah
Annette Hilty
Margot Knorr
Jenny Long
Johnette Luxeder
Gary Mancini
Laura Martin
Mary Eileen McCarthy
JoAnn Muir
Cynthia Lee Nyitray
Kathryn Olsen
Mary Ann Snieckus
Barbara Snyder